# 1
# FRANCES WRIGHT

## STUDIES IN HISTORY, ECONOMICS AND PUBLIC LAW

EDITED BY THE FACULTY OF POLITICAL SCIENCE
OF COLUMBIA UNIVERSITY

Volume CXV]                    [Number 1

Whole Number 256

# FRANCES WRIGHT

BY

WILLIAM RANDALL WATERMAN

AMS Press, Inc.

New York

1967

AMS Press, Inc.
New York, N.Y. 10003
1967

To

ELLEN MAGOON WATERMAN

Humankind, its condition, its nature, its capabilities, and its destinies, have formed the study of my life. To aid its progress has been at once my occupation and my passion.

*Course of Popular Lectures*, vol. ii, p. 27.

I have wedded the cause of human improvement; staked on it my reputation, my fortune, and my life.

*Course of Popular Lectures*, vol. i, pp. 71-72.

# PREFACE

At a moment when the women of the United States are rapidly bringing to a successful conclusion their long struggle for equal rights a study of the life of Frances Wright seems most fitting, for Frances Wright was one of the foremost pioneers in the cause, although never a participant in the organized movement. Her interest, indeed, was broader than the single issue of equal rights for women, for she is to be numbered among those fascinating early nineteenth century reformers who believed in the perfectibility of man, and dreamt of future Utopias in which contemporary evils would disappear and inequalities of race, wealth, sex, and birth would not exist. And to this larger object she devoted most of her attention. The women of the United States owe her much, however, for in her courageous lecture-tours throughout the country in the years 1828-1830 she not only pointed out to her somewhat scandalized audiences irrational discriminations against her sex, but inspired other brave women to follow in her footsteps.

Of the life story of this interesting reformer surprisingly little has been known, although writers upon the history of the women's rights movement have almost invariably made her work their point of departure. It was with the hope of making Frances Wright something more than a tradition, and of securing for her a definite niche in the social history of the people of the United States, that the present study was undertaken.

In the preparation of his life of Frances Wright the writer has been most deeply indebted to the Reverend William

Norman Guthrie, Rector of St. Marks-in-the-Bouwerie, New York City. Dr. Guthrie, who is a grandson of Frances Wright, most kindly permitted access to the Wright MSS. collection still in his possession, and made many valuable suggestions. To Miss Alice Jane Gray Perkins of New York City, author of *The Honorable Mrs. Norton,* the writer owes a debt of gratitude for much generous aid and the loan of valuable material which Miss Perkins gathered several years ago when herself contemplating a life of Frances Wright. Indeed, without access to the material in the possession of Dr. Guthrie and Miss Perkins it would have been quite impossible to reconstruct the early life of Frances Wright. The writer also wishes to express his appreciation of the courtesy of that part of the staff of the New York Public Library with which he came in contact, and particularly of the thoughtful consideration of Miss Miller and Mr. Taylor in the American History Room. Thanks are also due to the staffs of the Boston Public Library, the Columbia University Library, and the Dartmouth College Library. In the arduous task of proof reading the author has been fortunate in having the assistance of Professors Frank Maloy Anderson and Wayne E. Stevens of Dartmouth College.

To Professor Dixon Ryan Fox of Columbia University, at whose suggestion this study of Frances Wright was first undertaken and under whose direction the work has been pursued, the writer finds himself particularly indebted. Indeed, whatever of merit the work may possess is due to his kindly criticism and to his frequent and sympathetic encouragement.

WILLIAM RANDALL WATERMAN.

DARTMOUTH COLLEGE,
HANOVER, NEW HAMPSHIRE,
MARCH 1, 1924.

# CONTENTS

# CHAPTER I

## The Early Years

Few women have played a more interesting part in the life of their times than did Frances Wright in the first half of the nineteenth century. On this side of the Atlantic, where she spent the more active years of her life, she first attracted attention as the youthful author of an entertaining and enthusiastic description of the political and social institutions of the United States. Later, she aroused the interest of those who were beginning to look askance at the "peculiar institution" of the South by an experiment in gradual emancipation, through which she hoped to prove that the evil of slavery might be done away with in a "rational and natural" manner. But it was as a popular lecturer and the editor of a weekly paper devoted to free-thought doctrines and radical social reform that she became most widely known to the American peopple. A firm believer in the perfectibility of mankind, and of womankind also, she was quick to denounce existing evils and to plead for a better order of society. So closely, indeed, did she associate herself with the radicalism of the day that for a time "Fanny Wrightism" and "radicalism" were very nearly synonymous terms.

In Europe she was almost equally well known. In England her literary work caused Jeremy Bentham to seek her friendship, and welcome her to his home in Queen's Square Place where she met many of the liberal-minded Englishmen of the time. On the continent her enthusiasm for political liberty and the political institutions of the United States led

General Lafayette to make of her a confidante and aide in the conspiracies of the French Carbonari against the reactionary government of Louis XVIII. Indeed, in Europe as in America, Frances Wright became widely known as a champion of political liberty, social reform, and freethought.

Frances Wright was of Scotch parentage, and was born in Miln's Buildings, Nethergate, Dundee, the sixth of September, 1795. Her father, James Wright, was the descendant of a long line of wealthy merchants, who appear as large property holders in Dundee as early as the year 1500. On the mother's side she came of both Scotch and English ancestry. Her maternal grandfather was Duncan Campbell, an officer in the British army. Her uncle, General William Campbell, rose to prominence in the Indian service in which he eventually lost his life. Of her English ancestry the most interesting connections were her mother's uncle, Richard Robinson, first Baron Rokeby and Primate of Ireland, and the brilliant Mrs. Montagu, her mother's great-aunt.

Frances Wright derived much of her liberal turn of mind from her father, for on the mother's side the influences were wholly conservative and orthodox. James Wright was a man of no little ability. Left an orphan at an early age, he was placed in the care of a friend and fellow-townsman of his father's who saw that he had every advantage that the times afforded. He attended the best academies of Perth and Edinburgh, and brought his formal education to a close with advanced studies in the University of Dublin. This was followed by the two years of travel on the continent customary for the wealthy young Britisher of his day. Wright's literary and scientific activities early attracted attention, and while still very young he became a correspondent of Adam Smith, and of the Scotch physician and surgeon, Dr. William Cullen. His daughter tells us that he

had scarcely reached his majority before being admitted to
membership in a number of the scientific and literary societies of the United Kingdom.  Numismatics seems to have
been his chief interest, and in this field he became such an
authority as to be consulted by the Scotch antiquary and
historian, John Pinkerton, and by Joseph Planta, the assist-
ant librarian and antiquary of the British Museum.  He was
an extensive collector of coins and medals, ancient and
modern, and believed that through numismatics much could
be done to elucidate and to rectify history.  Most of his
rare and valuable collection he eventually donated to the
British Museum.

James Wright's interests were not entirely literary and
scientific, however.  He was also a keen student of government, and heartily in sympathy with the political liberalism
of his time.  Years later Frances discovered among his
writings a statement of his conception of law and government.  " The spirit of law and the tenor of the conduct of
governments," he wrote, " in order to be well adapted to
the mutable and every-varying state of human affairs, ought
continually to change according to existing circumstances
and the temper of the age."  A man with such views as this
naturally took the greatest interest in the liberal movement
in his own country, and in the progress and principles of the
French Revolution.  There is no evidence to show that he
was associated with any of the more radical political clubs
in the kingdom, but his activity in spreading throughout
Dundee and its neighborhood popular translations of French
political and philosophical works, and the promotion, in
1794, of a cheap edition of Thomas Paine's *Rights of Man,*
brought him under government espionage.  Fortunately for
himself and his family he was a man of some distinction
and wealth, and of sufficient discretion to avoid actually
bringing down upon his head the wrath of a terror-stricken

government, at a time when all too often the fate of the radical was Botany Bay. His personal reaction to this espionage is evidenced by a change in the motto on the family crest. *"Pro rege saepe"* it read, and to *" Patria cara carior libertas "* he changed it. Frances Wright came honestly by her independence and liberalism.

Sadly enough when Frances was but two and a half years old both James Wright and his wife died, leaving three little children, two girls and a boy. The boy, Richard, spent his childhood with his father's best friend and his own great-uncle, James Mylne, professor of Moral Philosophy in the University of Glasgow. At the age of fifteen he entered the service of the East India Company, as a cadet, but on the first passage out his ship fell in with a French war vessel, and in the encounter which followed he was killed. Frances speaks of him in her autobiography as a boy of uncommon promise. Frances herself, at the wish of her maternal grandfather, General Duncan Campbell, was taken to England, and brought up as a ward of chancery in the Campbell home in London, or at Luscombe in Devonshire. Camilla, the youngest child, remained for a time in Dundee, but a few years later was taken to London to join her sister.[1]

Although brought up in the midst of luxury with servants to attend her every wish, Frances Wright called her childhood " singularly calamitous." [2]  To the conventional, conservative, and orthodox British family of the upper class in which her early years were spent she must have seemed at times an impossible child. The liberal heritage and independent spirit received from her father seem to

[1] D'Arusmont, Frances Wright, *Biography, Notes and Political Letters of Frances Wright D'Arusmont.* In two parts. New York, 1844, pt. i, pp. 5-9, *passim.* The first part of this work is in reality a short autobiography sketching in outline the life of the author down to the year 1829.

[2] Wright MSS. From the dedication to Frances Wright's unpublished poem, " The Thoughts of a Recluse."

have been often in revolt, and misunderstandings were probably frequent. " Experience taught her," she says, " in very childhood, how little was to be learned in drawing-rooms, and inspired her with a disgust for frivolous reading, conversation, and occupation."[1] It was this " absence of all sympathy with the views and characters of those among whom her childhood was thrown " and " the heart solitude of orphanship " that led her to seek happiness in the rare and extensive libraries with which she was surrounded—perhaps to the relief of the family.[2]

The education of this precocious child must have been quite a problem. She tells us that care was taken to provide her with the very best masters to be had, and that she applied herself by turns to the various branches of science, to ancient and modern languages, and to the arts. She must have been an interesting and often a difficult scholar, for hers was not the passively receptive mind:

She was, at an early age, surprised at the inability of masters to answer her questions, which usually turned upon the nature, origin, and object of the subject submitted to her attention. Being checked on one occasion by a deep and shrewd mathematician and physician, who observed that her question was dangerous, she replied—" Can Truth be dangerous? " " It is thought so," was the answer. She learned in this experience two things: the one that Truth had still to be found; the other that men were afraid of it.

The same conclusion was ever more and more pressed upon her mind, when, in her solitary studies, she remarked the discrepancy of views and opinions existing in books; and again, in society, when she listened to those accounted authorities in learning, letters, and morals. If no *two* agreed, no *one* has discovered the Truth; and, if so, Truth has still to be found. But where?[3]

[1] *Biography*, pt. i, p. 15.
[2] *Ibid.*, p. 9.
[3] *Ibid.*, pp. 9-10.

The result of such a process of research and reflection was the wreck of the religious beliefs of her earlier years:

I may say [she wrote many years later] that I too in childhood was religious, devoutly, enthusiastically, yet I fear hardly savingly.  For love suited me better than fear, a sentiment to which, physically or morally, I never inclined, and moreover there awoke with my earliest faculties a something that drove to my lips on all occasions a little word most prophetical of future heresy, even a word which orthodoxy admits not in her dictionary, and to which masters usually give a frown in answer.  Still I loved the three letters, the more perhaps that they were forbidden or neglected, it mattered little which, and if my *why* was seldom audible it was none the less earnest.  Study, observation, reading, and perhaps more than all, reflection, gradually supplied the answers which the foolish could not and the wise perhaps would not give.

I was saved by temperament from the distressing fears of incipient doubts so common to young believers when first awakening to enquiry . . . , but I remember an uneasiness and restlessness of mind during the earlier states of enquiry which held me fast to the subject until I clearly saw to which side the solution inclined and can yet more distinctly recall the sweet composure which spread over my intellect when I finally drew my conclusions and felt satisfied with their truth.[1]

As she lost faith in the orthodox theology of the day with its emphasis upon rewards and punishments, and what seemed to her its superstitions, it is not surprising that she should have turned with increasing interest to the philosophical teachings of ancient Greece, and more particularly to the materialism of Epicurus.[2]  It was during a visit to Pro-

---

[1] *New Harmony Gazette*, July 23, 1828.

[2] *Biography*, pt. ii, pp. 5-6.  It was not until much later that she became familiar with the works of the French rationalists. The few sceptical works in English which she read at this time she found dull and uninteresting.

fessor Mylne in her eighteenth or nineteenth year that she first seems to have become acquainted with the Greek philosophers, and the outcome of her new studies was to make her an ardent and whole-souled disciple of the great Greek teacher of the Garden. It was a devotion which lasted throughout her life, and which more immediately produced the most charming and entertaining of all her writings, the little fragment " Epicurus," a defense of the doctrines of her new master.

If reflection and study had thus brought to grief the religion of her youth, observation could do no less for her faith in contemporary political and social institutions, stamped, as these were, with the reactionary spirit of post-Napoleonic Europe. In spiritual revolt at the coercion of liberal thought, as well as at the economic distress and oppression of the poor and helpless which she saw about her, she became convinced " that some strange secret—some extraordinary vice lay at the foundations of the whole of human practice." [1] What this strange secret, this extraordinary vice, was, she determined to make it her life work to discover and, if possible, to correct.

It was scarcely to be expected that this youthful sceptic and political radical should remain indefinitely in the conventional environment of the Campbell home. Upon reaching her majority she rather abruptly returned with her sister Camilla to the land of her birth.[2] In Scotland the sisters found a congenial home at Whitburn with Mrs. Rabina Craig Millar, the sister-in-law of Professor Mylne and the daughter of Dr. William Cullen.[3] Safe again in her native

---

[1] *Ibid.*, pt. i, p. 11.

[2] *Ibid.*, p. 13.

[3] *Dictionary of National Biography*, London, 1885-1901. See Millar, John, and Cullen, William. Mrs. Millar was a widow. As Miss Cullen she had married the eldest son of John Millar, Professor of Law in the University of Glasgow.

land, withdrawn from a world in which she was bitterly disappointed, Frances "poured to the mountains and the winds the complainings of a vexed and wounded spirit." [1]

The next few years were devoted to study and writing. Encouraged by the sympathetic little circle of friends at Whitburn she found an outlet for her feelings in plays on the theme of political liberty, poetic comments on unhappy Europe bowing its knee "to sceptered bigots' idiot tyranny," [2] and most notably in the little fragment "Epicurus" mentioned above. Of "Epicurus" which she published a few years later as *A Few Days in Athens*, and dedicated to her friend Jeremy Bentham, it seems advisable to speak in some detail, for the little book was much more than a clever compilation of the Epicurean doctrines woven into an attractive story.[3] It represented the earnest expression of an honestly thought out position upon the subject of religion which influenced the whole of her later life.

In the foreword to this interesting little work the reader is told that *A Few Days in Athens* is a translation from the Italian of an original Greek manuscript which had recently fallen into the hands of an eminent Italian Hellenist. Because of the hostility of the Austrian government toward all profane learning the scholar had asked Miss Wright to translate the manuscript into English and French, and to attend to its publication. It is needless to say that this innocent little fiction did not long conceal the fact of authorship. The literary merit of the book makes it very readable, while to the student of Miss Wright's life the story gives

---

[1] Wright MSS. Foreword to the "Thoughts of a Recluse."

[2] *Ibid.*, "Thoughts of a Recluse."

[3] Wright, Frances, *A Few Days in Athens; Being the Translation of a Greek Manuscript discovered in Herculaneum*, London, 1822. The change in the title was due to the fear of the publishers that the title "Epicurus" might frighten the conservative and hurt the sale of the book. The citations are from the New York edition of 1825.

an insight into the character and results of her early studies.
The search of the youthful Corinthian, Theon, for knowledge in the schools of Athens, and his ultimate conversion
to the doctrines of Epicurus, portray, no doubt, in story
form, the mental struggles and conversion of Miss Wright
herself, while throughout the story is found that spirit of
enquiry which seems to have been inherent in the character
of the author.  " I would wish you to think nothing good,
or bad either, upon *my* decision," says Epicurus to Theon.
" The first and last thing I would say to man is, *think for
yourself*.  It is a bad sentence of the Pythagoreans, ' The
master said so.' " [1]

The substance of the philosophy which made so strong
an appeal to Miss Wright is set forth in the form of a lecture, delivered by Epicurus to a gathering of his disciples
in the Garden.[2]  Why, he asks, do they enter the Garden?
Is it to seek happiness, or to seek virtue and knowledge?
In finding the first he assures them they will find all three,
for " to be happy we must be virtuous; and when we are
virtuous we are wise."  Of what then does true happiness
consist?  Happiness, says Epicurus, consists in the right
direction of our faculties, affections, and passions.  " Perfect pleasure, which is happiness, you will have attained
when you have brought your bodies and souls into a state of
satisfied tranquility."  To reach this, however, a skilled pilot
is necessary to steer us between the Scylla and Charybdis
of our carnal affections.  Such a pilot is Prudence who tells
us, " that a *happy life is like neither to a roaring torrent,
nor a stagnant pool, but to a placid and crystal stream, that
flows gently and silently along*."  And with Prudence comes
" the lovely train of the virtues."  Temperance, throwing a

[1] *Ibid.*, p. 17.
[2] *Ibid.*, pp. 102-109, *passim*.

bridle on our desires; Fortitude, to strengthen us "to bear those diseases which even temperance may not be efficient to prevent"; Justice, to give us security among our fellows, and satisfaction in our own breasts; Generosity, to endear us to others, and sweeten our natures; Gentleness, to take the sting from the malice of our enemies; Gratitude, to "lighten the burden of obligation, or render it even pleasant to bear"; and Friendship, to put the crown on our security and joy.

But, it may be urged, the virtues shown are modifiers and correctors of evil rather than actual and perfect good. We are told that "happiness consists in ease of mind and body; yet temperance cannot secure the former from disease, nor can all the virtues united ward affliction from the latter." True, replies Epicurus to this criticism, philosophy cannot change the laws of nature, but she may teach us to accommodate ourselves to them:

Examine the ills of life, are they not of our own creation, or take they not their darkest hues from our passions or our ignorance? What is poverty, if we have temperance, and can be satisfied with a crust, and a draught from the spring?— if we have modesty, and can wear a woolen garment as gladly as a tyrian robe? What is slander, if we have no vanity that it can wound, and no anger that it can kindle? What is neglect, if we have no ambition that it can disappoint, and no pride that it can mortify? What is persecution, if we have our own bosoms in which to retire, and a spot of earth to sit down and rest upon? What is death, when without superstition to clothe him with terrors, we can cover our heads, and go to sleep in his arms? What a list of human calamities are here expunged—Poverty, slander, neglect, disappointment, persecution, death. What yet remains? Disease? That, too, we have shown temperance can often shun, and Philosophy can always alleviate.

But there is, indeed, a pain that the wisest and best of men cannot escape; the loss of those nearest and dearest to them. And yet, if fate does deprive us of the friendship we prize so dearly, philosophy is always at hand to uphold us with fortitude:

And think, my sons, perhaps in the very evil we dread, there is a good . . . ; perhaps all our pleasures take their zest from the known possibility of their interruption. What were the glories of the sun, if we knew not the gloom of the darkness? What were the refreshing breezes of morning and evening, if we felt not the fervours of noon? Should we value the lovely flower, if it bloomed eternally; or the luscious fruit, if it hung always on the bough? Are not the smiles of the heavens more beautiful in contrast with their frowns, and the delights of the seasons more grateful from their vicissitudes? Let us then be slow to blame nature, for perhaps in her apparent errors there is hidden wisdom. Let us not quarrel with fate, for perhaps in our evils lie the seeds of our good. Were our body never subject to sickness, we might be insensible to the joy of health. Were our life eternal, our tranquillity might sink into inaction. Were our friendship not threatened with interruption, it might want much of its tenderness. This, then, my sons, is our duty, for this is our interest and our happiness; to seek our pleasures from the hands of the virtues, and for the pain which may befall us, to submit to it with patience, or bear up against it with fortitude. *To walk, in short, through life innocently and tranquilly; and to look on death as its gentle termination, which it becomes us to meet with ready minds, neither regretting the past, nor anxious for the future.*

With this exposition of the philosophy of Epicurus the more serious side of the book, as first published, was brought to a close. Several years later four more chapters were added, and given to the world through the columns of the

*New Harmony Gazette.*[1] Of these chapters the first three were planned at the same time as the original twelve, but were withheld from the public, owing to the desire of the author for a more mature consideration of their content— a discussion of the existence of the gods. Theon, the hero of the story, had brought before the master certain grave charges; namely that he denied the existence of the gods. To these charges Epicurus replied that, " To *deny* the existence of the gods would indeed be presumption in a philosopher; a presumption equalled only by that of him who should *assert* their existence." For, continued the sage, " As I never saw the gods, my son, . . . I cannot *assert* their existence; and, that I never saw them, is no reason for my *denying* it."

" But do we believe in nothing except that of which we have ocular demonstration? " asked Theon. " Nothing, at least," replied Epicurus, " for which we have not the evidence of one or more of our senses " :

I know but of one thing, that a philosopher should take for granted; and that only because he is forced to it by an irresistible impulse of his nature; and because, without doing so, neither truth nor falsehood could exist for him. He must take for granted the evidence of his senses; in other words, he must believe in the existence of things, as they exist to his senses. I *know* of no other existence, and can therefore *believe* in no other: although, reasoning from analogy, I may *imagine* other existences to be. This, for instance, I do as respects the gods. I see around me, in the world I inhabit, an infinite variety in the arrangement of matter;—a multitude of sentient beings, possessing different kinds, and varying grades of power and intelligence,—from the worm that crawls in the

[1] *New Harmony Gazette*, March 21–April 11, 1827. These chapters also appear in a London edition of *A Few Days in Athens*, published by Austin & Co., 18–(?). For the following quotations see pp. 68–71.

dust, to the eagle that soars to the sun, and man who marks
to the sun its course. It is possible, it is moreover probable,
that, in the worlds which I see not,—in the boundless infinitude
and eternal duration of matter, beings may exist, of every
countless variety, and varying grades of intelligence, inferior
and superior to our own, until we descend to a minimum and
rise to a maximum, to which the range of our observation
affords no parallel, and of which our senses are inadequate to
the conception. Thus far, my young friend, I believe in the
gods, or in what you will of existences removed from the
sphere of my knowledge. That you should believe with posi-
tiveness, in one unseen existence or another, appears to me
no crime, although it may appear to me unreasonable: and so,
my doubt of the same should appear to you no moral offence,
although you might account it erroneous.

For a nineteen-year-old girl it must be admitted that
Frances Wright had gone far on the road toward free enquiry. Her conversion to Epicureanism had robbed her,
not unnaturally, of all but a critical interest in the church,
as is shown in the following description of a chance visit
paid to the Anglican church in Whitburn. It was, perhaps, one of the last church services she attended:

It is now some years since I have assisted at divine service in
an English Episcopal Church. I entered one therefore this
morning with something of that feeling of respect and
*attendrissement* with which we revisit after long absence and
with a matured mind some haunt of our childhood. If I was
pleased with the gentler gravity and reverence of the tone
and manner of the English minister to those generally seen
in the clergy of Scotland, if I was pleased with this I was soon
wearied of the idle repetitions of the service and presently
disgusted with its absurdity, and yet worse with its blasphemy.
The creed called of St. Athanasius was read (this St. by the
way must have been as mad as a March hare and as brutal
as a Catherine of Medici . . .).

I shut my own little book and listened in wondering silence. The innocent congregation murmured nonsense and damnation after the Priest as if it had all been the wisest and most amiable occupation in the world. Well, all this was very well—as to the nonsense—if the heads could not follow it, perhaps there are many wise things that the same heads could not follow better—and as to the wickedness (the impious anathemas)—I am sure the hearts did not follow it. The lips muttered as the parrot does "pretty poll."

But we had a sermon on the Trinity!—on the creed aforesaid. The minister (by the bye a young good-looking gentle-looking creature) amused me very much at his outset. . . . The ingenuity with which he begged the question was admirable. [He passed a] calm, unlimited, unqualified sentence of damnation against all dissenters or heretics. All in fine who could not receive the T in the Unity and the U in the T, or who think doubtfully or blunderingly upon the hallowed incarnation are sine dubio ordained for eternal torments. Kind mercy, and this reverend Teacher would have us to love his God. For my share—if such were the state of things—I would make no sort of objection to his majesty with the tail and the cloven hoofs. I would rather live with him in his brimstone than with the unjust judge of my holy instructor in his streets of gold and walls of precious stones. Voltaire (if I remember right) well corrected the text "God made man after his own image" to "Man made God after his image." I think I have done with churches. When I can hear of one that does honor to God and good to man it shall have my presence and my love.[1]

One dominant interest she does appear to have had during this period, aside from her literary work, an ever-growing interest in what then seemed to her the land of promise, the United States. It was in her sixteenth or seventeenth

---

[1] Wright MSS. This seems to have been part of a diary. It is dated Whitburn, May 17, ——, Sunday. The year is not given. It may have been as late as 1821, but the years 1816-1818 seem more probable.

year that she made her discovery of America in the dramatic, and, to her, fascinating account of the American War of Independence by the Italian historian Botta, " the only work on a subject so politically heterodox which had found a place in the aristocratical libraries which surrounded my youth." [1]   That Botta's work should have made so tremendous an appeal to her imagination was due to the fact that her whole childhood had been spent in the heat of the great Napoleonic struggle.   Our own day has had ample opportunity to observe the depressing effect of war upon popular government and civil rights, but to the generation growing up in 1812 war must have seemed almost the normal condition of the world.   Botta awoke her to a new existence.   " Life was full of promise; the world a theatre of interesting observation and useful exertion.   There existed a country consecrated to freedom, and in which man might awake to the full knowledge and exercise of his powers." [2]   In the full tide of ecstacy at so wonderful a discovery she was suddenly seized, she tells us, with the apprehension that it was perhaps but a myth.   It was almost too good to be possible on this poor earth.   She flew to her atlases; the first was an old one and no such country appeared, but a second showed *United States* marked along the Atlantic littoral of North America, and she breathed more easily.   She now searched her history shelves, and finally, in Belsham's *History of Great Britain,* she found that her heroes were real men, and that the United States really existed.   It was not until reaching Scotland, however, that she became thoroughly conversant with the story of the

---

[1] Wright, Frances, *Course of Popular Lectures*, New York, 1829. The preface, p. 7.  The Italian work referred to is that of Botta, Carlo Giuseppe Guglielmo, *Storia della guerra dell' independenza degli Stati Uniti d'America*, Paris, 1809.

[2] *Biography*, pt. i, p. 11.

English colonies in America. In the libraries of the University of Glasgow Professor Muirhead put at her disposal material which enabled her to prepare herself for a more intimate examination of this remarkable people, for she had had from the first a fixed but secret determination to visit America.[1] The friendship with Mrs. Millar must have increased this determination, for Mrs. Millar had crossed the Atlantic in 1794 with her husband, a political refugee fleeing the persecutions of a government determined to crush all liberalism, in its fear of the principles of the French Revolution.[2] Here was direct proof that America offered asylum to the oppressed.

In the spring and early summer of the year 1818 Frances finally matured her plans for the first visit of the sisters to the United States. Down until the time of embarking the only person who knew of and encouraged the proposed adventure was Mrs. Millar. Only at the last moment was the Mylne family told of the proposed journey.[3] They were not wholly pleased, as a voyage to America in 1818 seemed rather a serious undertaking for two unprotected young ladies. Professor Mylne raised some objections and suggested, not unnaturally, that Greece and Italy would be more in unison with her early studies. To this Frances replied that a young country inhabited by freemen was infinitely more worth while than countries in ruins inhabited by slaves. " The sight of Italy, dear uncle, prostrated under the leaden sceptre of Austria, would break my heart." [4] To

[1] *Ibid.*, pp. 11-12.

[2] *Ibid.*, p. 11. See also the *Dictionary of National Biography* under Millar, John. The younger Millar was of pronounced Whig sympathies, and found it desirable to leave England in order to avoid persecution. He died of sunstroke in the United States in 1795.

[3] *Ibid.*, pp. 13-14. Also the Wright MSS. A letter from Mrs. Millar to Frances Wright in the autumn of 1818. No specific date given.

[4] *Ibid.*, pp. 13-14.

her explanations Professor Mylne listened with kindness, remarking that she was " the child of her father and must have inherited her views and principles in the blood." [1] It is interesting to know that of the two sisters the Mylne family were more fond of Camilla, whom they believed to be somewhat coerced by the more independent and masculine character of Frances.[2] This may have added to Professor Mylne's objections.

Early in August Frances and Camilla embarked at Liverpool in the New York packet ship, " Amity," Captain Staunton, and the great adventure had begun.[3]

[1] *Ibid.*, p. 14.

[2] Wright MSS. Comment in a letter from one of the Mylne family to Sylva D'Arusmont, Frances Wright's daughter, many years later.

[3] *Biography*, pt. i, p. 13.

# CHAPTER II

## THE PROMISED LAND

THE voyage across the Atlantic proved a quiet one, and on the third of September, thirty days after leaving Liverpool, 'the "Amity" reached New York.[1] Here friends of Mrs. Millar's, to whom the sisters had brought letters of introduction, recommended a suitable boarding house where Frances found life for a time most entertaining, as it enabled her to meet interesting people from all parts of this exciting new land.[2] But boarding house life finally grew wearisome. It also proved more expensive than was desired. In consequence the sisters arranged to make their home for the coming winter with a Scotch family, the Wilsons, a move which greatly relieved Mrs. Millar's fears for the comfort of the girls.[3] To Frances, the Wilson family must have been an interesting one, for Mrs. Wilson was the widow of the famous Irish patriot Theobald Wolfe Tone, the founder of the society of United Irishmen and the leader of the unsuccessful Irish revolutionary movement of 1798. In 1817 Mrs. Tone had contracted a second mar-

[1] Wright, Frances, *Views of Society and Manners in America; in a Series of Letters from that Country to a Friend in England, During the Years 1818, 1819, and 1820.* By an Englishwoman [Frances Wright], New York, 1821, pp. 1-3. The work consists of a number of entertaining and charming letters written by Miss Wright to her friend Mrs. Millar. For the arrival of the sisters in New York see the *New York Evening Post*, September 3, 1818.

[2] *Views of Society and Manners in America*, pp. 15-16.

[3] Wright MSS. Mrs. Millar to Frances Wright, Autumn, 1818.

riage with a Mr. Wilson of Dullater, Scotland, and shortly
afterward crossed the Atlantic with her husband to join her
son William Theobald Wolfe Tone, who had resigned his
commission in the French Army upon the final restoration
of the Bourbons, and sought his future in the United States
where he eventually took up his chosen profession again.[1]
As a friend of liberty, and one of an oppressed people,
young Tone seems to have made a strong appeal to the
sympathetic Frances.

The first winter in the United States the sisters spent in
New York City, where their brightness and intelligence, as
well as their enthusiasm for the country, soon made them
popular. They were fortunate, moreover, in possessing a
letter of introduction from Mrs. Millar to Charles Wilkes,
at that time cashier, and later president, of the Bank
of New York, which enabled them to meet in his home many
of the prominent New Yorkers of the day.[2] It was in the
Wilkes' home, very probably, that they became acquainted
with Cadwallader Colden, a lawyer of note who was soon
to be mayor of the city, Doctor Samuel L. Mitchill, the
" Nestor of American Science," Doctor David Hosack of
Columbia College, Colonel John Trumbull, the artist, and
many others. More intimate acquaintances, connections by

---

[1] Tone, William Theobald Wolfe, editor, *The Life and Adventures of
Theobald Wolfe Tone, Written by Himself,* Glasgow, no date of publication given. The editor adds a brief biographical sketch of his own
and his mother's life.

[2] Domett, Henry W., *A History of the Bank of New York,* New York,
1884, pp. 83-84. Charles Wilkes was the son of an elder brother of the
notorious John Wilkes of Parliamentary fame. He was born in London
in 1764. Twenty years later he came to the United States and entered
the service of the newly established Bank of New York of which he
ultimately became cashier, and, in 1825, president. His eldest daughter,
Charlotte, married Lord Jeffrey, the well known editor of the *Edinburgh
Review.* It was probably through Jeffrey's friendship for her father-in-
law, Professor Millar, that Mrs. Millar had first come in contact with
the Wilkes family.

marriage of Colden, were Harriet and Julia Garnett with whom there grew up a friendship lasting through many years.

But Frances' interests by no means centered exclusively in the activities of the social circle in which the Wilkes family moved. Her residence in the Wilson home brought her into contact with a number of the Irish refugees in New York, of whom the most interesting was Doctor William J. Macneven, an eminent physician, and an old comrade in arms of Theobald Wolfe Tone. It was in part, no doubt, the influence of Macneven and of William Theobald Wolfe Tone, stimulated by her own enthusiasm for the free institutions of the United States, that encouraged her to attempt in New York the production of one of several plays which she had written upon the theme of political liberty. She had tried to have one of her plays produced in England, but her efforts to interest the actor Kemble had resulted only in disappointment.[1] In America she hoped for better luck, although Mrs. Millar was rather apprehensive of the attitude of Mr. Wilkes on such a question. That gentleman, indeed, when sounded upon the possibilities of the American stage had had but little good to say of it:

Nothing can be—as far as I can judge—more degraded than our stage. The only passport to success here seems to be success in London, and I am very confident that the public taste here is to the full as much vitiated as it is with you. I have but very little acquaintance with the Manager of our Theatre who to say the truth is a person with whom I could not associate and whose tastes and talents of every kind are, I should think, much below mediocrity. He would be in-

---

[1] Wright, Frances, *Altorf*. Preface to the London edition of 1822. There were two editions of *Altorf*. The first was brought out by Mathew Carey and Son of Philadelphia, in 1819, and the second in London, in 1822. The latter was dedicated to Mrs. Millar. Citations will be to the American edition of 1819.

capable of judging of works such as you describe and incapable of relishing them even if he understood them.  Nor do I think he has any advisors who would do any better.[1]

About the time of Miss Wright's arrival, however, a capable company of English actors, including the elder Wallack, reached the United States, and this may have somewhat overcome Mr. Wilkes' objections, for, with much secrecy as to its authorship, the tragedy of *Altorf* was produced at the Park Theatre on the evenings of the nineteenth, twenty-fourth, and twenty-sixth of February, 1819, with Mr. Wallack in the leading role and Mrs. Barnes as the heroine.  The prologue of the play was written by W. T. Wolfe Tone.[2]

The theme of *Altorf* is the struggle of the forest cantons of Switzerland against the power of Austria in the early part of the fourteenth century.  The victory of Morgarten (1315) had just been won, and the victorious Swiss bands, under the leadership of Eberard de Altorf, were encamped upon Mount Sattel watching the movements of a second division of the Austrian army.  Werner, Count de Rossberg, the kinsman of Altorf and the loyal subject of Austria, takes this moment to seduce the patriotism of the young Swiss leader through the latter's love for his daughter Rosina de Rossberg.  Through the unconscious efforts of Rosina, who has sought her former lover in the Swiss camp, Rossberg succeeds, and with Altorf flees to his castle, only to have triumph turned to tragedy with the arrival of the Swiss forces and the death of Altorf.

The action of the play moves slowly, but the story is both interesting and well told.  Many of the lines are good, though, in general, their quality is rather uneven.  Through-

---

[1] Wright MSS.  Cited in a letter from Mrs. Millar to Frances Wright, Autumn, 1818.

[2] *New York Evening Post*, February 18, 23, 24, 1819.

out runs the author's intense enthusiasm for political liberty.
Perhaps a few brief selections will best give the reader an
idea of the character and sentiment of the play, and, incidentally, of its author. Rossberg has just informed
Erlach, the father of Altorf, that Leopold of Austria stands
ready to grant him full pardon if he will but return to
his old allegiance:

### ERLACH

Look at these locks, my lord! the snows of age
Have bleached them o'er and o'er.—Art not asham'd
To bear such message to so old a man?
Go! tell him that sent thee, not his empire
Could buy the voice of Altorf from his country.
Go to! I know the drift—I know you deem
My voice hath weight among this artless people.
And you are right: it hath: I'm proud to say it.
Tush! you have chosen ill—you should have sought
Some hot brained boy, fresh from his mother's apron,
To catch your bait—wealth, rank, station, count,
All these I had and freely parted with.
My wealth! I've poured it forth to arm my country;
My rank! I've learned to know it but a name,
And thrown it to the winds—My station! that!
Behold I've fled for aye the throne of kings,
And found it at the pedestal of freedom.

### ROSSBERG

This might be thought enough; yet I'll speak further.

### ERLACH

No further, count, if that your drift be treason.

### ROSSBERG

Treason? In Erlach's mouth that word sounds nobly,
Erlach, who's broken oath and loyalty,
And rung rebellion's clamour through the land.

ERLACH

Speak not of these things, count, they are beyond thee.
I tell thee, Rossberg, thou cans't not understand
The cause of freedom, nor the patriot's motives.
Why—did I show thee all I think and feel,
All I've done and would do in this cause,
Thou'dst call me moonstruck and beside my reason.
Rebellion?—Treason?—Thou'rt the rebel, Rossberg!
Thou, who prefer'st the interest of one man,
And that a base, and mean, and sordid interest,
Unto the weal of thousands. Thou, who stoop'st
A servile knee unto a thirsty tyrant,
Whose hands are dripping with thy country's gore,
And his vile coffers fill'd with plunder of its poor.
Oh, Rossberg! Rossberg!—Talk no more of this,
Thou'lt break my aged frame with indignation:
It ill becomes so old a man as me
To swell with anger.

\* \* \* \* \*

ROSSBERG

You do refuse, then, Austria's proffered bounties?

ERLACH

I wed in life or death the cause of freedom.[1]

Perhaps as interesting as any lines in the play are those
in which Erlach philosophizes upon human nature:

Why, what a riddle is the soul of man!
How grand and how contemptible!—Now shining
In such full majesty of godlike virtue,
In thought so high, in feeling so devoted,
In scheme so vast, in action so sublime,
It seems, upon earth's theatre, not less
Than the Creating Spirit, when it moved

[1] *Altorf*, pp. 11-12.

O'er the blank face of chaos, bringing light
And life, and joy, and loveliness to being—
And then again—and, oh my God, how frequent!
So petty in its aims, base in its feelings,
Gross in its pleasures, sordid in its service,
'Twould be as one with the unreasoning brutes,
Wer't not more rank and loathsome.—Oh, my country!
Remain but simple, frugal, and content,
Hold high in honor still the plow and distaff—
Still think the shepherd's crook more worthy honor
Than idle sceptres of more idle kings:
Then shall your hearts be pure, your conscience proud,
Your store be plenty, and your hearth set round
With smiling children and with grateful guests;
Then shall the blessings of your God be with you,
The love, the envy, and the praise of men.[1]

Notwithstanding the illness of one of the players, which made necessary an eleventh-hour change in the cast, the play went off very well. The audience was both large and appreciative, and, at the close, called lustily for the author, who, however, did not appear.[2] The press treated the effort kindly, due, perhaps, to the impression that *Altorf* was the work of an American. The *New York Evening Post* thought there was too little incident and too much dialogue, a criticism which seems perfectly just to the present-day reader.[3] A more extended criticism, which the *Post* endorsed, appeared in the *New York Columbian*. It was written just before the actual production of the play:

What . . . was our surprise in reading a work, which for the simplicity of the plot and action, the interest of the story, the elegant boldness of the style, never sinking into familiar

[1] *Ibid.*, p. 15.
[2] *New York Evening Post*, February 20, 1819.
[3] *Ibid.*

mediocrity—nor soaring into bombast, the warm and true delineation of natural passions; and above all, the purity and generosity of the principles and sentiments, may challenge competition with the best productions of the British stage. It is not indeed a work of the modern school—it reminds us of better ages. We advance this opinion without waiting for the fiat of an English audience, or an English review—and feel sure that it will be confirmed by all those of our countrymen who dare to think and judge for themselves.

The author is unknown. He has trusted his work to its own merits and to the unprejudiced liberality of an American audience. He has trusted a tale of freedom to the feelings of the only nation where the cause of freedom dare be asserted.[1]

It was, in part, the element of truth in the closing sentence of the foregoing quotation that had led the author to bring out the play anonymously. Perhaps, also, there was a feeling that the production of a play by a woman, at a time when woman's activity was supposed to be confined pretty closely to the home, might not be well received. *Altorf* seems mild enough when read today, but the production of a new drama on the subject of political liberty was a difficult and dangerous proceeding at a time when the fortunes of Europe were controlled by a Metternich or a Castlereagh.[2] If it were known that the author was an English-woman it might seriously endanger her literary future in Great Britain. It would, indeed, be difficult to find an illustration more impressive of the progress of a century from the day of *Altorf*

[1] *New York Columbian*, February 18, 1819.

[2] *Altorf*. Preface to the Philadelphia edition of 1819. "America is the land of liberty. Here is the country where Truth may lift her voice without fear;—where the words of freedom may not only be read in the closet but heard from the stage. England pretends to an unshackled press, but there is not a stage in England from which the dramatist might breathe the sentiments of enlightened patriotism and republican liberty. In America alone might such a stage be formed."

to that when England welcomed American aid to make the world safe for democracy. But alas, for the hope of secrecy. Due, apparently, to the indiscretion of the Wilkes family, knowledge of the authorship soon became public property.[1]

The authorship of the play being no longer a secret, Frances came to the conclusion that publication under her own name could do no further harm. *Altorf* was, therefore, brought out in the same year by Mathew Carey and Son of Philadelphia for the use of the Philadelphia green room. The published play was well received. Thomas Jefferson wrote to Miss Wright that he had read it with great pleasure and saw within it

that excellent moral which gives dignity and usefulness to poetry. The character of Altorf, the father, is a model of patriotism and virtue well worthy of the imitation of our republican citizens; and that of Giovanna is a proper study for both sexes. He prays mrs. Wright to accept the assurance of his high respect.[2]

It was shortly after the production of *Altorf,* in the spring of 1819, that Frances and Camilla began their journeys throughout the northern and eastern states of the Union; of which Frances has left us so delightful an account in the charming letters written to her friend Mrs. Millar. They were later published as her *Views of Society and Manners in America.*

Welcomed into the best of society wherever her travels took her, and mixing boldly and easily with the common people, in town and country, Frances Wright was able to gain a considerable knowledge of the manners and char-

[1] Wright MSS. Mrs. Millar to Frances Wright, 1819.

[2] Jefferson, Thomas, *Correspondence,* edited by W. C. Ford, Boston, 1916, p. 254. Thomas Jefferson to Frances Wright, Monticello, May 22, 1820.

acteristics of the American people. Her very enthusiasm seems to have aroused an answering enthusiasm in the bosoms of those with whom she conversed, and her eager questions met with ready and willing responses. " I verily believe," she says, " that you might travel from the Canada frontier to the gulf of Mexico, or from the Atlantic to the Missouri, and never receive from a native born citizen a rude word, it being understood always that you never give one." [1] One old veteran of the Revolution, with whom she crossed the Hudson River, remarked to her on parting, " You seem to be a foreigner. I wish you may soon become a citizen for I think you are worthy to be a citizen of our country." [2] No higher praise could Frances then have asked for. By whimsical and novel methods she proved the temper of the people, and found it to ring true. Imagine her starting out one bright September morning, shortly after her arrival, to visit the home of a friend in a distant part of the city :

I must confess that I was in no difficulty as to the line of my route. Meeting, however, a man whom, from his appearance, I judged to be a mason, I accosted him with " Friend! can you direct me to such a street?" He paused, and facing about, patiently explained the advance, in the straight line that I was to make, with all the turnings that I was to follow afterward. " But I *guess* you are a stranger to the city. I have nothing very pressing on hand, and can see you on your way." With all due acknowledgments I declined the offer as unnecessary. Pursuing my walk a little further, I overtook a woman who was about to cross the street. She had the air, I thought, of a servant, and the apparently well-stocked basket of provisions that she carried seemed to say that she was returning from market. I addressed her with the same query I had before put to the mason, and she, turning round, with words and signs replied

---

[1] *Views of Society and Manners in America*, pp. 226-227.

[2] *Ibid.*, p. 29.

as he had done, then checking herself, " But perhaps you are
a stranger."   " And a foreigner too," said I.   " Why then—
wait a moment."   And crossing the pavement, and placing her
basket upon the broad stone step leading into a shop, " I will
walk with you to the head of the next street, where I can
better point your way."   " But the basket," said I, eyeing it
over my shoulder, where it stood on the step.   " What harm
should come to it?   It will stand there."   " Will it?" said I,
" 'tis an honest city then."   " Honest enough for that," said
she.   I suffered the good woman to accompany me to the spot
she proposed, for I own I was curious to prove whether the
basket *would* stand as its owner reckoned upon.   We proceeded accordingly, and, reaching the angle of the street, my
kind informer repeated her directions and exchanged with
me a " Good morning."   I waited to trace her back with my
eye through the crowd of moving passengers, and soon saw
her in the distance crossing the street with the basket on her
arm.   You will think that I had practiced sufficiently on the
good nature of the public, but I made yet another trial of it.
I stept into a small but decent looking shop.   A man, the only
person in it, was seated at his ease behind the counter, reading the
newspaper.   To my query of " Can you direct me, &.," he rose,
and coming through the door, ran through the necessary directions.   " But stop!   I have somewhere a map of the city."
He sought and found it and spreading it on the counter, traced
upon it my route.   I thanked him and departed; and was disposed, from the experience of the morning to pronounce the
city quite as civil as any city in England, and perhaps a little
more honest; for, pondering upon the basket, I could not but
suspect that it would scarcely have stood as quietly upon an
English pavement, or, what I judged was undoubted, a woman
with her five senses would never have thought of placing it
there.[1]

Blessed with such a spirit, Miss Wright in her *Views of
Society and Manners in America* has none of that critical,

[1] *Ibid.*, pp. 24-25.

almost hostile tone, which characterizes the writings of
other contemporary English travelers in the United States.
Those incidents of American life which so annoyed Ashe,
Fearon, Captain Hall, and Mrs. Trollope, Frances Wright
passes over with scarce a comment.[1]  She had come to
America to see for herself whether this was indeed a land
of political liberty, happy and prosperous in the possession
of free institutions, and what she saw enchanted her, as,
perhaps, she had resolved to be enchanted.  It mattered not
that American society was often crude, and, at times, even
coarse; the all important and overwhelming fact was that
this people actually governed themselves.  Under the emotions produced by the vindication of her fondest hopes, it is
not surprising that her picture of the country should be one
glowing tribute to American men and government, and the
struggle for independence idealized until scarcely recogniz-
able.  It was an over-enthusiastic picture, as she admitted
herself some years later, but the error, due, as it was, to the
infatuation of a generous mind, should be readily forgiven.[2]

It is interesting to contrast the attitude of Frances Wright
with that of her friend, Mrs. Frances Milton Trollope, who
first came to this country with Miss Wright when she returned in the fall of 1827, and five years later published
her *Domestic Manners of the Americans,* a book which
aroused the indignation of her erstwhile hosts.[3]  Of the

[1] Ashe, Thomas, *Travels in America, performed in 1806,* London, 1808;
Fearon, H. B., *Sketches of America,* London, 1818; Hall, Basil, *Travels
in North America in the years 1827 and 1828,* Philadelphia, 1828; Trol-
lope, F. M., *Domestic Manners of the Americans,* London, 1832. Miss
Wright's contempt for the English travellers in America was great.
*Views of Society and Manners in America,* pp. 483-485.

[2] *Course of Popular Lectures,* p. 154; also pp. 7-8. "My own enthusiasm doubtless conspired to throw a claud [*sic*]-lorraine tint over a
country which bore the name of Republic."

[3] Trollope, Frances Milton, *The Domestic Manners of the Americans,*
2 vols., London, 1832.

two women Miss Wright was the more fortunate in her first impressions of the country, for it chanced that Mrs. Trollope entered by what was then the back door, New Orleans, and the two years of her visit were spent almost wholly in the growing West, which still exhibited much of the crudity of the frontier. Put to the test of actual experience, Mrs. Trollope's enthusiasm for democracy broke down, and, failing to find in the West the material and spiritual comforts to which she had been accustomed in London, she was prone to see in American society little but the roughness which must ever be inherent in a young and growing country. American democracy, with its intense spirit of individualism, appeared to her as license. It must be admitted that much of what Mrs. Trollope says of American life was true, but, in her annoyance at small shortcomings, she entirely overlooked many of the genuine social and political advantages that America had to offer in contrast with the old world. Frances Wright, on the other hand, entered the country through New York, and, bearing letters of introduction to people of prominence, was immediately taken up by the best society that America offered. Favorably disposed toward the United States even before her arrival, and possessed in no small degree of the courage and spirit of the pioneer, she was in a position to appreciate and evaluate, far better than was Mrs. Trollope, what this experiment in democracy meant for the world.

One cannot but admire the courage with which Frances and Camilla Wright pursued their travels through the country, for travel in the United States in 1819 presented hardships which might well have daunted less hardy spirits. But what were a few bumps and bruises to the joys of mixing at first hand with the people, and of discussing in stage coach and country inn the politics and institutions of the country. Everywhere she found the people courteous and

hospitable, and the welcome of the American "country gentleman " (a title which many an Englishman would have refused to any in this new land) charmed her beyond measure:

The American gentleman receives his guest in the true style
of old patriarchal hospitality—with open hand at the gate;
and leads you over the threshold with smiling greetings, that
say more than a thousand words. There is about him an
urbanity, and a politeness, breathing from the heart which courts
and cities never teach. Nothing seems to be disarranged by
your presence, and yet all is ordered for your convenience
and amusement; you find yourself, in a few moments one of
the family; frankness and friendliness draw forth the same
feelings from you; you are domesticated at the hearth and
the board, and depart at last with the heart overflowing, as
from some *home,* endeared by habit and sacred association.[1]

It was in New England that she found the old moral distinctions of the country best preserved, due, she thought, to
the rigidity of its early religious creed, and to its greater
separation from the rest of the nation. The harsh Calvin-
ism of the Puritan had given way to a religion less austere,
but, to Miss Wright, New England still showed, at times,
a degree of self-sufficiency and provincialism which, while it
did much to preserve the virtues of a simple state of society,
led the people to be more loyal to their own institutions than
to those of the nation. Moral, well educated, industrious,
and intelligent, but cautious, shrewd, and peculiarly far-
sighted where their own interests were concerned, the New
Englanders were the Scotch of America, but with this difference: the Scotchman traversed the world to return with
the wealth he had gained to his native hills, whereas the New
Englander carried his penates with him and settled as con-
tentedly on the banks of the Ohio as on those of the Con-
necticut. With but few industries—for in 1819 the indus-

[1] *Views of Society and Manners in America,* p. 184.

trial revolution had but begun in New England—and a poor soil, New England had become the nursery of backwoodsmen, sending out its thousands yearly into the new lands of the great West.[1]

Into the West she scarcely ventured, except as she found it in the still wild regions of New York State beyond the valleys of the Hudson and the Mohawk. Here she was distressed by the hardships of the pioneer settlers who had " to encounter fatigues, and but too frequently unwholesome vapours to which even a vigorous constitution may fall a sacrifice," but heartened by the cheerfulness with which they bore them.[2]

In the middle states Miss Wright found a liberality of sentiment which added dignity to all their public measures. This she felt was due perhaps to their greater wealth, or to their central position, which gave to them all the advantages of free intercourse, both with the states about them, and with foreigners from all parts of the world.[3]

Into the South, at this time, she had but little desire to extend her travels. " I own that, as regards the southern states, I have ever felt a secret reluctance to visit their territory. The sight of slavery is revolting everywhere, but to inhale the impure breath of its pestilence in the free winds of America is odious beyond all that the imagination can conceive." [4] In spite of this repugnance to the institution of slavery, however, Miss Wright treats it in a manner both just and fair, appreciating fully the seriousness of the problem which confronted the planters.[5] A few years later she was to attempt a solution of this most vexing problem her-

[1] *Ibid.*, pp. 376-377.
[2] *Ibid.*, p. 189.
[3] *Ibid.*, p. 379.
[4] *Ibid.*, p. 517.
[5] *Ibid.*, pp. 66-67.

self, but in 1819 she felt that only those thoroughly familiar with the history and character of the institution, as it existed in America, should undertake to suggest a remedy.

Of real poverty she found little in the course of her travels. American cities were still untouched by the terrible housing and unemployment problems of the industrial revolution, and, except for the more remote regions of New England and New York, the farming class appeared to her prosperous and contented. " Plenty at the board; good horses in the stable; an open door, a friendly welcome, light spirits and easy toil; such is what you find with the American farmer." [1]

In view of our present-day concern as to the strangers who sally forth from Ellis Island, Miss Wright's observations upon the abilities and character of the immigrants who were entering the United States in the early years of the nineteenth century are interesting. " Of all the European emigrants," she says, " the Dutch and the Germans invariably thrive the best, *locate* themselves, as the phrase is here, with wonderful sagacity, and this being once done, is done forever." Next in adaptability comes the Scot, but the Frenchman is " given to turn hunter, the Irishman drunkard, and the Englishman speculator. Amusement rules the first, pleasure ruins the second, and self-sufficient obstinacy drives headlong the third." [2] There were exceptions, of course, particularly among the more recent arrivals from England, among whom there were many men of property and serious purpose. Miss Wright, herself, advised no man to come to America not possessed of a clear capital of at least five hundred pounds. If Miss Wright may be believed, the immigrant who came to America in the early years of the nineteenth century was prepared to give benefits to, as well as to

[1] *Ibid.*, pp. 186-187.
[2] *Ibid.*, p. 176.

receive them from his adopted country. The Frenchman dreamed that he was " to new-model the civic militia, or at the least the whole war department in the city of Washington "; the Englishman that he was " to effect a revolution in agriculture by introducing the cultivation of the turnip and planting hedgerows "; the Scotchman that he was " to double the national produce by turning out the women to work in the fields "; and even the poor German " conceives, that he he is to give new sinews to the state, heighten the flavor of the Kentucky tobacco, and expand the souls of the citizens who smoke it." [1]

At the age of twenty-five, in open revolt at the unhappy position in which the rigid conventions of the time placed her sex, Frances Wright naturally observed with interest the condition of American women. What she saw encouraged her. Nowhere, did it seem, were women held in higher estimation and more appreciated than in this country. " The deference that is paid to them at all times and in all places has often occasioned me as much surprise as pleasure," and this was true not only of the well-to-do classes but of the farming and laboring classes as well. " I have myself often met with a refinement of civility from men, whose exterior promised only the roughness of the mechanic, or working farmer, that I should only have looked for from the polished gentleman." [2] The liberty enjoyed by American women startled Miss Wright, as it did other European travelers, but she admired it whole-heartedly. In another respect, however, she felt that the condition of her sex might be much improved. Female education should no longer be neglected, for the wonderful advance which this nation had made might " be doubly accelerated when the education of women shall be equally a national concern with that of the

[1] *Ibid.*, pp. 264-265.
*Ibid.*, p. 423.

other sex; and when they shall thus learn, not merely to
enjoy, but to appreciate those peculiar blessings which seem
already to mark their country for the happiest in the
world." [1]

Great, however, as was Miss Wright's interest in the
social conditions prevailing within the United States, her
real interest lay in the political life and institutions of the
nation, and it was primarily to observe these that she had
crossed the Atlantic. Just what she expected to find was
hardly clear, even in her own mind, for Europe at that time
regarded the radical experiment in government in America
with much the same feeling with which the western nations
regard present-day Russia:

I remember, that, on coming to this country, I had myself a
very confused notion of the people that I was to find in it;
sometimes they had been depicted to me as a tribe of wild
colts, chewing the bit just put into their mouths, and fretting
under the curb of law, carelessly administered, and yet too
strict withal for their untamed spirits; at others I understood
them to be a race of shrewd artificers, speculating merchants,
and plodding farmers, with just enough manners to growl an
answer when questioned, and enough learning to read a newspaper, drive a hard bargain, keep accounts, and reason phleg-
matically upon the advantages of free trade and popular government. These portraits appeared to me to have few features
of resemblance; the one seemed nearly to image out a Dutch-
man, and the other a wild Arab. To conceive the two characters combined was not very possible; I looked at both and
could make nothing of either. The history of this people
seemed to declare that they were brave, high minded, and
animated with the soul of liberty; their institutions, that they
were enlightened; their laws, that they were humane; and
their policy that they were peaceful, and kept good faith; but
I was told that they were none of these. *Judge a man by his*

*works,* it is said; but to judge a nation by its works was no adage, and, I was taught, was quite ridiculous. To judge a nation by the reports of its enemies, however, seemed equally ridiculous; so I determined not to judge at all, but to land in the country without knowing anything about it, and wait until it should speak for itself.[1]

Reaching the United States in the early years of James Monroe's first administration, and at a time when the tides of partizan politics were at a low ebb, she saw but little of that fierce political struggle which her friend Mrs. Millar had witnessed in the second administration of Washington. The disastrous opposition of Federalism to the recent war had left the Republicans without a rival in the field, for post war issues had not as yet resulted in new party alignments. Of party distinctions, indeed, Miss Wright could find nothing but varying shades of Republicanism. The individual Federalist scarce existed, although " a certain soreness upon some political topics, a coldness of manner in pronouncing the name of Jefferson, and, I have observed of Franklin, is what may sometimes enable you to detect a *ci-devant* member of the fallen party." [2] The war itself she found had not only given to the country a recognized position among the nations of the world, but had been a great nationalizing force which had firmly cemented its internal union. A common danger and a common success had made of the people a nation.

Wherever she journeyed she sought to discover what the people thought of the institutions of their country, and what they knew of them. If one-half of what she says is true, she found the American people possessed of a degree of political intelligence far beyond that of their countrymen of to-day. Rich and poor, gentleman and mechanic, all had

[1] *Ibid.,* pp. 311-312.
[2] *Ibid.,* p. 378.

the particulars of the history of their country, and of its
institutions, at their finger-tips, and were ever ready to discuss them with an enthusiasm which always surprised the
inquisitive stranger. " I have never yet," says Miss Wright,
" conversed with the man who could not inform you upon
any fact regarding the past history and existing institutions
of his nation with all the readiness and accuracy with
which a schoolboy, fresh from his studies, might reply to
your queries upon the laws of Lycurgus or the twenty-
seven years' war of the Peloponnesus." [1]   Not only did the
American citizen possess this excellent knowledge of his
country, but, what interested her even more, he actually
felt himself to be an essential factor in the successful operation of the national institutions:

I have observed, that it is usual for an American, in speaking
of political matters to say *our* president does so and so; *we*
passed, or shall bring forward, such a bill in Congress; *we* took
such and such a measure with a view, &. To speak in short . . .
I should say that it were impossible for a people to be more
completely identified with their government, than are the
Americans. In considering it, they seem to feel, *it is ours;*
*We created it, and we support it; it exists for our protection*
*and service; it lives by the breath of our mouths, and while it*
*answers the ends for which we decreed it, so long shall it stand,*
*and nought shall prevail against it.*[2]

To Frances Wright this enthusiasm of the American for
his political institutions seemed perfectly natural, for in her
own enthusiasm she herself considered those institutions as,
" perfect in their theory, of which the principle is change,
according to, and in union with, the progress of the sovereign popular mind, and perfect also in that provision of
their political framework which facilitates, at all times, the

[1] *Ibid.*, p. 26.
[2] *Ibid.*, pp. 26-27.

moulding of the constitutional code of practice, so as to keep
pace with that progress." Based upon such institutions, the
duration and growth of the United States appeared " placed
above the shock of accident, even by the very nature of man,
and by the nature of things as influenced by human power." [1]
The machinery making possible this principle of change,
which she considered the greatest glory of American government, she found in the representative system, which had
been developed first in England and then carried to perfection
in the United States; " by it the body of the people rule in
everything; by it they establish their constitutions; by it
they legislate according to constitutions already established;
and by it again they amend their constitutions according to
the gradual advance of the public mind in political wisdom." [2]

Thus, though the form of government may be sometimes
found deficient " yet as the door is ever left open to improvement, in system it may always be pronounced perfect." [3]    Although in 1819 it seemed to Miss Wright that
the theory of the American government was supported by
its practice, it must be admitted that her view was rather a
superficial one, for she appears not to have considered the
limitations on the franchise in many of the states.

Unfortunately Frances left for home before the presid-
ential election of 1820, but the state and local elections of
1818 and 1819 gave her a good opportunity to observe the
operation of the electoral machinery of the country.   To
her surprise, and contrary to her English experience, she
found that American elections, with all their importance,
passed off very quietly, even though a glimpse at the political
press would lead the stranger to believe that in the success

[1] *Biography*, pt. i, p. 20.
[2] *Views of Society and Manners in America*, p. 116.
[3] *Ibid.*

of the opposition nothing less than political chaos faced the state or nation. Indeed, Miss Wright thought the campaign tone of the press quite scandalous, although the good sense of the people rendered it comparatively harmless, " for they no more regard all the noise and sputter that it occasions than the roaring of the vapour on board their steamboats." Public opinion, after all, she concluded, was the best, " and indeed the only efficient censor of the press: and in this country it is found all sufficient: while in other countries, fines, imprisonments, and executions, are had recourse to in vain.[1]

Nevertheless the intense interest of the American people in politics deluged the country with newspapers, and, if the more violent declamations of these made but little impression upon the voters, she found that their sound reasoning was followed with the closest attention and exercised the greatest influence. America, indeed, offered little opportunity for the demagogue, for its electorate was far too intelligent, and demanded of its leaders clear and well thought out arguments. It was this that had made Thomas Paine's *Common Sense* such an influence in the early days of the Revolution, and, later, the *Federalist* papers in the critical months before the adoption of the present Constitution.

As a fitting and necessary climax to her study of American life and institutions, Miss Wright visited Washington. Here she met a number of the prominent men of the day, and had an opportunity to observe Congress at work:

Never shall I forget the feelings with which I first looked down from the gallery of the hall upon the assembled representatives of a free and sovereign nation. Is there, in the whole range of this peopled earth, a sight more sublime! . . . Were I curious to try the soul of a European, I should wish to see him enter the house of the American congress. I defy a native of that continent who has a soul not to find it at that

[1] *Ibid.*, p. 405.

moment. Yes, my dear friend, while this edifice stands, liberty has an anchorage from which the congress of European autocrats cannot unmoor her.[1]

At the time of her visit the House of Representatives was in debate upon the tariff measure of 1820, and she was so fortunate as to listen to the eloquence of Henry Clay in its defence. He did not disappoint her expectations:

He seems, indeed, to unite all the qualifications essential to an orator, animation, energy, high moral feeling, ardent patriotism, a sublime love of liberty, a rapid flow of ideas and of language, a happy vein of irony, an action at once vehement and dignified, and a voice full, sonorous, distinct, and flexible; exquisitely adapted to all the varieties of passion or argument —without exception the most masterly voice that I ever remember to have heard. It filled the large and magnificent hall without any apparent effort on the part of the orator. In conversation, he is no less eloquent than in debate; and no sooner does he kindle with his subject, than his voice and action betray the orator of the hall; yet so unpremeditated is his language, that even in a drawing-room, the orator never appears misplaced.[2]

At the capital Miss Wright's travels in the United States came to an end. Perhaps it would be best to let her sum up in her own words the results of many months' study of the American character:

It is difficult to make observations upon the inhabitants of a particular district that shall not more or less apply to the nation at large. This is the case in all countries, but more particularly in these democracies. The universal spread of useful knowledge, the exercise of great political rights, the ease, and comparatively, the equality of condition, give to this

[1] *Ibid.*, pp. 504-505.

[2] *Ibid.*, pp. 507-508.

people a character peculiar to themselves.  The man of leisure, who is usually for the most part the man of *pleasure*, may, indeed, find himself somewhat alone in this country.  Every hand is occupied, and every head is thinking, not only of the active business of life (which usually sits lighter upon this people than many others), but of matters touching the general weal of the empire.  Each man being one of a sovereign people, is not only a politician, but a legislator—a partner, in short, in the grand concern of the state: and this not a *sleeping* partner, but one engaged in narrowly inspecting its operations, balancing its accounts, guarding its authority, and judging its interests.  A people so engaged, are not those with whom a lounger might find it agreeable to associate: he seeks amusement and he finds business; careless wit and he finds sense; plain straight-forward sober sense.  The Americans are very good talkers, and *admirable listeners;* understand perfectly the exchange of knowledge, for which they employ conversation and employ it solely.  They have a surprising stock of information, but this runs little into the precincts of imagination; facts form the ground-work of their discourse.  They are accustomed to rest their opinions on the results of experience, rather than on ingenious theories and abstract reasonings; and are always wont to overturn the one by a simple appeal to the other.  They have much general knowledge, but are best read in philosophy, history, political economy, and the general science of government.  The world, however, is the book which they consider most attentively, and make a general practice of turning over the page of every man's mind that comes across them; they do this very quietly and very civilly, and with the understanding that you are at perfect liberty to do the same by theirs.  They are entirely without *mauvais honte* and are equally free from effrontery and officiousness.  The constant exercise of the reasoning powers gives to their character and manners a mildness, plainness and unchanging suavity, such as are often remarked in Europe in men devoted to the abstract sciences.  Wonderfully patient and candid in argument, close reasoners, acute observers and original thinkers, they understand little the play of words, or, as the French more distinctly express it, *badinage* . . . . This people have nothing of the poet in them, nor of the *bel esprit,* and I think are apt to be tiresome when they attempt to be either. . . . On the other hand, they are well informed and liberal philosophers, who can give you, in half an hour, more solid instruction and enlightened views, than you could receive from the first *corps literaire* or *diplomatique* of Europe by listening to them for a whole evening. It is said that every man has his own *forte,* and so, perhaps, has every nation: that of the American is clearly good sense; this sterling quality is the current coin of the country. . . .

I must also remark of this people, that they possess an uninterrupted cheerfulness of mind, and an imperturbable evenness of temper, and, moreover, a great share of dry humor, which is the weapon they usually employ when assailed by impertinence or troublesome folly of any kind.[1]

It must be admitted, of course, that at times in her letters Miss Wright lets her enthusiasm quite run off with her, for the United States in 1819 was hardly the social and political paradise she pictured it. Society, outside of the Eastern cities, still showed much of frontier crudeness, and from our modern standpoint the government was far from being as representative as the reader of her work would gather. But after all she is to be excused, for, whatever one might say of cultural shortcomings, in its more even distribution of wealth, and the consequent economic contentment of its people, and in the greater liberality of its political institutions, the United States certainly presented a striking contrast to contemporary England.

As a closing comment upon these interesting letters it might be well to quote what she wrote eight years later in summing up her first experience in America:

[1] *Ibid.,* pp. 119-121.

A foreigner, I have looked round on this land unblinded by
local prejudices or national predilections; a friend to humankind, zealous for human improvement, enamoured to enthusiasm,
if you will, of human liberty, I first sought in this country to
see in operation those principles consecrated in her national
institutions, and whose simple grandeur had fired the enthusiasm and cheered the heart of my childhood, disgusted
as it was with the idle parade and pride of unjust power inherent in European aristocracy.   Delighted with the sound of
political liberty, the absence of bayonets, and constrained taxation, I spake and published, as I felt, in praise of American
institutions; and called, and, I believe, first generally awakened
the attention of the European public to their study and appreciation.[1]

This, for a girl of twenty-five, was no mean achievement.

[1] *Course of Popular Lectures,* p. 154

# CHAPTER III

## THE FRIEND OF LAFAYETTE

SHORTLY after their visit to Washington the sisters returned to England.[1]  Their somewhat hasty departure was
due to the picture of impending political revolution in that
country, as gathered from their London newspapers, and
even more vividly from the correspondence of Mrs. Millar.[2]
Mrs. Millar's pleading, added perhaps to the thought that
an ardent enthusiast for freedom and reform might well
play a more important rôle in the coming revolution than
in a country where the government was already " the very
palladium of liberty," led Frances to embark for home, with
high hopes, doubtless, of witnessing the end of the post-
Napoleonic reaction and the triumph of democratic principles.

England, indeed, in the winter of 1819 and the early
spring of 1820, appeared to be upon the verge of a great
upheaval.  The years immediately following the close of
the Napoleonic wars had been years of the most acute economic distress that the country had experienced since the
dawn of the industrial revolution.  The collapse of the war
industries accompanied, as it was, by that economic phenomenon known as over-production brought on an amount of
industrial unemployment before unheard-of.  Nor were the
agricultural classes better off than the factory workers, for

[1] *Views of Society and Manners in America*, p. 485.  The sisters left
New York about the middle of May, 1820.

[2] Wright MSS.  Mrs. Millar's correspondence, 1819-1820.

the very abundance of the crops during the last two years
of the war had made farming unprofitable. Whole parishes
were deserted by the destitute and starving laborers, and
"the crowd of paupers increasing in numbers as they go
from parish to parish spread wider and wider their awful
desolation." [1] With a distress so widespread and so serious
outbreaks of violence were inevitable, and with them the
radical reformers made their appearance, crying out for relief not in the economic measures of revenue and of industrial control that the situation really demanded, but in the
expected panacea, political reform. Universal suffrage, the
ballot, equal electoral districts, and annual parliaments
formed the radical remedies throughout these trying times.
So alarmed did the conservative Tory government of Lord
Liverpool become in the spring of 1817 that the Habeas
Corpus Act was suspended, and, although nothing was done
to ameliorate the actual economic distress of the people, every
effort was made to suppress the demands for a change in the
basis of government. During the year 1819 the discontent
and unrest reached its height, and in one huge meeting after
another the demands of the " Radicals," as they now openly
called themselves, grew bolder and bolder. The climax
came in the great Manchester meeting of the sixteenth of
August, when a vast concourse of between fifty and eighty
thousand workers gathered in St. Peter's Field on the outskirts of that city, to petition for reform, and to listen to
the eloquence of " Orator " Hunt, the most popular of the
radical speakers. [2] Here the stupidity of the city magistrates
in attempting the arrest of Hunt, after he had begun speaking, brought on a conflict which resulted in the death of
several, and in injury to hundreds of the assembled working-

[1] Hansard, *Parliamentary Debates*, vol. xxxiii, p. 671. Quoted in
Wallas, Graham, *The Life of Francis Place*, London, 1898, p. 114.

[2] Shortly after this affair Henry Hunt was imprisoned for sedition.

men. The indignation and bitterness which followed this wretched affair was intense, and for months revolution was in the air.

"Education and starvation have made their way with the people," wrote Mrs. Millar to Frances Wright shortly after the Manchester Massacre. Alarm and terror were everywhere, accompanied by the wildest stories of a coming division of property. "To give you a specimen of our alarm, for a month there was not a shilling to be got in Newcastle, Shields, or Sunderland—from fear making everyone hoard all the silver they could collect." [1] Thoroughly frightened, and lacking the legislation necessary to cope with the situation, the government summoned Parliament. "The temper of the Members on the first meeting of Parliament," again wrote Mrs. Millar, " was ferocious beyond measure." [2] Indeed, in passing the celebrated " Six Acts " of 1819, this Parliament well merited the name of the " Savage Parliament." By aid of these acts the government eventually suppressed political radicalism, although the early months of 1820, marked by renewed rioting, and the infamous Cato Street Conspiracy against the very lives of the Cabinet Ministers, were anxious and trying ones for the conservative. [3]

Such was the condition of affairs which was reported to Miss Wright as she made her way amid the peace and plenty

[1] Wright MSS. Mrs. Millar's correspondence, 1819. No specific date given.

[2] *Ibid.*

[3] For England between the years 1815 and 1820 see *The Annual Register;* Martineau, Harriet, *A History of the Thirty Years' Peace,* 4 vols., London, 1877. Volume I covers the period 1815 to 1822; *The Cambridge Modern History,* London, 1902-1912, see vol. x, ch. xviii; Mathieson, William Law, *England in Transition,* London, 1920; Wallas, Graham, *Life of Francis Place;* Walpole, Spencer, *A History of England from the conclusion of the Great War in 1815,* 5 vols., London, 1878-1886.

of America, and such the condition that she found on reaching England in June of 1820. She went directly to Allonby, a little place on the coast in Cumberland, where Mrs. Millar and her sister were then living. Here she eagerly awaited the revolution which never came, for the true nature of the recent unrest now became evident. With the return of good harvests and better business discontent gradually disappeared, and what little remained was rendered leaderless and harmless by the effective activities of the government under the Six Acts. Had the trouble been predominantly political, as Miss Wright seems to have hoped and believed, rather than what it really was, essentially economic, the result might have been very different. We can well imagine her disgust when the chief interest of the summer months proved to be not political revolution, but the divorce proceedings of the new king, George IV. England must have seemed just about hopeless.

The revolution having failed her, Miss Wright turned her attention during the long hot summer to literary work. She considered writing some articles for the *North American Review*, two numbers of this earliest of American reviews having recently fallen into her hands and met with her approval, as possessed of a " high character as well for liberality as for ability." [1]  This plan, however, seems to have been given up, for no article from her pen appeared in the *Review* either in this year or the following. The work which occupied most of her time throughout the fall and winter was a revision of the letters written to Mrs. Millar from the United States, with a view to their publication in the form of a book upon American society and manners.

By the early spring of 1821 her *Views of Society and*

---

[1] Wright MSS. Letter to the *North American Review*, dated Allonby, June 21, 1819. This date should read 1820 as she was not in England in 1819.

*Manners in America* was ready for the press, and through
the efforts of a friend, the London publishing house of
Longman, Hurst, Rees, Orme, and Brown offered to bring
out the work, take all the expense, and share the profits.[1]
Upon its appearance the book met with a very favorable reception from the English liberals, due, in large measure, to
the author's enthusiastic description of American political
institutions; an enthusiasm which no previous writer upon
the United States had shown.   Coming at a time when
political reform in England was much in the minds of
thoughtful men, although its actual progress had been temporarily checked, the assurance that American democracy
was not the failure they had been led to believe, but in
reality a thriving success, must have proved not a little
stimulating.   Miss Wright herself says of the appearance
of the book that it "changed the tone and somewhat corrected the views of leading British periodicals, while they
[the letters] revived, on the European continent, old reminiscences of the country of Franklin and Washington,
and a new ardor in the cause of political and religious
liberty."[2]   The work was "translated without her agency
into most of the continental languages."[3]

On this side of the Atlantic the *North American Review*
commented favorably on it in the January number of 1822,
although some of Miss Wright's statements were considered
as being a little too sweeping in their character, and unwarranted by the extent of her observations and travels.   "The
work is in fact," said the reviewer, "an eulogium on our
country and its character a panegyric of the warmest kind."[4]

The publication of this book soon brought into Miss

[1] *Ibid.*, Thomas Thornely to Frances Wright, March 6, 1821.

[2] *Biography*, pt. i, p. 15.

[3] *Ibid.*

[4] *North American Review*, January, 1922, p. 15.

Wright's life new interests and new friends. It "brought her," she tells us, "into relation with the prominent reformers of Europe."[1] In England it attracted the attention of Jeremy Bentham, the famous philanthropist and philosopher, and the great authority on jurisprudence. Bentham's interest led him to seek the friendship of the author, and to offer her the hospitality of his home in Queen's Square Place—no slight tribute to her personality and intelligence.[2] Here we find her often during the next few years, enjoying the society of "her Socrates," as she affectionately called the old man, and meeting in his evening symposiums that small group of "philosophical radicals" who were doing so much for England politically and intellectually, and who looked to Bentham for their inspiration: James Mill, well known as political economist and historian; Francis Place, the "radical tailor" of Westminster, and one of the most astute politicians of his day; George Grote, the brilliant author of the *History of Greece*; and the jurist, John Austin. From little comments here and there in her letters we gather some idea of the life in Queen's Square Place. Bentham, always an indefatigable worker, spent most of the day in writing and study, devoting the evenings to conversation with his friends. "It is now seven, the dinner hour of my P[hilosopher]," writes Frances Wright in one letter, "till that time I seldom see him, but from that hour I remain in his study till eleven."[3] Bentham's growing deafness seems to have made these talks somewhat of a trial, as well as a pleasure, to his friends:

I dine [to-day] with my old P[hilosopher] who carries his years

---

[1] *Biography*, pt. i, p. 15.

[2] Bentham, Jeremy, *Works*, John Bowring literary executor, 11 vols., Edinburgh, 1843, vol. x, p. 526.

[3] Wright MSS. Frances Wright to General Lafayette, February 25 (?), 1822.

as bravely as ever except that he is, I think, more deaf. This infirmity is a greater trouble to me than it appears to be to him. You may remember the difficulty I find in raising my voice. An hour's conversation with my Socrates leaves me more fatgued than does a walk of six miles.[1]

Just how great an influence the utilitarian doctrines of Bentham and his circle had upon the intellectual development of Miss Wright, it is hard to say. There is little trace in her writings of any interest in the philosophy of utilitarianism. Practical utilitarianism, however, "the greatest happiness of the greatest number," to be achieved by the application of rational principles to human behavior, and furthered by effective state legislation, undoubtedly made a strong appeal, and its influence may well be seen in her later activities as a political and social reformer in the United States. As freethinkers and anti-clericals the Benthamites made a more immediate impression, and it was apparently at the suggestion of Bentham that she brought out the little fragment, *A Few Days in Athens,* which, as we have already remarked, she dedicated to the Master, " As a testimony of her admiration of his enlightened sentiments, useful labours, and active philanthropy, and of her gratitude for his friendship."

Important and stimulating as the contact with Bentham proved to be, a much more interesting friendship was that formed with another admirer of her American letters, General Lafayette. At sixty-three the passion for political liberty burned as strongly in the bosom of the old veteran, as in those glorious days when, side by side with Washington, he had fought for the independence of the United States. Nor had he forgotten the country he had served so nobly in those trying years, for every book which described its later history was eagerly acquired.[2] It was in this way that he

---

[1] *Ibid.,* Frances Wright to General Lafayette, February 15-18, 1822.

[2] Morgan, George, *The True Lafayette,* Philadelphia, 1919, p. 410.

became acquainted with Miss Wright's work. Pleased, no doubt, with the freshness and charm of the narrative, as well as the enthusiasm of the writer for the cause of liberty, he wrote her a congratulatory letter, and expressed the wish that he might meet her.[1] This letter must have reached her in the late summer of 1821, for early in September we find her in France for the purpose of meeting him. It is not hard for us to understand the enthusiasm with which she relates to Bentham the story of that first interview with the hero of the French and American revolutions, whose life was, indeed, the epitome of everything she thought most worth while:

Having passed a day in Paris, I set out for La Grange (about forty English miles from hence). Imagine my dismay, on finding that General Fayette had crossed me on the road, having been summoned on business to Paris. His family (which comprises three generations,—sons and daughters, with their wives, husbands, and children, to the number, in all, of nineteen) received me with every possible demonstration of respect and regard, but were in despair at the absence of the General,—as I was in the same. I determined to return next day, to meet him here which I did. You will say again, " giddy goose," why did you set off for La Grange, without having written beforehand? There are reasons for everything, great philosopher. I had found a letter in Paris notifying the approach of some English friends, who were coming to see all the sights of this gay city, in the short space of ten days. Civility, therefore, constraining, for this period, my presence in Paris, I was obliged to seize the only day that remained to me before their arrival, for my journey into the country. Returning late at night, I sent a note, early the following morning, to General LaFayette, who soon answered it in person. Our meeting was scarcely without tears (at least on my side), and whether it was that this venerable

[1] *Biography*, pt. i, p. 16.

friend of human liberty saw in me what recalled to him some of the most pleasing recollections of his youth (I mean those connected with America), or whether it was only that he was touched by the sensibility which appeared at that moment in me, he evidently shared my emotion. He remained about an hour, and promised to return in the evening (he was engaged to dine with Constant). My sister, and all the rest of the family, escorted to Beaujours (a sort of Vauxhall) our English friends, while I remained to receive General LaFayette. We held an earnest tête-a-tête until after midnight. The main subject of our discourse was America, although we wandered into many episodes and digressions.

The enthusiasm and heart affection with which he spoke of our Utopia, the high respect he expressed for the character of its people, the ardent love of liberty which breathed through all his discourse, found, I need not say, an answering note of sympathy in me. He told me he had been particularly interested by the allusions in my work to the history of the American Revolution: " You have made me live those days over again." In speaking of the revolutionary army he exclaimed, " We were an army of brothers; we had all things in common, our pleasures, our pains, our money, and our poverty." At another time he observed, " No historian could render justice to the virtues of that army, no words could paint their sufferings, still less could they paint their fortitude, their disinterested, and sublime patriotism." He observed, also, upon the simple manners, warm hospitality, and pure morals of the American nation. " You have only rendered justice to them," he added smiling, " truly they are the best and happiest people in the world." I need scarcely say that we talked of you often, and that General LaFayette expressed the highest respect and admiration for the philosopher and philanthropist, to whom, as he observed, the whole human race owes a debt of gratitude.[1]

[1] Bentham, *Works*, vol. x, p. 526. La Grange was Lafayette's country seat near the village of Rosnay in the department of the Seine-et-Marne. Benjamin Constant was one of Lafayette's liberal colleagues in the Chamber of Deputies.

This was the beginning, Frances Wright tells us, " of a friendship of no ordinary character." [1]   A few weeks later she was asked to visit La Grange, the beautiful country home of the Lafayettes in the department of the Seine-et-Marne.   Here, during the next three years, she spent many happy months, devoting herself to writing a life of her hero, and often playing the part of his secretary and confidante. The friendship so happily begun in Paris ripened into real affection, upon her side almost to infatuation and upon his to a paternal tenderness delightful in its sympathy and feeling.   Perhaps one of her letters written while Lafayette was absent from La Grange will enable us the better to appreciate that friendship:

My beloved and honored friend—tomorrow I shall have a letter from you, n'est-ce-pas?  In truth I don't know what to make of myself without my paternal friend.   I look round for you, listen for your foot, and your voice twenty times a day, but I look and listen in vain.   You are in Paris and I am forty miles from it.   La Grange looks very lovely and all its inmates are kindness and goodness personified and my little Cam. is sweetly affectionate and so is Harriet also, but still I am alone without you.   Tell me when you expect to be released from that vile chamber and viler M. P. that I may know when to make my journey to Paris to return with you—unless indeed you should come for me—which would be very sweet but I fear very impossible.   And indeed I know not that I wish it—or that I ought to wish it for the journey would be long and fatiguing seeing that you could only stay one day. . . .

I do not ask if you sometimes think of me.   I know you do —very very often—even while you are looking at M. de Peyronnet.   My friend, my father, and if there be a word more expressive of love, and reverence, and adoration I would fain use it.   I am only half alive when away from you.   You see

[1] *Biography*, pt. i, p. 16.

you have spoilt me. In truth you have been and are too good
to me. You must continue to love me, however, in spite of
my little worthiness for in truth I love you very, very, much.
I have nothing as you see to tell you except this, and as you
knew it before was it worth the writing? I know you will
answer yes.

I put my arms round the neck of my paternal friend and
ask his blessing.

Little Cam's kind love and Harriet's and Fanny's but indeed
as for the last she has no more love to give you—you have
all her heart has to give.[1]

Her acquaintance with Lafayette, so delightful in itself,
soon brought her into contact with many interesting Frenchmen of the period, most of them of a liberal turn of mind.
At La Grange, among the immediate family, were George
Washington Lafayette, the son and devoted follower of the
General, of whom Miss Wright seems to have had a high
opinion, and Charles Philibert de Lasteyrie, the French publicist and philanthropist.[2] There also she met the celebrated
French painters, Ary and Henri Scheffer, the former at that
time the teacher of the children of the Duc d'Orleans. No
doubt there were many others unmentioned in her letters.
But not all her time was spent at La Grange. When the
Chambers opened she followed Lafayette to Paris there to
take up lodgings with her sister in the Rue St. Maur, or the
Rue de la Pépinière. Here she held a little *salon* of her own,
as Camilla Wright tells us in one of her letters to her cousin
James Mylne:

[1] Wright MSS. Frances Wright to General Lafayette, July 18, 1822.
M. de Peyronnet, Keeper of the Seals in the Villèle ministry, was a
strong reactionary. Camilla was often at La Grange with her sister,
and so occasionally was Harriet Garnett, whose family had removed to
France on the death of Mr. Garnett in 1820.

[2] Charles Philibert de Lasteyrie was the brother of Louis de Lasteyrie,
the husband of Lafayette's daughter Virginie.

If the sum of their [Mylne's friends] ambition be indeed to meet F. your letters will ensure them, and at our house they will chance to encounter such public characters as liberal foreigners would most wish to stare at. We have followed the prevailing custom here which I think is a good one of choosing one evening in the week for being at home to such of your friends and acquaintances as may feel disposed to assemble at your house, take a cup of tea and chat, and come and go without ceremony.[1]

In that *salon* one might have met such public characters as Jean Pierre Pagès, liberal and publicist, and the intimate friend of Lafayette, Benjamin Constant, one of the most prominent of the liberal deputies, Laffitte, the great banker and the financial backer of more than one of the conspiracies against the governments of Louis XVIII and Charles X, Augustin Thierry, author of *The History of the Conquest of England by the Normans,* and the Comte de Ségur, who was just then publishing his monograph on Napoleon in 1812. No doubt, also, many of Lafayette's colleagues of the *côté gauche* made their way to that little *salon,* for Miss Wright was from the first an interested follower of the activities of the parties in the Chamber of Deputies, and often attended the sittings at the invitation of her friend.

Indeed, as the friend of Lafayette, and an ardent enthusiast for political liberty, she found French politics intensely exciting, for, during the years 1821-1824, the liberal opposition to the government of Louis XVIII reached its height in a series of alarming, although eventually unsuccessful, conspiracies. The spirit of political toleration which the government had wisely inaugurated, after the White Terror of 1815-1816 had brought the ultra-royalists into disgrace, came to an abrupt end with the assassination of the Duc de Berry, the king's nephew, by a fanatical liberal

[1] Wright MSS. Camilla Wright to James Mylne, February 17, 1823.

in the spring of 1820. This unfortunate affair was immediately followed by the fall of the moderate royalist ministry, and the initiation by its successor of harsh reactionary measures. The opposition to the Bourbons which up to this time had confined itself largely to protests in the Chamber of Deputies now took a more dangerous turn. Encouraged by the success of the Spanish and Neapolitan revolts in the early months of 1820, and fearing that the infamous Carlsbad Decrees, which had been inflicted upon Germany in 1819, might be adopted by the French government, the French liberals believed that the time was ripe for subversive measures. The result was the hatching of a military conspiracy known as the plot of Vincennes, which, however, failed disastrously, as the government was forewarned. In this affair Lafayette took no active part, although cognizant of the plans of the conspirators. Had they succeeded he would probably have been made the head of the provisional government.

Though the collapse of this revolutionary effort, and the failure of the uprisings in Naples and Piedmont temporarily discouraged the liberals, they were ready for a fresh effort in the fall and winter of 1821-1822, when the chance of success looked much brighter. For one thing they now had the support of the widespread organization of the Carbonari. The secret society of the Carbonari (charcoal burners) had first appeared in Italy, where it had already been responsible for the liberal movements in Naples and Piedmont. In 1821 lodges of the society were established in France, where they rapidly increased in numbers and in size, attracting chiefly the politically disaffected among the middle classes. Although initiated by obscure men, the society soon included within its lodges many of the more prominent liberals, and among those to be found in the supreme lodge were the two Lafayettes. The object of this secret organization in France

was the expulsion of the Bourbons, and the setting up of a
provisional government which would allow the people to
decide for themselves the type of rule they really wanted.
The historian Lamartine in his *Histoire de la Restauration*
intimates that Lafayette was the soul of the society, but this
remains uncertain. Certainly, however, his share in its
activities was large. Besides the advantage derived from
this powerful secret organization the liberals believed that
the contemporary political situation favored their plans.
Under the modified electoral law of 1820 the subsequent
elections had given the royalists a comfortable majority in
the Chamber, but the ultras were not satisfied with the for-
eign policy of the Duc de Richelieu, feeling that not enough
was being done for the cause of legitimacy in the disaffected states of Europe. The liberals too were opposed to
it on the ground that too little was being done to support
liberalism abroad, and on the slender basis of their general
opposition the extremes combined against the government.
The liberal leaders accepted this strange alliance the more
readily, as, in view of the conspiracy at that moment maturing, it was hoped that the triumph of ultra-reaction would
serve to alarm the country and dispose the people to look
with favor upon revolution. The hopes of the coalition were
realized; the ministry fell, and a still more reactionary one
took its place headed by M. de Villèle.[1] Of this triumph
of reaction Frances Wright was an interested observer, and
has left us a letter, written to Bentham, commenting upon
the change of ministry:

[1] Lamartine, A. de, *Histoire de la Restauration*, 8 vols., Paris, 1851-
1852. See also for this period in French politics: Maurin, Albert, *Histoire de la Chute des Bourbons*, 6 vols., Paris, 1849-1852; Charavay,
Étienne, *Le Général LaFayette*, Paris, 1898; *Annuaire Historique Universel*, Paris, 1818-1824; Hall, J. R., *The Bourbon Restoration*, London,
1909.

We went yesterday for the first time to the Chambre des Dé-
putés and saw the entrance of the new ministers drawn from
the ultra benches. The ultras have had a hard fight for the
victory. There has been for the last three weeks a most
amusing union of votes between the extrême droite and extrême gauche. Indeed, all parties seem agreed in flouting the
government however different their ground of quarrel. The
King, finding it impossible to carry anything, his speech cen-
sured by the C[hambre], and his bills thrown out—struck his
colors three days since and gave to Monsieur, the Comte
d'Artois, the nomination of the ministers upon which occasion
he is reported to have said, " Je ne suis pas fâché de cette
occasion assez curieuse de voir de mon vivant comme les
choses se passeront après ma mort."

When the present Boeotian race of ministers made their first
bow to the King—after some gracious speeches (which the
cunning old gentleman can always say to those he dislikes),
he nodded his head and cried " macte animo."

" Le Roi nous a très bien reçu," said one of the party as they
left the presence.

" Comment bien reçu," exclaimed the Duc de Bellune.
" Marchez animaux. Je ne trouvais rien de bien poli là." [1]

But Miss Wright could not have attended the sessions of
the Chamber of Deputies many times in December of 1821
at the invitation of Lafayette, for about the twentieth of
the month he left Paris for La Grange, ostensibly to be
there on the anniversary of the death of his wife, the
twenty-fourth, but also to allay the suspicions of the police
and prepare for the part he was to play in a Carbonari conspiracy.[2] How much Frances Wright knew of his real

---

[1] Wright MSS. Frances Wright to Jeremy Bentham. No date given,
but from internal evidence it would appear to have been written on
December 15, 1821, three days after the King had struck his colors on
December 12, 1821. The Duc de Bellune is perhaps better known as
Marshal Victor. At this time he was Minister of War

[2] Charavay, *Le Général La Fayette*, p. 422.

object in leaving Paris her letters do not inform us, as it would have been scarcely safe to have intrusted even veiled hints in the mails. She tells us in her autobiography, however, that she possessed " his most intimate private and personal confidence," and so it would seem probable that she did know somewhat of the Carbonari plans.[1] Although the following letter written just after his departure does not throw light upon the adventure on which her friend was now embarked, it is of some interest from the attendant circumstances :

After a sleepless night your note did me good, my most valued and revered friend. I rose half expecting to receive a little word from you, half intending to address one to you, but then I reasoned with myself that you might set off early and that my messenger might not find you, and that the same cause might prevent your sending one to me. While hesitating what to do and chiding myself into composure, your parcel was brought to me.

I like to think of you at La Grange, my excellent friend— although it deprives me of your society. You have need of a few days repose after all your fatigues in this city. I am indeed unreasonable enough to lament that I do not pass them with you and to envy those who enjoy the good that is denied to me. I am anxious to hear how you made out your journey and how you found all the dear inmates of the chateau. What sweet hours I have passed in those walls! I must pass many more there, my good friend—and (receive the threat for good and true) shall pass many more there. Hitherto my life has had so much of bitterness in it that I am sure there must be now much good in store for me and for all those connected with me. Much therefore for you, my excellent friend. May heaven grant it—grant every wish of your heart. And would not all the human race echo the prayer. Yes—for all the human race would be the gainer.[2]

[1] *Biography*, pt. i, p. 16.
[2] Wright MSS. Frances Wright to General Lafayette, December 27, 1821.

This letter could scarcely have reached the General at La Grange, however, for on Tuesday, the twenty-fifth, he had left the chateau, accompanied by his son George Washington Lafayette and his servant Bastien, and on the evening of the twenty-seventh, when the above letter was written, he was far on the road to Belfort, where, as one of the leaders of the French Carbonari, he was to take part in the opening scene of a long planned insurrection. The plans of the conspirators called for the initial outbreak among the garrison at Belfort on the night of January first, to be followed by similar risings in other garrison towns, and, if successful, the establishing of a provisional government composed of the liberal deputies Lafayette, Koechlin, and Voyer d'Argenson. Unfortunately for the plotters the unusual activity among the troops quartered at Belfort aroused the distrust of some of the officers, and, guessing at the truth, the gates were ordered shut and all suspicious persons arrested. In the confusion the leaders escaped, and two of them hastened to meet the approaching Lafayette to tell him that all was lost. He turned back, and to deceive the police went immediately to Grey, the home of M. Martin, a liberal colleague and ex-deputy from the Haute-Saône. A few days later he returned to La Grange, and soon after was again in his place on the *côté gauche* in the Chamber of Deputies, together with the other liberal deputies who had been implicated in the plot, apparently perfectly secure, thanks to the loyalty of his fellow Carbonari.[1]

About a month after the Belfort affair Miss Wright left Paris for London upon one of the longer of her occasional visits. This visit in the spring of 1822 was made partly with a view to overseeing the publication of several of her literary works, but more particularly for the carrying out

[1] Charavay, p. 422; Lamartine, *Histoire de la Restauration*, vol. vii, p. 31; Hall, *The Bourbon Restoration*, pp. 299-300.

of certain missions entrusted to her care by Lafayette.[1] Just what the nature of her " friend's business " was she does not tell us, for her letters traveled to and fro in the portfolio of the French Minister Chateaubriand, and many things could only be hinted at, or suggested, by remarks totally unintelligible to the present-day reader. But she does intimate that a good part of her activities in London were in connection with the political refugees who had fled from France following the discovery and failure of the various plots in the years 1820 and 1821.

It was a curious mixture of society in which Miss Wright moved while in London. On the one hand there were the English liberals with whom she came in contact through her friendship with Bentham and her residence in his home: James Mill, already mentioned as one of the Bentham circle; Major John Cartwright, the " Father of Reform," and founder of the Hampden Clubs which had so alarmed the government by their political activities in 1816; Joseph Hume, one of the few liberals in the House of Commons, and famous for his emphasis upon financial " retrenchment ", a word which he added to the radical program; Mr. Coulson, the editor of the *London Traveller*; the poet Campbell, and others—while at the same time we find her in close touch with the political refugees who had flocked to London from all over western Europe, and, strangely enough, were tolerated by the government in spite of the fact that by the close of the year 1820 Tory reaction in England was triumphant, and the native radical leaders imprisoned, exiled, or in hiding.[2] Indeed, English apathy, in general, to the

A second edition of her *Views of Society and Manners in America*, and a first English edition of *Altorf*. She was also bringing out *A Few Days in Athens*.

[2] All of these are mentioned in her letters to Lafayette written during February and March, 1822.

sacred cause of liberty, whether at home or abroad, did not please Miss Wright:

The game now cannot be won by long-headed calculators: we want hands of steel and hearts of flame. But all countries are richer in these than this dull England. My Socrates has just been all but cursing it. Truly it makes the blood boil as one walks among a nation ground to the earth with oppression until it be too spiritless even to groan beneath the burden. Men here hug their chains, with you they shake them—the despised Spaniards break them. Nothing is talked of here but the state of the Treasury.[1]

After reading this letter it is not hard to decide which group Miss Wright found to be the most stimulating and interesting. In the following letter she comments upon her activities, and upon the masculine independence of character which enabled her to be of such material assistance to her friend:

It is not four hours since I sealed my last letter to you; since which time I have been walking far and wide in this overgrown city, and as I had before made a quick march of three miles I am privileged to sit down in an arm chair and feel myself tired. Among other performances I have paid this day no less than three visits to the war office. What to do there, you will say? Not to enquire into the army expenses, nor to sue for a commission, but only to see a gentleman upon the subject of my friend's business. An old saw has it that the third time brings luck: and so I found, for I found my man. I dare say you marvel sometimes at my independent way of walking through the world just as if nature had made me of your sex instead of poor Eve's. Trust me, my beloved friend, the mind has no sex but what habit and education give it, and I who was thrown in infancy upon the world like a wreck upon the waters have learned, as well to struggle with the elements as any male child of Adam. Dearly valued friend, I find myself alone at the fireplace in the house of my good old Socrates where I returned this morning, and which I shall quit again to-morrow. I am too tired to do anything useful and therefore it is that I am talking nonsense to you. I wish I had your second letter. I know there is one on the road. Methinks I would have one every day, and had I the arranging of the mails and portfolios it should be so. But you will have no time to listen to this idle chattering. Farewell my— friend. Take care of yourself. Think of me sometimes— love me always, and drive the côté gauche out of the Chambre.[1]

Perhaps the most interesting of the revolutionists whom Miss Wright met in London was the hero of the recent unsuccessful liberal movement in Naples, General Guglielmo Pepe. Of Pepe she apparently saw considerable, and while admiring his courage and spirit she was not so favorably impressed with his statesmanship. He is described in one of her letters to Lafayette as " a fine warm hearted patriot but a very crude legislator . . . . I doubt if the head be as deep as the heart is warm, but then it is not every country that is blessed with a Lafayette . . . . Oh, would to Heaven we could x you by 12, and then by the square of 12, and then by the cube of the square, and spread you abroad among the nations of the earth." [2]   She found indeed that the political ideas of many of the revolutionists were very vague and uncertain. With another of these " hands of steel and hearts of flame " she appears to have fallen in love, a not unnatural outcome of her admiration and enthusiasm for the cause they represented. Unfortunately, we know little of the hero of this affair, except

[1] *Ibid.*, February 11, 1822. The last sentence refers to a suggestion that the liberal deputies leave the Chamber of Deputies in a body, as a protest against the reactionary measures of the government..

[2] *Ibid.*, February 18, 1822.

that he was, perhaps, one of General Pepe's aides, and that later he left London to join the cause of revolution in the Spanish peninsula.[1]

But, even in the midst of the excitement in London, her thoughts were often in Paris with her friend, who appears to have been having troubles of his own with his brother Carbonari:

It is very painful to me to be absent from my best friend in these threatening times. I have many disquieting thoughts which the sight of your hand-writing alone dissipates. And yet I like not all that you hint to me. " Ces contrariétés d'intérieur," are calculated to pain your heart—so kind, so heavenly tempered as it is, more perhaps than any other species of vexation. And now you have not your young friend to soothe and cheer you after the vexations of the day. Did she not cheer you? Yes, I am sure she did. But still she feels with her good friend though she cannot tell him so—yes, and still she is with him tho' he cannot see her—Indeed I love you dearly, you never had a child that loved you more tenderly, never a friend who felt your interests to be more her own.[2]

Early in April she returned to Paris, and soon afterward went with her sister Camilla and her friend Harriet Garnett to La Grange for a six-months visit. Here she worked upon a life of General Lafayette which she had laid out as a sacred task, and followed with interest and concern the course of contemporary European politics.[3] In France,

[1] Wright MSS. Of this incident we know only through a few verses of mediocre poetry and some references, half apologetic, in her correspondence with Lafayette.

[2] Wright MSS. Frances Wright to General Lafayette, February (?), 1822.

[3] The uncompleted manuscript of this work still exists among the Wright MSS.

Carbonarism, as a serious menace to the stability of the government, had about run its race. During the spring the government had greatly strengthened its position by meeting successfully the military plots at Saumur, La Rochelle, and Colmar, and by apprehending a number of the conspirators, the most prominent being the Napoleonic general, Berton. In carrying the trials of these men to a successful conclusion, and executing the death penalty upon eleven of them, the government effectually crushed the Carbonari movement, discredited it before the nation, and caused the rank and file of the society to lose faith in the ability of its leaders. The fate of General Berton, the hapless leader of the futile attempt at Saumur, particularly aroused the sympathy of Miss Wright. "Poor Berton," she wrote to Lafayette, who was then in Paris, where with the other liberal deputies in the Chamber he was meeting with defiance and denial the open accusations of complicity in the conspiracies, and demanding investigations which the government would not concede, "would to Heaven there were any means of rescuing him from the clutches of those monsters."[1]  But Lafayette and his fellow Carbonari were helpless, and Berton went to his death, sending, as one of his last acts, his star of the Legion of Honor to Lafayette. The shock to the General's young guest remained long in her memory, and finally found expression in verse:

> Cold is the heart which beat beneath thee, star
>   Of Gallic honor! Cold, forever cold!
> Oh! had the blood flowed in the tide of war
>   Which stains thy motto, and thy rays of gold!
>
> .   .   .   .
>
> And there are those who dare blaspheme his name,
>   And call him Traitor whom a Traitor sold,
> Speak! answer for the dead, thou star of fame!
>   "Honor and country"—Berton's life is told.
>
> .   .   .   .

[1] Wright MSS. Frances Wright to General Lafayette, June, 1822.

Sleep on that heart as on a holy shrine
Where liberty in secret hoards her flame
Where graved in characters more deep than thine
The sons of fame behold their country's name.[1]

The disastrous collapse of Carbonarism, followed by the unsuccessful opposition to the intervention of France in the internal affairs of Spain in the year 1823, proved death blows to French liberalism. In the elections of 1824 but nineteen liberal deputies were returned, and among the defeated were the two Lafayettes. More than twenty years afterward, when writing her autobiography, Frances Wright summed up the causes of the liberal failure as they then appeared to her:

Though familiar with all the movements of the revolutionary party, and deeply interested in the fate of leading individuals, she had but seldom anticipated success to efforts of which the object appeared to her ill-defined, and those who pursued it far from agreed among themselves. The general want of political knowledge and political experience, the frequent vanity and frivolity of individuals, the confidence placed in more than suspicious characters, the absurd drawing-room intrigues and fashionable conspirators, contrasted strangely and painfully, though sometimes almost ludicrously, with the serious character of a struggle in which human lives, and often those of the young and the chivalrous, were the stakes of the game.[2]

Discredited for his share in the military conspiracies, defeated in the elections for the Chamber in his own constituency, and approaching bankruptcy, it was probably with relief and pleasure that Lafayette accepted the invitation of the Congress and President of the United States to visit

[1] *Free Enquirer*, December 5, 1829. Miss Wright states that this poem was written upon the presentation of the cross to General Lafayette at La Grange.

[2] *Biography*, pt. i, p. 18.

that country in the summer of 1824.[1]  A more personal
reason for welcoming the proposed visit was, perhaps, the
somewhat mysterious crisis which had arisen in the Lafayette
family in consequence of the General's intimate friendship
with Miss Wright.  Led by the paternal affection for " ma
bien aimée, adorée Fanny, la tendre fille de mon choix" [2] with
which the General returned her passionate devotion, Frances
Wright seems to have hoped to become his adopted
daughter.  To such a step the family of Lafayette was
strongly opposed, and the position which Miss Wright occupied at La Grange, became, in the spring of 1824, an
impossible one.  An illness of the General's which followed
this crisis,[3] however, seems to have caused the family to
seek a reconciliation, and even to urge Miss Wright to make
the visit to America with him.  Of this we are told in a
letter from Frances to Camilla, who was then in Whitburn.

Today's post has brought me letters from my friend Virginie
and our dear and esteemed M[e]. Charles.  Their contents
seem to open again a prospect of better accommodation and
reconciliation than I had thought possible, and I must state
to my Camilla and our two mothers as far as can be done by
letter and that hastily too, what has passed and how things
stand.  The explanations that have taken place between our
friend and his family (of which only the general result has
yet reached me, the full details coming by another conveyance

---

[1] That Lafayette was in financial straits at this time, I gather from
Vincent Nolte, *Fifty Years in Both Hemispheres*, New York, 1854, pp.
307-308.  Nolte states that in the summer of 1824 Lafayette desired to
visit the United States but had no money.  His debts in France amounted
to one hundred thousand francs.  Not wishing to mortgage La Grange
he asked Nolte to secure an advance for him from the Barings in London.
As the Barings refused the loan, Nolte says that he interested the American Minister in Paris, James Brown.  How the  matter was finally
settled he did not know.

[2] Wright MSS. Lafayette to Frances Wright, April 26, 1824.

[3] *Ibid.*  Francis to Camilla, May 24, 1824.

than the post) have led to much contrition and a warmly
expressed desire that we should be with our friend, much regret also at my having left Paris without having seen them.
M<sup>e</sup>. Charles adds [secret] admiration of my conduct in this
instance, however, as in others. Of this I know not. I believe, however, the contrition to be sincere, and the mortifica-
tion deep. It appears that there have been mischief makers
and busy bodies at work—of whom too we know little, perhaps nothing. Meddling politicians jealous of my supposed
influence who had asserted to the son that nothing was done
or said without my approbation, etc., and that the family was
held in leading strings—silly and ill-natured women who supposed intentions of another nature and the Lord knows what.
All this operating upon little minds and petty jealousies produced all and more than we saw. Fully convinced that they
have wounded the feelings and marred the happiness of our
friend they are now as anxious to cement the tie as they were
before to break it, and will therefore form no impediment but
the contrary to any plan we may decide on. It now remains to be seen what we may decide on. Our friend's coun-
sellors in Paris urge our making the voyage, but to humor the
folly of those who are supposed to misinterpret things to
make it separately. To this I have replied in a letter which
goes by the return post. I believe I had better quote (I
must observe that the proposal made by my friend does not
originate with him and that he, I doubt secretly, concurs with
it). After stating minor objections I continue thus, " There
is yet another consideration which weighs with me much more.
I am at Havre. I have been in France, and that in a private
and somewhat singular manner, that is to say if I immediately
go away again. I do not embark with you. Why? Because we are conscious of having excited justly or unjustly
(and in these cases the world puts always the worst interpretation) the ill nature of the public or of individuals. Therefore as if admitting the truth or at least the importance of such
remarks we adopt an underhand mode of doing what we desire. My honest friend, I need not enter into details to ex-

plain my idea. You will seize it, and then I may add that not only does my character repugn from a covert way of proceeding but that I think such a way of proceeding totally inconsistent with yours, liable to cover you with reproach and both parties—if I dared use the word as applied to one—with ridicule. No one will believe that Frances and Camilla will go to America at this time merely to go there. Our intimate connection is too well and universally known in both hemispheres. No, my honest friend, should I give an opinion, it is this. If our union is to continue, it can only do so with honor to you and without prejudice to us by your assuming openly and avowedly the air and character of a protector. You must be our father not in a doubtful and covert way but in an open and manly one. I blush, my honest friend, at this seeming arrogance—but it is not to you but rather to our mutual friends and to your family that I address these arguments. Forgive me then if I say that if you and yours approve I will call my Camilla to me. I will place her under your protection—we will assume together the place of your children—we will call you father—we will be with you as children, and dispising and confronting slanders which thus met in the face will slink away—we will go, and stay, and return with you. If not this, honest friend, late as it is to renounce engagements which my heart will ever acknowledge to be more sacred than any ever made on earth—we must part. Our position otherwise would be embarrassing, painful, doubtful, and even absurd. I foresee also that even this cruel alternative of relinquishing what our peace of mind requires will also seem to sanction silly gossip. It will be said that I left you because I dared not stay, that your family objected or that we have quarrelled. Reflect on this—consult with Pages to whom I shall explain my ideas also, and give me your answer." You see, my beloved Camilla, how I have ventured to dispose of you. Our London friend, good and kind as he is, would doubtless censure me, but I know your generous heart better than he does and that in venturing to consider you as part of myself I shall best consult your wishes. Write to me immediately

what you think. If you and our mothers think and feel with
me. . . . Perhaps you should now set out for London. . . .
There you will be on the spot to join me here or for me to
join you there according to what may be decided.[1]

Apparently the family of Lafayette continued their soli-
citations that she should go to America, for she wrote
again to Camilla a few days later:

I believe the family perfectly repentant—nay full of remorse
so far as regards the father—as regards me I care not to imagine what their feelings may be, but none good doubtless.
They desire sincerely our going to America, but perhaps have
real or pretended scruples as to our accompanying him—perhaps also to avoid an open avowal of an adoption and effecting
of that complete union which appears to me alone consistent
with dignity or comfort.[2]

Camilla Wright, in a letter to her cousin James Mylne,
who was then at Oxford, tells us of the outcome of this
crisis in the affairs of Frances and the General. Before
Lafayette's departure from Havre, on the thirteenth of July,
the sisters visited La Grange at the earnest request of the
family, and there it was decided that they should go to
America, although it was too late for them to go by the
same vessel:

When I parted from you in London, my dear James, it was
my intention to have written to you soon after my arrival at
Havre had not a variety of unforeseen events arisen to interfere with this and many other plans for the future. I had

[1] *Ibid.* Frances to Camilla, June 10, 1824. Virginie was Lafayette's
daughter. Me. Charles was probably Madame Charles de Lasteyrie. By
"our two mothers" Frances referred to Mrs. Millar and her sister Miss
Cullen. "Our London friend" may have been Bentham.

[2] *Ibid.* Francis to Camilla, June 14, 1824. It is to be regretted that our
knowledge of this crisis comes only from Miss Wright's letters. Whether
Lafayette ever considered such an adoption as Miss Wright hoped for
there is not sufficient evidence to determine.

hardly time to recover from the fatigue of my rapid journey
from the North of England when we received letters from
our paternal friend General Lafayette that his visit to America
was definitely fixed for the fifteenth of the month and en-
treating us to come to Paris and meet him in the midst of his
family previous to his departure.    On our arrival we found
a plan which we had almost abandoned pressed upon us with
such increased earnestness both by him and his family that
we would accompany him in his voyage to America that tho'
time no longer admitted of our making the voyage together we consented to hasten our arrangements so as to follow him if possible by the first of next month.    This we
now expect to accomplish and have indeed written to our
friends the Garnetts to secure our passage for that day in one
of the regular sailing packets established on the same plan and
conducted in a similar manner with those at Liverpool.    Much
as I dislike the thought of another voyage across the ocean to
which experience has only tended to increase my aversion I
cannot but anticipate much satisfaction from witnessing the
reception of this veteran of American and European liberty
by a people who have never ceased to evince the most heart-
felt gratitude for his services and are at the present moment
vying with each other how best to testify their love and veneration for his presence and character.

As his absence will certainly not exceed a twelve month our
parting from our European friends will merely be temporary
and I hope you, my dear James, will not allow the Atlantic to
interfere with our correspondence—by addressing your letters
to our friend Charles Wilkes, Esq. of New York they will be
sure at all times to find us. . . . You have probably seen in the
papers the very flattering reception of General Lafayette by the
very respectable body of merchants at Havre who as many as
could procure horses, about sixty in number, went forward several miles into the country to meet and escort him into the town
where the streets and walls were crowded with inhabitants
who received him with cries of " Vive Lafayette." The military and gens d'armerie in vain interfered to repress their ardor

and the only means they could devise for venting their spleen
was by shutting the gates on the gentlemen who had gone
forth to meet him and refusing them entrance for the space
of several hours. We shall pass two days longer with the
family here and leave Paris for Havre on Sunday morning.[1]

A few days later Camilla wrote to her cousin from Havre:

We arrived here yesterday, my dear James, and I am already
so heavily engaged in preparations for our voyage that I have
only time to tell you our passage is engaged for the first
on the London, Captain Moran, which is not in the regular
line of packets established between this and New York but is
an equally good ship with excellent accommodations and has
the advantage of being cheaper for each of us—only twenty-
four pounds.[2]

On the sixteenth of August the good ship " Cadmus,"
Captain Allyn, safely brought General Lafayette and his
party into the port of New York. After four delightful
days in the city he journeyed north through the New England states, returning to New York early in September,
where a great celebration in his honor had been planned at
Castle Garden. Of the mysterious postponement of that
festivity, and of the arrival of the Wrights and their reception, we will let Camilla tell us in another of her letters

[1] *Ibid.* Camilla to James Mylne, La Grange, July 20, 1824. It will be
noticed that Camilla speaks of a return to Europe within a year. There
is some evidence, however, that Frances had contemplated settling in the
United States if the General decided to remain there. Vincent Nolte, pp.
308-309, states that in the summer of 1824 he met the Wright sisters at the
request of Lafayette, and that they turned over to him one hundred and
twenty thousand francs for investment in Louisiana. Why they should
have wished to place so heavy an investment in the United States, just at
this time, is not wholly clear, unless the explanation lies in the following
note, added by Frances to a letter from Harriet Garnett to Camilla, June 2,
1824. In this note she says, " I have in part engaged in the event of his
[Lafayette] being constrained to remain in that country, and of his son's
return that we should join him."

[2] *Ibid.*, Camilla to James Mylne, Havre, July 28, 1824.

to her cousin James Mylne.[1]  Unfortunately, Frances' own letter to Professor Mylne, which Camilla mentions and which described these events, is missing from the Wright manuscript collection:

My time has been so fully occupied since my arrival in this city I have not found the moments to acquaint you, my dear James, with our safety after a tedious passage of forty days during the greater part of which time I suffered most severely from sea sickness and lost many pounds of flesh in consequence. Our reception by Mr. Wilkes and his family was all that was kind and affectionate, and as they would not hear of our going into lodgings and we could not conveniently leave the city even for the near neighborhood of their summer quarters we acceded to Mrs. Colden's (the mother-in-law of our friend Nancy Wilkes) kind request that we become her guests.  The afternoon of our arrival General Lafayette was engaged with a public dinner and the Theatre in the evening so that he could not come to us till past midnight.  He had been most anxiously awaiting our arrival for some days that we might be present at the grand festivity to be given in his honor by the city, and he had thro' various ways procured its delay and thus afforded us one of the most splendid and gratifying sights I ever before witnessed.  As I have no time to attempt a description I must refer you to that given at length by Frances to your father who she thought might like to have some notion of the reception of our valued friend by this generous people which has indeed been grand and touching in the extreme, and when we reflect that all they have done and are yet to do is the spontaneous effort of their own free will, without even the possibility of interference on the part of the government of the country his triumphs assume a character unsurpassed in history.  Dinners, balls, and fêtes everywhere await him—multi-

[1] *New York Evening Post*, September 8, 1824. The *Post* states that the fête planned for the tenth would have to be postponed until the thirteenth, as the weather had prevented the necessary preparations from being made.  Castle Garden is now the aquarium in Battery Park.

tudes crowd around him and press upon his steps: proudly
happy those who can say they have taken his hand while many
of the lower order of citizens are seen to approach him with
reverence and laying their hand on his arm or the skirts of
his coat, retire with an air of satisfaction and delight.  His
reception in this city is said by those who witnessed it to have
been grand and beautiful in the extreme—we hope shortly to
be present at that prepared for him in Philadelphia where
thirty thousand militia are said to be already assembled to receive him with military honors.  He left this city on his
journey thither yesterday and intends devoting three days to
the Jerseys where in each town thro' which he passes military
and civic honors are prepared for his reception.  We leave
this tomorrow morning for Philadelphia where we shall arrive
the same evening, lodgings having been already secured for us
by Mrs. Lewis—the daughter of Mrs. Washintgon by her first
marriage and once a celebrated toast in Virginia—as the lovely
Nellie Custis.

From Philadelphia we shall proceed to Baltimore, Washington, and so on to Yorktown where a fête is prepared for
the hero of the day that is to last for three days, and where the
taking of Lord Cornwallis [in] which he bore a conspicuous
part is to be acted over again.  You will thus readily believe our
time for some months to come will be very little at our own
disposal—nor can you reasonably marvel if I prove a very
tardy correspondent. . . .

Since our return from an excursion up the North River
. . . we have been spending a quiet week at Greenwich with
Mr .Wilkes and his family, and I have already derived so much
benefit from the care and kindness of my friends here, all
the bad effects of my sea voyage have disappeared.[1]

[1] Wright MSS, Camilla Wright to James Mylne, September, 1824.
The *New York Evening Post* of Saturday, September 11, 1824, reports
the ship "London," Captain Moran, in the lower harbor.  From Camilla's
letter it is evident that the sisters came up to the city in a small boat that
same afternoon.  On that afternoon Lafayette attended a banquet given
in his honor by the Frenchmen of New York, and then went to the
theater where he remained until the close of the performance.  This
would fit in with Camilla's account of his late arrival at the Colden home.

Following a journey up the Hudson to Albany and Troy, upon which, it would seem from Camilla's letter, the sisters accompanied him, General Lafayette left New York for the Yorktown peninsula, where the pageant mentioned by Camilla was in preparation.  Two days later Frances and Camilla followed him, overtaking his party in Philadelphia.  Here the sisters witnessed the celebration and attended the functions in honor of the General, at one of which that indefatigable diarist John Quincy Adams mentions seeing them.[1] From Philadelphia they went with Lafayette through Baltimore and Washington, and so on to the fête at Yorktown. Upon leaving Yorktown Lafayette proceeded to Monticello, the home of his old friend Thomas Jefferson.  Jefferson also seems to have anticipated the visit of Miss Wright, whom he had not as yet met, but in whose work he had taken considerable interest.  *Altorf* he had read with pleasure, and Lafayette himself had sent him the *Views of Society and Manners in America* and *A Few Days in Athens*.[2]  In the following note to Lafayette he welcomed Miss Wright to Monticello:

You mention the return of Miss Wright to America, accompanied by her sister; but do not say what her stay is to be, nor what her course.  Should it lead her to a visit of our University, which, in its architecture only, is as yet an object, herself and her companion will nowhere find a welcome more hearty than with Mrs. Randolph, and all the inhabitants of Monticello.  This Athenaeum of our country, in embryo, is as yet but a promise; and not in a state to recall the recollections of Athens.  But everything has its beginning, its growth, and end; and who knows with what future delicious morsels of

[1] Adams, John Quincy, *Memoirs,* Philadelphia, 1874-1877, vol. vi, p. 421. According to Adams, this was at General Cadwallader's..

[2] Jefferson, Thomas, *Writings,* edited by P. L. Ford, 10 vols., New York, 1892-1899, vol. x, p. 282.  Jefferson to Lafayette, Monticello, November 4, 1823.

philosophy, and by what future Miss Wright raked from its ruins, the world may, some day, be gratified and instructed.[1]

Unfortunately, Frances Wright has left us no record of the visit paid to the homes of Jefferson and Madison at this time,[2] but from the account given by Lafayette's secretary Levasseur, in his *Lafayette en Amérique,* we know that many interesting hours were spent in the discussion of political and other questions. It was in their talks on Southern slavery that Miss Wright found the inspiration for the experiment in gradual emancipation, which she carried out at Nashoba during the next four years, and of which we shall have more to say in the following chapter.

They were back in Washington again for the opening of the second session of the eighteenth Congress, and a few days later Frances and Camilla were among those present when Lafayette was formally received by the Senate:

General Lafayette was received by the Senate today [observed the *Washington Gazette*] in the most distinguished manner. The Senate Chamber was crowded on the occasion. Many ladies were present; among whom we noticed the lady of General Jackson and others of the city and the celebrated English authoress Miss Wright and her sister. General Lafayette's Son and Secretary accompanied him.[3]

This reception was followed a few weeks afterward by a congressional grant of two hundred thousand dollars in money and a township of land to the old hero of the Revolution, in appreciation of his services to the United States.

During the winter of 1824-1825, which General Lafayette spent in the city of Washington, Miss Wright appears to

[1] Jefferson, Thomas, *Writings,* edited by H. A. Washington, 9 vols., Washington, 1853-1854, vol. vii, p. 379.

[2] For Miss Wright's visit to Montpelier, Madison's home, see Madison, James, *Writings,* edited by Gaillard Hunt, vol. ix, pp. 209-210.

[3] *Washington Gazette,* December 9, 1824.

have enjoyed both the social and political life of the capital. Adams met her again at one of Mrs. Adams' alternate Tuesday evening parties, when the General was also present. " Miss Wright," he says, " told me that she had seen a friend of mine in London, who had often spoken of me— Mr. Jeremy Bentham." [1] At the house where Lafayette boarded she had the opportunity of meeting General Jackson and his wife, and Jackson's friend, General Sam Houston, later the hero of the Texan revolution. She was also much at the capitol, observing with interest the procedure of the American Congress, and comparing it, not improbably, with that of the French Chamber of Deputies. " They [the sisters] very frequently attended the debates, and the most distinguished members were always crowding round them. For this unwonted gallantry they apologized to their beautiful countrywomen by saying that if they took an equal interest in the debates, the galleries would always be thronged by the members." [2]

On the twenty-third of February, 1825, General Lafayette left Washington for his trip through the Southern states. For a short time Frances and Camilla remained in Washington, after which they started west to rejoin their friend, visiting on their way the Rappite communities at Economie, Pennsylvania, and Harmonie, Indiana, the latter village having been recently purchased by the English philanthropist, Robert Owen, for the site of his proposed communistic experiment. After a brief trip to the English settlement at Albion, Illinois, established by Morris Birkbeck, the sisters proceeded down the Mississippi to meet Lafayette at New Orleans. Tradition has it that this journey was made on a flatboat.

[1] Adams, *Memoirs*, vol. vi, p. 443.

[2] Trollope, Frances Milton, *Domestic Manners of the Americans*. vol. ii, p. 18.

Whether Miss Wright and her sister came up the river in Lafayette's party we do not know. There is a local story that she landed at Memphis, and visited with the General the site of her future social experiment at Nashoba, near Memphis, but this seems improbable. From this point Miss Wright's movements are not very clear, although there is no reason to believe that she did not remain in close touch with the General until the first of August, when he retired to the White House at the invitation of President Adams, there to rest until his departure for France.[1] During the closing days of his visit to the United States Miss Wright was not with him, nor was she present when he finally left for home.

Why she should have failed to bid farewell to her friend seems rather hard to comprehend. During the last month of his stay we know that she was intensely absorbed with a new enthusiasm, the solution of the American slave problem, and that, in view of an experiment in gradual emancipation which she planned, and in which Lafayette, Jefferson, and Madison were all much interested, she was busily engaged in observing community methods at Economie, the Rappite settlement in western Pennsylvania, and in consult-

[1] That they were with Lafayette at the time of the Bunker Hill celebration in Boston, in 1825, would seem to be indicated by the following comment of the Duke of Saxe-Weimar, who arrived in Boston about a month after that event. "In these peregrinations about Boston I made inquiries after Miss Wright who some years ago published letters on America which excited attention in Europe as well as in America. I was told that this lady with her sister, unattended by a male protector, had roved about the country, in steamboats and stages, that she constantly tagged about after General Lafayette, and whenever the General arrived at any place, Miss Wright was sure to follow the next day; as but little notice had been taken of this lady in Boston, a literary attack was expected from her pen. She is no longer young, and is of tall stature and masculine manners. In general her letters are not much esteemed, and the flattering terms in which she speaks of Americans and all their institutions are regarded as overstrained." Bernard, Duke of Saxe-Weimar Eisenach, *Travels through North America during the Years 1825 and 1826*, 2 vols., Philadelphia, 1829, vol. i, pp. 41-42.

ing with Benjamin Lundy, the well known editor of the
*Genius of Universal Emancipation,* in Baltimore. But it
may not have been wholly the new interest which kept her
away. Perhaps both desired to avoid a painful parting,
especially as we know from a letter written by Lafayette
some months later that there had been an unhappy interview while they were in Philadelphia. Just what was discussed we are not told, but it does not seem improbable that
Miss Wright was then forced to give up whatever hopes
she still had of a legal adoption.[1] If such was the case, it
is not altogether surprising that she should have decided to
remain in America, for to return to France and La Grange
would have been manifestly impossible. It must not be
supposed, however, that with Lafayette's departure his interest in Frances and Camilla Wright came to an end. Indeed, he appears to have been a better correspondent than
was Frances, and there exist many of his letters indicating
his interest in the experiment at Nashoba, and in the wel-
fare of the two sisters.[2]

[1] Wright MSS. Lafayette to Frances Wright, February 24, 1826.

[2] Wright MSS. Lafayette to Frances Wright, October 10 [directed in
care of Charles Wilkes], 28, December 28, 1825; February 24, March 29,
July 27 [directed in care of Henry Clay], 1826. It is interesting to note
that in these letters the general still refers to Frances and Camilla as
" mes chères bien aimées filles."

# CHAPTER IV

## Nashoba Begun

THE absorbing interest which occupied the time and attention of Frances Wright during the closing weeks of General Lafayette's visit in the United States was, as has already been mentioned, her search for a solution of that most perplexing of American social problems, negro slavery.

With slavery in the South she first came in actual contact during the course of her visit to Virginia with Lafayette in the fall of 1824, when the sight of the oppressed race aroused all her sympathies.[1] At Montpelier, the home of ex-President Madison, she listened, doubtless with intense interest, to those discussions of slavery which Lafayette held with his host and the neighboring planters.[2] From these talks, and her own observations, she learned that while many Southerners deplored the evil none could suggest an adequate remedy. With her interest in the question thus aroused, it probably needed very little encouragement upon the part of her friend to induce her to turn with enthusiasm to a study of slavery, with the hope of finding some way out of the difficulty in which the South found itself.

Upon returning to Washington for the winter of 1824-

[1] Four years earlier, it will be recalled, she had avoided extending her travels into the southern states, so painful to her feelings did she believe would be the sight of human slavery in a land devoted to political liberty.

[2] Levasseur, A., *Lafayette en Amérique, en 1824 et 1825*, 2 vols., Paris, 1829, vol. i, pp. 482-483. In the pages referred to he notes the discussions, but not the presence of Miss Wright. Indeed no trace of Miss Wright appears in his entire account of Lafayette in America.

1825 she lost little time in attacking the problem. That it was capable of solution she concluded from the "conduct of the master race toward the slave in which she found as much to admire as to anathematize, and which inclined her to expect that, if the complex difficulties which surround the subject could be satisfactorily met, the will to act justly would not be wanting." [1]  Determined to understand the situation in all its details, she thoroughly examined the laws of the southern states upon slavery, and followed this up with careful survey of conditions in the south: [2]

[She] visited familiarly the planters, and consulted them on her object and her views; seeking the aid of their experience, and discussing with them the dangers for the country, the disadvantage to the master race, the pernicious example to youth, the monstrous anomaly in the institutions presented by a state of things which associated labor—the source of all that is good and great in man—with social degradation, political nullity, and brutal ignorance. On the other hand, she readily admitted the impossibility, even the absurdity, the danger to American institutions—alone fitted to guide and re gulate the bodies politic, endowed with intelligence, and habituated to the exercise of sovereign power—the common ruin, in short, for the two races, of an act of simple enfranchisement similar to that which had passed in the northern States. She knew from observation the evil effects produced by mere governmental abolition of an evil which has its seat in the mind, the habits, and through hereditary influences, in the very physical organization of a race. She had distinguished, at an early age, that human enfranchisement,—which is but another name for civilization—is, in its beginnings, a slow, gradual, and complex operation, and that, to ensure its certain advancement, it must be made to move forward simultaneously in the soil of

---

[1] *Biography*, pt. i, p. 22.

[2] Gilbert, Amos, *A Memoir of Frances Wright: the Pioneer Woman in the Cause of Human Rights*, Cincinnati, 1855, p. 21.

the internal man, and in the external influences which surround him.[1]

If, then, emancipation could come with safety to both
races, and to American political institutions, only through the
slow education of the subject race in an environment of
stimulating influences, the success of her own efforts would
depend upon whatever experiment she essayed meeting those
requirements.  At the same time, in order to meet the most
pertinent of the objections to emancipation, she must assure
the South against financial loss, and provide for the colonization of the freed negroes.

In her autobiography Frances Wright tells us that her
first conception of the mode whereby the gradual emancipation of the slaves might be effected came from an inspec-
tion of the religious communities of the German Pietists
established by George Rapp at Harmonie, Indiana, and afterward at Economie, Pennsylvania, but in this the writer feels
that she fails to give due credit to two other sources of inspiration.[2]  Many years before, her friend Lafayette had
attempted an experiment in gradual emancipation on his
estate of La Belle Gabrielle at Cayenne in French Guiana,
an experiment unfortunately cut short by the outbreak of
the French Revolution, and this effort he must have dis-

[1] *Biography*, pt. i, pp. 24-25.  These discussions must have occurred
during her trip into Virginia with Lafayette, and in the course of her
journey into the South and West in the spring of 1825.

[2] *Ibid.*, p. 28.  For an account of the Rappite communities see, Nordhoff, Charles, *Communistic Societies of the United States*, New York,
1875, pp. 63-91.  George Rapp was a German Pietist who had migrated
to the United States with his followers early in the nineteenth century.
The Rappites, as Rapp's followers became known, first established a
" community of equality " in western Pennsylvania.  In 1815 they moved
west to Indiana where they settled on the banks of the Wabash, and built
their little village of Harmonie.  When this village was sold to Robert
Owen in 1825 Rapp returned with his people to Pennsylvania and built
the village of Economie, just outside of Pittsburg.

cussed many times with her. In its broad outlines, at least,
it seems to have been entirely in sympathy with her own
ideas.[1] The other influence was that of the famous English
philanthropist and Utopian socialist, Robert Owen. Owen
arrived in the United States late in the fall of 1824 to complete his purchase of the great Rappite estate at Harmonie,
Indiana, where he hoped to prove to the world, by a practical demonstration, the truth of his theory that man was
entirely the product of his environment. After a brief visit
to his new property, he went to Washington to lay his plans
before the assembled representatives of the nation. It is
probable that here Miss Wright met him, and attended the
public lectures in the Hall of Representatives, where he set
forth his principles in detail, exhibited a model of one of
his proposed communities, and invited to New Harmony, as
he called his newly purchased village, all those who wished
to become members in the Preliminary Society about to be
started there.

Searching, as she was, for some means whereby the slaves
could be freed gradually without financial loss to the planters, Owen's schemes for a cooperative community no doubt
greatly interested her. It may have been at his suggestion
that she made a study of the Rappite community, which
had been singularly successful in its financial aspect, for on
leaving Washington she took occasion to pay a brief visit to
Harmonie. Two months later she witnessed the departure
of the Rappites for their new home at Economie, near Pittsburg, which she also visited in the summer of 1825. What
she saw at Harmonie and Economie proved very suggestive:

Upon inspecting all the departments of industry, and more
especially the agriculture, which formed necessarily the large
base of the growing wealth and prosperity of the property,
she was forcibly struck—not merely with the advantages of

[1] Morgan, *The True Lafayette*, pp. 224-225.

united and organized labor, which may be seen at any time
in a cotton mill, or in any other public work or institution
whatsoever—but with their peculiar appropriateness to the
object which, at the time, engrossed her attention.  Nor was
there, indeed, much difference in the point of intellectual advancement between the mass of the German laborers, there submitted to the spiritual and temporal control of astute leaders,
and that of the southern negro.[1]

To the valuable hints on cooperative labor given her by
the Rappites, and to the knowledge of slavery and the negro
gained from her talks with the planters, Miss Wright added
the advice afforded by Benjamin Lundy's wide experience
in the cause of anti-slavery.  By the late summer of 1825
her plan had taken definite shape.  Before his departure
Lafayette had an opportunity to examine it, and to submit
it for consideration to his friends Madison and Monroe,
and to Chief Justice Marshall.  The observations of the
first two must have been not a little encouraging, as both
augured well for the plan, particularly in view of the fact
that the proposed experiment was to be tried in the South,
and that the emancipated slaves were to be colonized.[2]
Lafayette himself approved it on the ground that it satisfactorily met the pecuniary objections of the planters.[3]  It is
of interest to know that Frances Wright not only sought
the advice of Thomas Jefferson, but his actual participation
in the plan, an honor which he felt it wise to decline because
of advanced age and the necessity of conserving his energies

[1] *Biography*, pt. i, pp. 25-26.

[2] Wright MSS. Lafayette to Frances Wright, Washington, August 26,
1825.  Lafayette remarks, " Chief Justice Marshall has, under seal of
secrecy, your prospectus, and will shortly write me his opinion con-
fidentially.  You know he is nominal head of the Colonization Society."
This letter is also to be found in Brown, Anne B. A., " A Dream of
Emancipation," *New England Magazine,* June, 1904.

[3] *African Repository*, vol. i, pp. 285-286.

for his labor in behalf of the University of Virginia. Of her efforts, however, he heartily approved, and considered her plan as holding a very good prospect of success " even should it not answer fully to calculations in figures." [1]

The prospectus of the proposed experiment was made public in a pamphlet published in Baltimore early in September.[2] Briefly, the plan set forth was one of gradual emancipation based upon a system of cooperative labor somewhat similar to that which had proved its worth financially in the Rappite and Shaker communities. Such a plan, it was urged, would entail no pecuniary loss upon the South, as the labor of the slaves would pay for their cost and keep, plus interest on the capital invested, and would meet the prevailing objections of the planters to the presence of the free negro by providing for the colonization of those emancipated. Should the scheme prove its success in one instance it was hoped that it would be generally adopted throughout the South, and lead eventually to the entire disappearance of slavery.

To prove the feasibility of the scheme its projectors planned to purchase lands in the upland cotton region of Tennessee, Alabama, or Mississippi, the location to be somewhat isolated in order to prevent any hostility on the part of the surrounding planters. Upon this purchase would be placed from fifty to one hundred slaves, and a system of co-operative labor introduced, holding out as a stimulus to the negroes, the hope of freedom, together with the liberty and education of their children. For the last purpose, a school of industry, on the Lancastrian principle, was to be opened

---

[1] Jefferson, Thomas, *Letters and Addresses of Thomas Jefferson*, edited by William B. Parker and Jonas Viles, New York, 1908, pp. 285-286. Thomas Jefferson to Frances Wright, Monticello, August 7, 1825.

[2] Wright, Frances, *A Plan for the Gradual Abolition of Slavery in the United States without Danger of Loss to Citizens of the South*, Baltimore, 1825. The *Plan* was also printed in the *New Harmony Gazette*, October 1, 1825.

which should carry order and cooperation from school-
room to field:

the children working, under the direction of their monitors,
with such intermission as shall keep their minds cheerful, and
their bodies vigorous. It is believed on a cotton plantation,
such a system will raise the value of youthful to nearly that
of mature labor. The same may apply, also, to such establishments as shall hereafter combine manufactures with agriculture.

Discipline was to be maintained by explaining to the slaves
that any misconduct would mean a lengthening of their term
of service. How long this would be in the first instance
would have to be determined by experience, but it must cover
the purchase cost of the slave, losses through sickness and
accident, and the expense of colonization. Five years, it was
believed, ought to suffice for a good laborer to return his
purchase money with interest, but, in order that families
might not be broken up, labor was to be valued by the family
rather than by head, keeping the children with the parents
until the former had reached a certain age. As to the place
of colonization the prospectus was indefinite, suggesting as
possibilities, Haiti, Texas, or California. It is interesting
to note that Miss Wright believed that free white labor
would flow into the South to fill the gap created by the departure of the blacks.

The first cost of such an experiment was estimated at
about forty-one thousand dollars for an establishment of
one hundred slaves, and it was expected that at the end of
the first year, after deducting an interest charge of six per
cent on the capital invested, there would be a net profit of
close upon ten thousand dollars:

This plan, proposed in a spirit of equal good will to master
and slave, is intended to consult the interests of both. To pre-

pare the latter for liberty, before it is granted, and in no case
to grant liberty, but in accordance with the laws of the state.
—To remove, by gradual and gentle means, a system fraught
with danger, as well as crime—To turn labor to account, which
is in many places, worse than profitless, and everywhere to
heighten its value—To assimilate the industry of the south to
that of the north, and enable it to multiply its productions, and
improve all the rich advantages of the southern soil and
climate—To open also the field of industry to free white labor,
now in great measure closed throughout a large portion of this
magnificent country.

Late in September of 1825, Miss Wright, accompanied by
George Flower, one of the founders of the English settlement at Albion, in Edwards County, Illinois, and an ardent
advocate of emancipation, started south to seek a location
for the great experiment.[1]   Flower's hostility to slavery had
originated in the fierce struggle over the question of slavery
in Illinois, and his sympathy for the unfortunate free negroes
of that state had led him in 1823 to finance the migration
of a number of them to the island of Haiti, a plan which he
appears to have been the first to adopt.   He met Frances
Wright in Washington where he had probably gone to greet
his old friend General Lafayette, and there his introduction
to her plans seems to have come about in the following
rather interesting manner: [2]

La vue d'un batiment dans un port de la Virginie, chargé et
surchargé de malheureux enchainés deux à deux destinés pour
le marche de la Savannah—au moment de mon débarquement,
eveilla tout ma sympathie . . . .

[1] *New Harmony Gazette*, October 1, 1825.  For the story of George
Flower see Flower, George, *The History of the English Settlement in
Edwards County, Illinois*, Chicago, 1882.  Unfortunately nothing is said
in this work of the association of Flower with Frances Wright.

[2] *The History of the English Settlement in Edwards County, Illinois*.
It appears that Flower had visited La Grange in 1815.  There are letters
from Lafayette to Flower in that year given in the appendix of the book.

Je rencontre M. Flower occupé du même objet, Je parle de mon ideé, et M. Flower me donne sa parole de se vouer corps et âme a la realization de nos projets.[1]

Whether George Flower had any part in drawing up the plan which has just been described is not clear, but it is probable that Miss Wright drew freely upon his extensive knowledge of Western farming methods and lands, and was only too glad to enlist his services in the cause.

Flower and Miss Wright first journeyed to Nashville, Tennessee, where they hoped to learn of available lands in the upland cotton region of that state. There, their attention was directed, perhaps by General Jackson, to whom Miss Wright would naturally turn for advice, to the recently acquired Indian lands on the Wolf River in western Tennessee, not far from the town of Memphis.[2] On horseback they traveled across the state to inspect them, and from the first entry in the " Nashoba Book," the journal of the institution, we learn that on Saturday, October eighth, 1825, " Frances Wright and George Flower arrived at Memphis by way of Nashville in search of land," and on the twelfth that, " Frances Wright and George Flower, having seen the lands, now of Nashoba, left Memphis for Nashville." [3]  At Nashville she purchased a few slaves with which to start her experiment.[4]  A month later she was again in Memphis,

[1] Wright MSS. From a letter of Frances Wright dated Memphis, December 26, 1825, which was published in *Le Globe* of Paris, January 23, 1827.

[2] The lands first acquired by Miss Wright were conveyed to her by William A. Lawrence and William A. Davis, assignees of General Jackson.

[3] Wright MSS. " The Nashoba Book." This was the official journal of the institution. It was kept by James Richardson, a gentleman who became closely associated with Miss Wright in her enterprise.

[4] *Ibid.* From the letter of Frances Wright published in *Le Globe* of Paris, January 23, 1827.

where she "purchased the three hundred acres from William Lawrence and contracted for the building of two double cabins."[1] To this first purchase she added lands which eventually increased her holdings to about two thousand acres. These lay on both sides of the Wolf River some thirteen miles from Memphis. She describes the lands acquired as "two thousand acres of good and pleasant woodland, traversed by a clear and lovely stream, communicating thirteen miles below with the Mississippi at the old Indian trading post of Chickasaw Bluffs," and again, as "dry, rolling, and second-rate soil. I trust we shall secure health, while we shall be within convenient distance of the western navigation. The soil and climate are well suited to cotton, and will admit also of good northern farming."[2] To her new property Miss Wright gave the name of Nashoba, the old Chickasaw Indian name for wolf.

George Flower now returned to Illinois to make arrangements for taking his family and Camilla Wright to Nashoba in the spring. During his absence Miss Wright remained at Memphis and Nashoba writing, superintending the construction of the cabins, and adventuring with her horse about the countryside.[3] In a letter to a friend, Jeremiah Thompson of New York, she gave an excellent summary of the progress made during the winter, and of the modifications which it had been deemed advisable to make in the original plan:

When I was induced to confer with yourself and others on the plan which had occurred to me for the gradual abolition

[1] *Ibid.* "The Nashoba Book," November 18, 1825.

[2] Wright MSS. Extract from a letter of Frances Wright to a gentleman in Boston. The letter was published in the *Genius of Universal Emancipation*, April 1, 1826.

[3] *Ibid.* Letter of Frances Wright published in *Le Globe* of Paris, January 23, 1827.

of slavery it was rather in compliance with the opinions of
others than my own. I could rather have wished to prosecute
my own views on a confined scale and in privacy, and to have
given the more general views, contained in the pamphlet of
which you will have received a copy, at some future period,
than claimed public attention and assistance for them before
I could bring any practical experience in support of their
efficiency. With the hope held out to me that such assistance might be obtained as would render the experiment more
complete than my slender means could attain, I thought it
right to make the attempt recommended to me. Should it
hitherto have met with little success I am perhaps chiefly to
blame. The part required of me, I am ill fitted to act.
There is an awkwardness in suing for assistance—although in
a good cause. With yourself and a few other friends I felt
at ease. I knew my motives would not be doubted, and that
I should escape even the charge of presumption and vanity
which the world at large is usually disposed to make against
any purposes of reform of old abuses or alleviations of
human sufferings. Whether I shall have incurred this charge
I know not. Should it appear so I shall not on that account
desist from my efforts or slacken my zeal although from a
distaste and disqualification for the office of subscription
raising I shall confine them within the narrow limits prescribed by my own fortune and that of the friends who may
voluntarily unite their efforts to mine.

Aware, however, of the risks to be run—of the possible and
probable difficulties that may present themselves I am fully
convinced of the necessity of proceeding with caution. The
sum of $17,000 which I at first proposed to embark with I
shall restrict to $10,000, and place out with due circumspec-
tion, not exceeding $8,000 the first year which sum will fur-
nish out a small farm worked by ten hands—Mr. Flower
adding live stock and food for the first year to the value of
$2,000. Thus our first object will be to raise the common
necessaries of life, and as soon as possible to make all the
clothing within ourselves, and when this is done to extend our

views gradually, employing young hands in simple manufactures and organizing a practical school of industry. Proceeding with this caution I shall hope in the course of time to see such an experiment tried as I explained to you. But sufficient for the day, etc.

I have been led to this determination by several weighty considerations. It will be sufficient to mention—the high price of provisions this year and the expected fall in the price of negroes which, although already slightly affected by the depression of the cotton market, is still unusually high. The only business which we desire to connect in the first instance with our farm is a small store. The profits of merchants—as they are styled in the south and west are exorbitant, unwisely so as it appears to me, since they are based on a ruinous system of long credits. We shall propose to ourselves here the practice of the old Harmonists—a reduced per cent for ready money of the United States, paying as we buy and receiving as we sell. I purpose to vest in the store $1,000 reinvesting the profits that may arise in the same way. This business not only promises success, but will assist us greatly towards procuring necessary supplies for home consumption at a cheap rate until we can manufacture ourselves. Of course all we are necessitated to draw from the store we shall pay for so as to keep untouched its funds. You see I write to you as a friend interested in my undertaking, and should you encourage me I shall from time to time report progress. I have now to state that I do not desire the loan of which I wrote to you. I could not have immediately raised $17,000 without the sale of some stock to a disadvantage from the depression of the stock market (the stock alluded to is vested in the old Louisiana State Bank). Having decided that it is better to begin on as small a scale as possible I have enough at command.

But now, my dear sir, you can render me, as I imagine—an important service, and one I hope not troublesome. Your city is the best for the supply of many articles used in the common trade of this country. I know not who to apply to as a man of honesty and judgment. Can you point one out to me—who for the usual commission will procure and forward good articles at the lowest prices with care and punctuality either by the way of New Orleans or Wheeling as is judged best? My agents in New Orleans are Messrs. Dick, Rooker, and Co. We shall want in the first place some pieces of stout domestic shirting cotton and sheeting, cotton checks, stripes, and plaids, assorted of various patterns and qualities, blankets and flannels, white and red. The blankets should be thick and heavy—what are called the Mackindue, and of different sizes. Among the flannels may be included one piece of common green beige, six pieces of printed calicoes, two or three dozen of fulled thick woolen socks men's size. The same of coarse men's shoes and some boy's size.[1]

To this letter the excellent Quaker to whom she had written answered by not only undertaking her commission, but by making to the institution a present of the goods ordered, as his share " in aid of thy good efforts," adding with the thriftiness of his people, " I cannot too much applaud your excellent and exemplary intention of selling for cash only." [2]

With the opening of February the experiment began in earnest. First appeared a gentleman from South Carolina,

[1] *Ibid.* Frances Wright to Jeremiah Thompson of New York, Memphis, December 9, 1825. There appeared an article in Lundy's *Genius of Universal Emancipation,* December 12, 1825, commented upon in the *United States Gazette,* December 16, 1825, to the effect that Lafayette had contributed ten thousand dollars to the plan of Miss Wright. This, however, Miss Wright denied in a letter to Lundy dated Memphis, January 10, 1826: " In your paper of the 10th ult. which has just reached me I find an article headed 'Frances Wright's new Institution for the Abolition of Slavery.' The statements which appear therein respecting the funds at command or likely to be employed, are, I regret to say, incorrect. The individuals concerned in this at present very slender and imperfect undertaking, have no funds to rely on but their own, and those too limited to admit of anything like a fair experiment of the Plan as published in your paper." Wright MSS.

[2] Wright MSS. Jeremiah Thompson to Frances Wright, January 28, 1826.

Robert Wilson, who desired to place a family of slaves under the care of Miss Wright.[1]  Two weeks later Camilla Wright, with George Flower and his family arrived on a flatboat from Illinois, having been delayed for some time by ice in the Ohio.[2]  On the first of March, the slaves purchased in Nashville, five males and three females, reached Memphis, and a few days later all hands set out for Nashoba where the whites took up their residence in one of the newly erected double cabins, and the slaves were quartered in the other.[3]  Shortly afterward the party was joined by two gentlemen who were to play a large part in the fortunes of the experiment, James Richardson, a Scotchman, whom Miss Wright had met at Memphis, and one Richeson Whitby whose experience had included some years in a Shaker community, and more recently a residence at New Harmony as a disciple of Owen.

The next few months were devoted to desperately hard and wearying work.  " We have raised buildings for immediate use," wrote Miss Wright to a friend at New Harmony, " cleared and fenced round them, cleared thoroughly, planted, and fenced an apple orchard of five acres, planted in potatoes a vegetable garden—opened fifteen acres for corn and planted two of old ground in cotton." [4]  In this arduous labor she bore her part with the others and " might have been seen with her swarthy companions, piling brush, rolling logs, &c., &c., from early dawn to dusky eve."[5]  Absolutely unprepared by early training for such a life of physical activity it was not surprising that, in spite of the rest afforded by a few weeks spent in New Harmony, she should

[1] *Ibid.*, " Nashoba Book," February 8, 1826.
[2] *Ibid.*, February 27, 1826.
[3] *Ibid.*, March 5, 1826.
[4] *Ibid.*, Frances Wright to the Reverend Hugh McMillan, May 3, 1826.
[5] Gilbert, pp. 27-28.

have fallen a victim to the burning heats of a southern sun and the malarial climate of the Wolf River lands. So serious was her illness that for a time even her life was despaired of, but the constant care of Camilla, aided by the medical knowledge of James Richardson, finally won the day. Upon the fever leaving her, however, it was felt that entire restoration of health could come only with complete rest in a more salubrious climate.[1] Thus, almost before it was under way, the experiment faced disaster in the failure of its projector's health.

It was partly to meet this situation, and partly the result of a visit to New Harmony in the preceding summer, that she now made a profound change in the control and character of the institution. By a deed of trust signed the seventeenth of December, 1826, the lands of Nashoba and all her personal property thereon were conveyed to ten trustees — General Lafayette, William Maclure, Robert Owen, Cadwallader Colden, Richeson Whitby, Robert Jennings, Robert Dale Owen, George Flower, Camilla Wright, and James Richardson — " to be held by them, and their associates, and their successors, in perpetual trust for the benefit of the negro race. . . ." By the deed it was provided that " a school for colored children shall always form a principal part of the plan, and provided further that all negroes emancipated by the trustees, shall, on quitting the lands of the institution, be placed out of the limits of the United States." [2] The slaves were also deeded to the trustees " on

[1] *Biography*, pt. i, pp. 29-31.
[2] Wright MSS. Deed of the Lands of Nashoba, West Tennessee. Miss Wright also reserved for herself a trusteeship in the institution. With Lafayette, Robert Owen, Colden, Whitby, Richardson, Flower, and Camilla Wright, the reader is already familiar. William Maclure was the partner of Robert Owen in the community venture at New Harmony, Jennings was an educational theorist whom Miss Wright had met at New Harmony, and Robert Dale Owen was the eldest son of Robert Owen.

the condition that, when their labor ... shall have paid, to the institution of Nashoba a clear capital of $6,000, with six per cent interest on that capital, from the first of January, 1827; and also a sum sufficient to defray the expenses of colonization,—these slaves shall be emancipated and colonized . . . ."

The future control of Nashoba was placed entirely in the hands of the trustees, of whom those in residence at Nashoba were to constitute a quorum for the conduct of business, provided they numbered not less than three.

To this point there was nothing unusual in the deed of trust, but other provisions profoundly modified the original character of the institution. From a simple experiment in self-emancipation under the guidance of intelligent leaders it now became a cooperative community modeled somewhat after New Harmony, but with the negroes doing the heavier and more laborious work. John H. Noyes in his *History of American Socialisms* has rather aptly described the scheme as providing for a sort of Brook Farm plus a negro basis.[1] Membership in the community could be secured only upon a vote of the resident trustees after a trial residence of six months, and so careful was the selection of members to be, in order to prevent the gathering of any such conglomeration of cranks as had inconvenienced Owen at New Harmony, that the admission of a husband did not include that of the wife, nor that of the wife the husband, nor did the admission of the parents secure that of any children over fourteen years of age. All must be considered individually, but once admitted each was entitled to the comforts afforded by the institution, that is, " to food, to clothing, to lodging, to attention during illness, and to protection in old age." The children of the members were to be raised and edu-

[1] Noyes, John Humphrey, *History of American Socialisms*, Philadelphia, 1870, pp. 66-72. " Nashoba."

cated by the institution until twenty years of age, when they were to be voted in or helped to establish themselves elsewhere.

It is interesting to note the clever manner in which Miss Wright endeavored to bring her original plan into harmony with the new community scheme. In asking the planters to give up their slaves, and change their whole mode of life, she says, they must be shown how it can be done without compromise of their ease and comfort:

Let us, then, propose to them to unite their property, to pursue such occupations as their previous habits may bend to, and to continue to impose the harder tasks of labor, during their lives or necessities, upon the present generation of slaves; conferring such an education on the children of their slaves, as shall fit them for the station of a free people.—Let them, at the same time, train their own children in the habits worthy of free men; rendering them independent of the labor of others, by a complete and practical education, that shall strengthen the body equally with the mind, render just and amiable the opinions and feelings, and introduce at once, in a new generation that complete equality of habits and knowledge, alone consistent with the political institutions of the country. . . . It will be seen that this community is founded on the principle of community of property and labor; presenting every advantage to those desirous, not of accumulating money, but of enjoying life, and rendering services to their fellow-creatures; these fellow-creatures, that is, the blacks here admitted, requiting these services, by services equal or greater by filling occupations, which their habits render easy, and which to their guides and assistants might be difficult, or unpleasing. No life of idleness, however, is proposed to the whites. Those who cannot work, must give an equivalent in property. Gardening or other culivation of the soil; useful trades practiced in the society, or taught in the school; the teaching of every branch of knowledge; tending the children;

and nursing the sick—will present a choice of employments sufficiently extensive.[1]

This reorganization of Nashoba upon a community basis was the result of a new influence in her life, an influence that was to affect profoundly its whole future tenor—that of Robert Owen and his theories for the social reform of mankind. It was during a visit to New Harmony in the summer of 1826 that she first came fully under the spell of Owen's ideas.[2]  Both were humanitarians, but Frances Wright, up to this time, had envisaged human happiness as the outcome of political liberty. It was Owen's part to push her thought one step farther, to show that the attainment of political liberty and equality was but half the victory, and that in mental liberty alone lay the panacea for all human ills.[3]  Could men but break the fetters of false conventions, superstitions, and prejudices, which now held their minds in thrall, and guide their lives by rational principles, the millennium would be attained. It was to prove that society could reach this millennium through the medium of a proper environment that he had established his community at New Harmony, where in theory, at least, all were to be free and all equal, and the ills that afflicted contemporary society nonexistent.

As a humanitarian and a philosopher it is not hard to see how these theories would appeal to Frances Wright, especially as at New Harmony, in the summer of 1826, she appeared to have before her what seemed to be a striking in-

[1] Wright MSS. Deed of the Lands of Nashoba, West Tennessee.

[2] There is no evidence in Miss Wright's letters or published works that prior to meeting Owen in Washington, in 1825, she had had any connection with the man or his doctrines.

[3] It was at New Harmony, July 4, 1826, that Owen made his famous Declaration of Mental Independence. It is not improbable that Miss Wright was in New Harmony at the time.

stance of their successful application. Why should she not combine with her experiment in emancipation an experiment in the moral regeneration of the race, avoiding, if possible, the mistakes made by Owen? The Nashoba community, as outlined in the deed of trust, was the outcome of her enthusiasm, and the choice of trustees gives evidence of how large a part New Harmony had played in its creation, for of the ten appointed, five were then, or had been, associated with Owen's experiment: Robert Owen, Robert Dale Owen, Robert L. Jennings, Richeson Whitby, and William Maclure.[1]

One immediate result of the change must be noted. George Flower, who had done so much to aid in founding Nashoba, now withdrew his active support and returned to Illinois. This was unfortunate, for Flower was a man whose sound judgment and sterling common sense might well have avoided the unfortunate occurrences which very nearly wrecked the institution during the next year.

[1] For a full discussion of the New Harmony movement see Lockwood, G. B., *The New Harmony Movement*, New York, 1905.

# CHAPTER V

## NASHOBA CONCLUDED

IN the spring of 1827 the community experiment at New Harmony came to an end, and, at the invitation of Miss Wright, Robert Dale Owen, the eldest son of Robert Owen and his enthusiastic disciple, joined the resident trustees at Nashoba.[1] Gifted with charm of manner, no little literary ability, and with a head brimfull of all sorts of liberal theories, young Owen was a type which would naturally appeal to Frances Wright. At Nashoba he hoped to carry on, in a happier environment, the experiment started at New Harmony, trusting "there to find more cultivated and congenial associates than those among whom, for eighteen months past, I had been living."[2] Apparently he anticipated a little Eden, where "a few kindred spirits . . . should have their small, separate dwellings, contribute to a common fund enough for their support, and spend their time in 'lettered leisure,' "[3] for it was the lighter side of community life which appealed most strongly to him. What he found quickly disillusioned him; "the land, all second-rate only, and scarcely a hundred acres of it cleared;

[1] Robert Dale Owen had come to the United States with his father in 1825. At New Harmony he taught school, helped edit the weekly paper, and assisted in the management of the community. An interesting account of his early life is to be found in his brief autobiography, *Threading My Way*, New York, 1874.

[2] *Threading My Way*, p. 303.

[3] *Ibid.*, p. 299.

three or four squared log houses, and a few cabins for
the slaves, the only buildings; slaves released from the
fear of the lash working indolently under the management of Whitby, whose education in an easy-going
Shaker village had not at all fitted him for the post of
plantation overseer," presented a discouraging prospect
to one who had hoped to spend his time in "lettered
leisure."[1] To add to this dark outlook the health of
Miss Wright was wretchedly poor.

The forbidding appearance of Nashoba probably made
Owen quite ready to accept the proposal that he accompany Frances to Europe, for it was now decided that she
must immediately seek rest and health abroad. In
Europe, too, they encouraged themselves to believe,
might be found recruits for their community. Camilla
was to remain at Nashoba with Whitby and Richardson,
owing to the feeling on Whitby's part that the control
of the slaves would be almost impossible without the
presence of one of the sisters.[2]

About the middle of May, Frances and young Owen
left Nashoba for New Orleans, where, after a few days
spent in arranging business affairs, in securing a maid to
attend Miss Wright, and in interviewing colored folk interested in Nashoba, they finally embarked for Havre.[3]
Until fairly out to sea, Owen tells us in his autobiography, he had grave fears for the life of his companion,
but she gradually recovered, and by the end of the long
two months' voyage was again quite herself.[4]   From

[1] *Ibid.*, p. 303.

[2] *Ibid.*, p. 304.

[3] *Ibid.*, p. 304; Wright MSS. Robert Dale Owen to Camilla Wright,
New Orleans, May 29, 1827; Off Balize, June 1, 1827.

[4] *Threading My Way*, p. 304; Wright MSS. Frances Wright to James
Mylne. On board the "New England," in the British Channel, July
26, 1827.

Havre they went to the home of the Garnetts in Paris, and a few days later were with Lafayette at La Grange.

Hardly had Frances reached La Grange than disquieting rumors of conditions at Nashoba began to reach her, for, unfortunately, neither Camilla, Whitby, nor Richardson possessed the personal qualifications necessary for carrying on the work they had undertaken in her absence. Camilla, always dependent upon the stronger mind of her sister, lacked character and decision; while Whitby, who ought to have assumed the leadership, though amiable and conscientious, lacked the force and aggressiveness needed to handle successfully a plantation of slaves and dominate his co-trustees. Both fell completely under the influence of the powerful, but impracticable and visionary, mind of James Richardson whose amazing indiscretions soon brought the institution into widespread ill repute.

James Richardson was an interesting personality. A Scotchman, he had left his native land for the United States, where he had finally settled in Memphis. It was here in the winter of 1825 that Frances Wright met him, and thought so well of his abilities that she made him a partner in her enterprise. Perhaps the fact that in Scotland he had studied medicine made him doubly acceptable. Of his character, Owen says that "he was upright, impracticable, and an acute metaphysician of the Thomas Brown school."[1] In opinion he was an atheist and a materialist, with a curious mixture of the sensual in his make-up. It was this last strain in his character, added to his hostility to the institution of marriage, which brought disaster.

As the trustee in charge of the correspondence of Nashoba, he sent to Benjamin Lundy, shortly after the

---

[1] *Threading My Way*, p. 391.

departure of Owen and Miss Wright, extracts from the records of the society, with "permission to give every degree of publicity to them" through the columns of *The Genius of Universal Emancipation*. He did this, he says, because "Mr. Lundy had in his letters to Frances Wright requested from time to time, to be informed of our proceedings. The extracts which I sent to him were perused by both the other trustees neither of whom objected to this measure."[1]   But how Camilla and Whitby could have acquiesced in the open publication of the selections sent is beyond comprehension, the only explanation lies in Richardson's complete ascendency and their own unworldliness:

Tuesday, May 15, 1827.
Mamselle Lolotte, a free colored woman, and family, arrived from New Orleans.

Sunday Evening, May 20, 1827.
Camilla Wright and James Richardson, resident trustees. Met the slaves—Camilla Wright repeated to them how the work was to proceed in Mr. Whitby's absence. She also informed them that to-morrow, the children, Delila, Lucy, Julia, and Alfred, will be taken altogether from under the management of the parents, and will be placed, until our school is organized, under the management of Mamselle Lolotte; that all communication between the parents and children shall, in future, be prevented, except such as may take place by permission, and in the presence of the manager of the children.

Saturday Evening, May 26, 1827.
Agreed, that the slaves shall not be allowed to receive money, clothing, food, or indeed anything whatever from any person resident at, or visiting this place, whether trustee, coadjutor, probationer, or stranger; and, that any article so

[1] Wright MSS. "Nashoba Book." The extracts were sent to Lundy, June 25, 1827.

received, shall be returned to the giver in the presence of the slaves and trustees.  If the giver be absent, the article shall be destroyed by the receiver, in the presence of the trustees and the slaves.

Agreed, that the slaves shall not be permitted to eat elsewhere than at the public meals, excepting in case of such sickness as may render confinement to their cabins necessary.

Sunday Evening, May 27, 1827.

Met the slaves—Camilla Wright informed them of the regulations agreed to yesterday evening.

Dilly having given utterance a day or two ago, to some grumbling at having so many mistresses James Richardson stated to them, that it is very true they have many mistresses as well as many masters, and that in all probability, they will soon have many more of both; as every free person who shall reside here, whether black, white, or brown, will be, in some sort, their master or mistress; that this is just the difference between a free person and a slave; and that they can get rid of these masters and mistresses in no other way than by working out their freedom, when they will be transformed into masters and mistresses themselves, but that, in the meantime, they will gradually find out, that this multiplicity of superiors, so far from being a hardship, is of palpable advantage to them, in preventing them from being at the mercy of the temper of any one individual, and in rendering the concurrence of at least a majority of the resident trustees, an indispensable preliminary to the infliction of even the slightest possible punishment, for the greatest possible offense.

Friday, June 1, 1827.

Met the slaves at dinner time—Isabel had laid a complaint against Redrick, for coming during the night of Wednesday to her bedroom, uninvited, and endeavoring, without her consent, to take liberties with her person.  Our views of the sexual relation had been repeatedly given to the slaves; Camilla Wright again stated it, and informed the slaves that, as the conduct of Redrick, which he did not deny, was a gross in-

fringement of that view, a repetition of such conduct, by him,
or by any other of the men, ought in her opinion, to be punished
by flogging.  She repeated that we consider the proper basis
of the sexual intercourse to be the unconstrained and unrestrained choice of *both* parties.  Nelly having requested a lock
for the door of the room in which she and Isabel sleep, with
the view of preventing the future uninvited entrance of any
man, the lock was refused, as being, in its proposed use, inconsistent with the doctrine just explained; a doctrine which
we are determined to enforce, and which will give to every
woman a much greater security, than any lock can possible do.

### Sunday Evening, June 3, 1827.

Met the slaves—Willis having, a few days ago, complained
to Camilla Wright, of Mamselle Lolotte's children beating his
children; thinking it was allowed because hers were a little
the fairest.  James Richardson took the opportunity of endeavoring to explain to the slaves, our views on the subject of
color.  He told them that, in our estimation all colors are equal
in rank, and that whatever distinctions may be established on
this place, color shall form the basis of none of them.

### Sunday Evening, June 10, 1827.

Met the slaves—Stated to them that, as some of them have
on two occasions broken the swing by using it in a riotous
manner, they shall no longer be permitted to use it at all—we
added, that they cannot be allowed to partake with us of any
such amusement, until their habits shall become more refined
than at present.

### Wednesday, June 13, 1827.

Willis having reported to us that Henry declined coultering
(ploughing) to-day, on the plea of pain in his knee joint, to
which he is subject—we met the slaves at breakfast time, and
told them that, though we did not doubt that Henry's knee
gave him more or less pain, we had not sufficient confidence in
his veracity to trust in his statement regarding the degree of
ailment; that we would, therefore, take their votes respecting

the capacity of Henry to follow the oxen to-day. From this
vote we stated that, we would exclude Willis, because he now
acts as director of their work, and Maria, because she now
cohabits with Henry. There were ten votes, five each way.
We gave our opinion as the casting vote, in support of Henry's
capacity to coulter (plough). He was therefore ordered to
attend to it.

Sunday Evening, June 17, 1827.

Met the slaves—James Richardson informed them that, last
night, Mamselle Josephine and he began to live together; and
he took this occasion of repeating to them our views on color,
and on the sexual relation.[1]

Could any more evidence be wanting than the above
extracts to prove the absolute incompetency of the resident trustees to manage an ignorant people! Whatever
might be said for the advanced ideas which had come to
prevail at Nashoba, to expect the slaves to understand
them and live in accordance with them revealed a faith
that was grounded in stupidity. To add to the confusion, Camilla and Whitby fell in love, and were married. When put to the test Camilla found Richardson's
free-love ideas too much for her.

It is hardly surprising that these unhappy extracts in
the *Genius of Universal Emancipation* should have
caused consternation among the friends of the sisters.
Lundy himself protested against anything at Nashoba
which in any way resembled the libidinous practices of
the slaveholders, while one of his correspondents went
so far as to term Nashoba " one great brothel." [2] This
statement was heatedly denied by Richardson, although

[1] Extracts from the " Nashoba Book " published in Lundy's *Genius of
Universal Emancipation*, July 28, 1827. Mamselle Josephine was a
quadroon daughter of Mamselle Lolotte.

[2] *Genius of Universal Emancipation*, August 18, 1827.

he crushed the hopes of Lundy that things were not so
bad as they seemed by asserting that the "language of
the records is not, I think, equivocal; nor have I observed any typographical errors of importance. Let the
records, then, speak for themselves."[1] From her old
friend, Charles Wilkes, of New York, Camilla received a
kindly letter, begging an explanation of what had appeared in Lundy's paper, and adding :

I cannot express the pain which this publication has given to
your friends here who have seen it for I find it was known to
many persons before I saw it, who would not communicate it
to me, and I dare not tell you what inferences are drawn from
it. I cannot believe they are fairly drawn.[2]

Camilla's answer to this letter must have proved a
shock to Wilkes and her New York friends, and a month
later to the Garnetts and Lafayette, for, after thanking
him for his kindly interest, she called his attention to
the change in the character of the institution made by
the deed of trust, and added that as to the question of
the marriage relation, which had aroused so much discussion, she frankly expressed her

entire disapproval of the marriage tie, which I regard as not
only in the utmost degree irrational, in requiring of two individuals to love each other during life, when they have not the
control of their affections for one hour, but in the highest
degree pernicious in compelling these individuals to continue
united, when the feelings which brought them together may
not only have changed, but, as I have known in several instan-
ces, have turned to utter aversion. I also view marriage as
forming one of the most subtle inventions of priestcraft for
poisoning the purest source of human felicity and fostering

[1] Wright MSS. James Richardson to Lundy, September 16, 1827.
[2] *Ibid.*, Charles Wilkes to Camilla Wright, New York, August 15, 1827.

and perpetuating the sad catalogue of misery and crime which more or less darkens the records of all nations wherein the law has undertaken to interfere in a matter utterly beyond its control, that is, in the supposition that it had for its object the promotion of human happiness.

The conduct of my friend Mr. Richardson in forming a connection in the manner [stated]—so far from exciting my reprobation, or that of any individual associated here—had their sanction and approval.

While I cannot refer to any writings of my sister giving her views on the sexual relation I should judge from the tenor of your letter that you are unacquainted with some of the opinions which she has lately published not less in opposition to the usually received opinions of the world than the one above mentioned. I allude to the second part of "A Few Days" published in the Harmony Gazette in which after discussing her intention of treating that of morals, wherein she will give at large her views of the sexual relation, and was only prevented from doing so by the state of her health obliging her to seek a change of climate.

So far from wishing [illegible], I request you communicate the contents of this letter to all friends who are likely to be interested. I send by the same post a copy of your letter and my answer to the Garnetts with the request that they will communicate them to General Lafayette, and others of my European friends.[1]

There is only one thing to be said for Richardson and Camilla in this business—their frankness and honesty in declaring to the world the new principles on which Nashoba rested, for there is no doubt but that in principle, at least, Camilla was right in ascribing to her sister the ideas which she so crudely expressed. But it was a frankness which wrecked what chance of future success the institution may have had in its original object, and

---

[1] *Ibid.*, Camilla Wright to Charles Wilkes, Nashoba, September 13, 1827.

placed upon its projectors a stigma which never wholly disappeared. Fifty years later Robert Dale Owen, writing his autobiography, remarked that the course of his life might have been very different had he not come under the influence of Frances Wright at this time; but great as may have been the influence of Miss Wright on young Owen, it is the author's belief that that of the Owens, father and son, upon her was infinitely more damaging.[1]

If it was true that Frances held the opinions ascribed to her by Camilla, she would never have risked the fate of her experiment in such a manner. Her patience with Richardson and Camilla under the circumstances was remarkable. Upon the rumor of what had been done at Nashoba reaching her at La Grange, she wrote the former, pleading for moderation and caution in the public expression of opinions so contrary to those then accepted by society:

Intimate as is our friendship, indebted as I have been to your affection and judgment for much valuable counsel, I feel it were utterly superfluous to preface any observations it may occur to me to address to you with an apology. Were an apology necessary, indeed, I should not make the observations. I conclude the letter referred to by my [illegible] to have been a private one, at all events not prepared for publication. Whether prepared or not however I will say, from my [illegible] quotation that I judge it to be very unfit for publication. Were our own happiness our sole object it might be indifferent in what manner we addressed ourselves to the world we had left—though in that case I should say it were wiser not to address it at all. Each of us, however, must decide on this differently and act accordingly. But surely, Richardson, that is not our only object, at least it is not mine. I am far from the conceit that it lies with us to convert the world. But I do

[1] *Threading My Way*, p. 323.

believe it is in our power to influence it. I do believe it lies with us to attract slowly and gradually much attention and to command not merely for our theory but for our practice the respect of our fellow creatures. Of opposition we shall have enough. Of abuse, of misconception, of misinterpretation enough and more than enough. All this must come as matter of course and can certainly as little mortify our vanity as it can flatter it. To shrink from criticism would mark us indeed as unfit for the work we have undertaken. But to provoke abuse would mark us for equally unfit. If we have in view the conversion of men or if we have simply in view our own happiness and dignity, the manner of all our communications is of equal import with the matter. Let us not throw stones at the world we have left. In declaring opinions new to many, as supported by practice startling to all, let us do so with composure as well as fearlessness; let us show the base on which we rest them and in all our arguments let us have in view their just explanation if not the conversion of mankind. It appears to me that the manner in which you have notified our opinions in the letter from which my [illegible] quotes must be calculated to increase the irritation which the opinions themselves are sufficiently likely to excite. Do they not merit a statement temperate in its language and complete in its reasoning? Do they not furnish arms which, if used with temper and self command must put their adversaries on the defensive? Do we not owe it to them and owe it to ourselves to weigh well our words in all communications with the world and is it advisable to launch our principles naked and defenseless in the midst of the enemy leaving to that enemy itself the task of developing them?

I am not questioning of course our right each to his own opinion, and to his own mode of expounding it. But it appears to me that each and all of us bear a double character —as an individual and as one of a society associated for certain objects which in the circle of Nashoba we may speak in our individual character—but it will be difficult for us hereafter to speak so in the world. Any impression there given by us in-

dividually will be received as given by the society and does it
not therefore behoove us to be cautious in provoking unnecessary hostility and misconceptions? You will not understand
me as counselling the holding back of opinions or dissimulating
their extent. I would fain see them stated distinctly in detail,
—in language impossible to be misunderstood. But I would
fain see them also stated in language calculated to persuade
but certainly not to irritate. It is one thing to state a truth and
another thing to prove it. But when we give the proposition
should we not subjoin the Q. E. D. Although all may not be
called upon to do this I think we are. All principles are liable
to misinterpretation but none so much as ours. If good taste
and good feeling do not dictate their expression and guide
their practice they will fall into (at all events momentary)
contempt. I could dwell much on this subject for I feel its
importance both for Nashoba and for all that Nashoba may
influence. Should you not think with me—you will not, I am
sure see any other motive in these observations than that arising out of the deep interest I feel in our success and in the
triumph of our principles.[1]

But unfortunately these words of wisdom were wasted,
for the damage had already been done.

Still unaware of how seriously her plans had been com-
promised at home, she left France for England, whither
Owen had already preceded her. Here their efforts to
arouse interest in Nashoba and its principles were not
altogether successful, at least from the standpoint of recruits, although Owen seems to have believed for a time
that they might be joined by Leigh Hunt and Mary Shelley.[2] Probably it was during the two short months
spent in England that Frances learned fully what had

[1] Wright MSS. Frances Wright to James Richardson, La Grange,
August 18, 1827.

[2] *Ibid.*, Robert Dale Owen to Frances Wright, August 29, September 6,
and September 15, 1827.

been done by Camilla and Richardson, for a letter from
Lafayette, cautioning her against the unwisdom of some
of her new ideas in the present state of society, would
seem to indicate that Camilla's letter to Charles Wilkes
had at length reached Europe.[1]  At any rate she found
it advisable to prepare a circular letter in French, for
distribution among her friends, in which was announced
the new basis of the Nashoba experiment.

One recruit she did gain, and a most interesting one.
Upon her arrival in England she had gone to Harrow,
to the home of Mrs. Frances Milton Trollope, well known
to Americans a few years later as the author of *The
Domestic Manners of the Americans*, and as the mother
of the English novelist Anthony Trollope.  Mrs. Trollope had first met Frances Wright at La Grange six
years before, and during the old refugee days in London
had opened to her the hospitality of her home, for Mrs.
Trollope "loved society, affecting a somewhat liberal
*rôle*, and professing an emotional dislike of tyrants,
which sprung from the wrongs of would-be regicides
and the poverty of patriot exiles."[2]  Naturally, at that
time, the activities of Miss Wright much appealed to
her.  But, in 1827, it does not appear that she was half
so much interested in the theories of her guest, as in the
need of recouping the family fortunes, and establishing
in life some of her growing family.  Strangely enough
Frances Wright was able to convince her that Nashoba
was just the place for them.[3]  In consequence Mrs. Trollope planned that residence in the United States, the

---

[1] *Ibid.*, Lafayette to Frances Wright.  Only a fragment of this letter
remains, and the date is missing.  Probably October, 1827.

[2] Trollope, Anthony, *Autobiography*, New York, 1883, pp. 19-20.

[3] Trollope, Thomas Adolphus, *What I Remember*, New York, 1888, pp.
106-108.

description of which, five years later, so aroused the ire
of all good Americans.

It may have been during the visit to Harrow that
Thomas Adolphus Trollope, the eldest son of Mrs. Trollope, remembered Miss Wright as a woman of a hand-
some masculine type of beauty, a commanding presence,
and a superb figure.    In some London magazine, he tells
us, there still exists a picture of her in which she stands
with her hand upon the neck of her horse, and clad, " if
I remember rightly, in Turkish trousers."[1]

On the fourth of November, Mrs. Trollope, accompanied by her son Henry and two daughters, embarked
with Miss Wright, at London, on the ·"Edward" for
New Orleans.    They reached New Orleans on Christmas
day, and, after spending a few days in the city, proceeded
directly to Nashoba where they were received by Camilla
and her husband; Richardson having left the institution
to return to Memphis.    One glance was sufficient to
convince Mrs. Trollope that a residence at Nashoba was
impossible.    Only the intense enthusiasm of Miss Wright,
an enthusiasm approaching religious fanaticism, could
have led her for a moment to believe that her European
friends could enter there, "and not feel dismayed at
the savage aspect of the scene."[2]    Desolation was the
only word Mrs. Trollope found to describe it, and to her
conventional English mind, the little clearing, with its
few log huts buried deep in the primeval forests of western Tennessee, must have been vividly dreadful.    Not
even " had they as yet collected round them any of those
minor comforts which ordinary minds class among the
necessaries of life."[3]    But Miss Wright's was not an or-

[1] *Ibid.*

[2] *Domestic Manners of the Americans*, vol. i, pp. 33-42.

[3] *Ibid.*

dinary mind, as Mrs. Trollope admitted, for in those surroundings she appeared perfectly at home, "nor was
there any mixture of affectation in this indifference; it
was a circumstance really and truly beneath her notice.
Her whole heart and soul were occupied by the hope of
raising the African to the level of the European intellect."[1] This was an enterprise too arduous for Mrs.
Trollope, however, and at the end of ten days she departed for Cincinnati, where for the next two years she
strove unsuccessfully to better the family fortunes, and,
incidentally, to lay the foundations for her observations
upon American manners.

Shortly after her return Frances carried out the suggestion in her letter to James Richardson, and made
public her famous "Explanatory Notes, respecting the
Nature and Object of the Institution at Nashoba, and of
the principles upon which it is founded: Addressed to
the Friends of Human Improvement, in all Countries
and all Nations."[2] In this remarkable document she
plainly stated that it was now the purpose of Nashoba to
carry into practice certain principles which had been long
advocated by liberal thinkers, but which the world would
never receive unsupported by experiment. At Nashoba
it was hoped to convince mankind of their moral beauty
and their utility, and within herself Miss Wright felt
there existed the qualifications necessary for successfully
carrying on such an experiment—mental courage and a
passion for the improvement of the human race.

Observation had taught her that "men are virtuous in
proportion as they are happy; and happy in proportion

[1] *Ibid.*

[2] This was written on board the "Edward" on her return from Europe,
and is dated December 4, 1827. It was published in the *New Harmony
Gazette*, January 30, 1828.

as they are free!'" In the present state of society, however, they were not free, but bound by a thousand unhappy conventions and conditions, which prevented the attainment of true happiness and virtue. An unequal division of labor separated them into artificial classes, condemning the greater half to a life of physical toil, and the lesser to one of pernicious idleness, or to mental exertion only, so that nowhere could one find "even a single individual, male or female, whose mental and physical powers have been fairly cultivated and developed." A false economy conceived of men as but so much machinery for the creation of wealth, and held a nation rich, "not in proportion to the number of its individuals who enjoy, but to the mass of ideal wealth, thrown into commercial circulation." The most necessary occupations were considered degrading, while those which throve upon the quarrels and credulity of men were exalted. The repressive force of public opinion too often failed to influence those classes most needing it, and crushed those "whose feelings and intellects have been most cultivated, and who consequently, are best fitted to a healthy and intellectual race." And finally there was the unfortunate effect of present institutions upon women, for "in what class do we find the largest proportion of childless females, and devoted victims to unnatural restraints? Certainly among the cultivated, talented and independent women, who . . . shrink equally from the servitude of matrimony, and from the opprobrium stamped upon unlegalized connexions."

Something, indeed, men had done to throw off the bonds which fettered their progress to freedom. In one country, at least, political liberty had been achieved; but political liberty, "the liberty of speech and of action, without incurring the violence of authority, or the pen-

alties of law," was only half the victory. True freedom
—"universal in all the objects it embraces and equal for
all classes of men"—could come only with the attainment of moral liberty—"the free exercise of the liberty
of speech and of action, without incurring the intolerance of popular prejudice, and ignorant public opinion."
With political liberty attained, a people had but "to will
it," to secure moral liberty, and with moral liberty men
might rationally enquire into their institutions, without
fear of popular prejudice, and free society from the ills
which burdened it. "It is much to have declared men
free and equal, but it shall be more, when they are rendered so—when the means shall be sought, and found,
and employed to develope all the intellectual and physical
powers of all human beings, without regard to sex or
condition—class, race, or color." It would be even
more when men learned "to view each other as members of one great family, with equal claims to enjoyment
and equal capacities for labor and instruction—admitting
always the sole differences arising out of the varieties
exhibited in the individual organization." To show that
moral freedom could produce so happy a result was the
duty of Nashoba.

For the times these were radical views, but they were
not very dissimilar to those avowed by Owen at New
Harmony, and it seems probable that had it not been for
an effort to apply them to the racial problem but little
attention would have been paid to them. However, in
establishing at Nashoba a cooperative community, based
upon principles of moral freedom, Frances Wright had
to consider the original object of her experiment. To
raise the slave to the level of the European intellect, and
an appreciation of the theory and practice of voluntary
cooperation, seemed impossible. The benumbing men-

tal effects of slavery were too great a handicap.  It was,
therefore, decided that the best interests of the negro
race would be consulted by limiting the number of slaves
at Nashoba to the original purchase, and by admitting
to membership, upon terms of absolute equality, respectable free negroes, whose children would receive a rational
education in the school of the institution, thus raising
the intellectual and moral character of the race.  In self-
emancipation, as a solution of the slave problem, Miss
Wright had apparently lost faith.  Slavery, she now believed, was destined to disappear in a comparatively few
years, due to economic causes, leaving behind it a serious race problem.  Then, "the principles avowed at
Nashoba may . . . attract the national attention, and
the olive peace of brotherhood be embraced by the
white man & the black, and their children approached in
feeling and education gradually blend into one, their
blood and their hue."  Indeed, it was in the amalgamation of the races alone that she could now see a solution
of the problem which she had so vigorously attacked two
years before:

It [emancipation] can only be progressive thro' the feelings; and, thro' that medium, be finally complete and entire,
involving at once, political equality, and the amalgamation of
the races. . . . The only question is, whether it shall take
place in good taste and good feeling, & be made at once the
means of sealing the tranquility, & perpetuating the liberty
of the country, and of peopling it with a race more suited to
its southern climate, than the pure European,—or whether it
shall proceed, as it now does, viciously and degradingly,
mingling hatred and fear with ties of blood—denied, indeed,
but stamped by nature on the skin.

In view of her frank advocacy of the amalgamation of
the races in a country where race feeling ran high, it is

no wonder that Miss Wright's name became anathema
in the South, and that gentlemen should intimate that
they would "not be surprised if Miss Wright should, one
of these mornings, find her throat cut!"[1]  Madison
wrote to Lafayette that with all her rare talents, and still
rarer disinterestedness, "she has I fear created insuper-
able obstacles to the good fruits of which they might be
productive by her disregard or rather open defiance of
the most established opinion & vivid feelings.  Besides
her views of amalgamating the white & black population
so universally obnoxious, she gives an eclât to her notions on the subject of Religion & of marriage, the
effect of which your knowledge of this Country can
readily estimate."[2]  By the few papers of liberal tendencies the "Notes" were well received, although they
commented upon the daring of the author, and the New
York *Correspondent* felt that it might be wise, at first,
to confine the practice of the views set forth to a community.[3]

In again taking up the task at Nashoba, the resident
trustees soon came to the conclusion that their hope of
establishing a cooperative labor community was impracticable, as the adults of the present generation were
totally unfitted by early environment to take up any serious physical work without danger of injuring their
health.   Hence the cooperative community was given

[1] Wright MSS. Mary Carroll to Frances Wright, New Orleans, February 4, 1828.  Miss Carroll was a young lady of New Orleans who had
given up her millinery business to start a "philosophical bookshop."  She
was a friend of Owen and Maclure, and was much interested in Miss·
Wright.

[2] Madison, James, *Writings*, edited by Gaillard Hunt, 9 vols., New York,
1900-1910, vol. ix, pp. 310-313.

[3] *New Harmony Gazette*, January 30, 1828; The New York *Correspondent*, February 29, 1828.

up for a Preliminary Social Community, composed of small capitalists, of whom each should furnish a certain sum of money yearly for their support.[1]  But in spite of this change, and a last effort made to open the school, which had always been one of Frances Wright's fondest hopes, the Nashoba experiment was drawing to a close. "My dear Jennings," wrote Frances to her friend and co-trustee, Robert L. Jennings, "co-operation has well nigh killed us all," and it was true.[2]  She herself was incapable of further physical exertion, and the break-down of Whitby now rendered necessary his departing from Nashoba with his wife, leaving the slaves in the care of an overseer, John M. Gilliam.[3]  Richardson had left the institution even before the return of Miss Wright, and young Owen, upon reaching the United States, spent but a few days at Nashoba before going on to New Harmony, from whence he wrote, urging Frances to join him in carrying on the *New Harmony Gazette*.  After a spring spent alone at Nashoba, except for the presence of the slaves and transient visitors, she finally departed on the fourth of June to join her sister in New Harmony, leaving the property in charge of Gilliam.[4]

Under the mismanagement of the overseer, Nashoba ran down so rapidly that by fall Miss Wright found it necessary, either to return and devote herself exclusively

[1] Wright MSS. Communication from the Trustees of Nashoba, February 1, 1828.

[2] *Ibid.*, Frances Wright to Robert L. Jennings, Memphis, February 24, 1828. In this letter Miss Wright asked Jennings to take charge of the proposed school.  Unfortunately the letter never reached Jennings, and was later made public without Miss Wright's consent in certain New York newspapers, for the purpose of embarrassing her.  See the *New York Courier and Enquirer*, June 19, 1830.

[3] *Ibid.*, "Nashoba Book," January 30, 1828.

[4] *Ibid.*, June 4, 1828.

to the institution, or to give it up entirely. Already deeply interested in the editing of the *New Harmony Gazette*, and in her lecture work, she decided upon the latter course, although it involved a financial loss of something like $16,000, more than half of her fortune at that time.[1] Until the slaves could be conveniently removed, and the experiment brought to a formal close, Whitby and Camilla assumed charge of the plantation.

Eighteen months later Frances returned to carry out her promise of emancipating and colonizing her slaves, now numbering thirty. Following in the footsteps of George Flower and Benjamin Lundy, she decided to place them on the island of Haiti under the protection of President Boyer. Not desiring to trust them to the care of an agent, she personally directed their removal, chartering the brig "John Quincy Adams" of Boston, and sailing from New Orleans about the middle of January, 1830.[2] In Haiti, President Boyer placed them on one of his own estates, and supplied them "with tools, provisions for the first months, and other encouragements. The whole free of all charge and rent so long as they choose to remain and prove good occupants." If their conduct was good, and they desired to become proprietors, they were to receive a grant of government land. President Boyer, moreover, generously assisted in the expense of the removal.[3] So ended Frances Wright's experiment in self-emancipation. "For the first time she bowed her head in humility before the omnipotence

---

[1] Owen, Robert Dale, "An Earnest Sowing of Wild Oats." An article by Owen which appeared in the *Atlantic Monthly*, July, 1874.

[2] "An Earnest Sowing of Wild Oats."

[3] Wright MSS. Frances Wright to Lafayette, Port au Prince, Haiti, February 15, 1830. For further information in regard to this subject see her letter to the *Free Enquirer*, February 13, 1830.

of collective humanity.   Man Species is alone capable of
effecting what I, weak existence of an hour, have thought
myself equal to attempt." [1]

In theory, at least, Miss Wright's project of self-
emancipation had started out with a fair chance of success.   Cooperative labor had proved its financial possibilities in the United States, in more than one instance,
under the direction of skillful leaders, and there appeared
no good reason why it could not be made the basis of a
satisfactory plan of emancipation.   At Nashoba, however, a number of factors contributed to its failure.   In
the first place, although Miss Wright possessed an un-
bounded enthusiasm for her project, and exercised great
energy in its promotion, she lacked the wisdom and
managerial experience necessary for its successful operation.   Then too, the location chosen was unfortunate,
for the amount of physical toil and pioneer hardship involved in clearing the mosquito-infested woodland of
western Tennessee could not but prove altogether too
much for the strength and health of those whose previous experience had totally unfitted them for such a life.
The consequent illness of Miss Wright at a crucial moment in the career of her experiment, making it necessary to leave Nashoba in charge of the incompetent
Whitby and the visionary Richardson, was well-nigh
fatal, but the most important cause of failure, in the
writer's opinion, was the unhappy attempt to combine
the original project with a cooperative community
scheme, based upon the Owenite plans for the moral regeneration of mankind.   This effort not only diverted
the attention and energy of Miss Wright from her pri-
mary object, and caused her to lose contact with the re-
alities of her original experiment, but gave free rein to

[1] *Biography*, pt. i, p. 32.

the eccentricities of her associates. In consequence, Nashoba fell into ill repute, and its mistress found herself forced to defend her institution, in a document which could not but alienate the sympathy of a public quite unprepared to accept with her own enthusiasm the principles and implications of mental or moral freedom, however much, in theory, they might conduce to the perfectibility of man.

As to the cooperative community, it never really existed except upon paper, for at no time were there more than six or seven whites resident at Nashoba, and these consisted only of Miss Wright and her immediate associates. Indeed, as Mrs. Trollope remarked, only the intense enthusiasm of Miss Wright could have led her to believe for a moment that people brought up amidst the refinements of society could have found contentment in the pioneer life and forbidding environment of Nashoba.

Of the sincerity of Miss Wright there can be no question. Her experiment in self-emancipation was one of the very few real efforts made to solve the problem of American slavery, and it deserved a better fate. For her community scheme not so much can be said. At best, it was an honest but impracticable attempt to better the condition of mankind.

# CHAPTER VI

## The Popular Lecturer

EARLY in June, 1828, Frances Wright left Nashoba for New Harmony, where she planned to spend the summer months with Camilla. Nashoba had been a disappointment and a failure, and she soon became convinced that further efforts there would be futile. Managerial and financial difficulties, as well as poor health, were sufficient causes for giving up the experiment, but more important was the feeling that Nashoba, as a single, small, and isolated experiment, could never hope to command for the principles upon which it was based the popular attention its founder felt indispensable. She had " envisaged a practical experiment when she might have been more usefully employed in preparing the popular mind for the exercise, with knowledge, of popular power " : [1]

I finally became convinced, that there are but two remedies for all our evils—for those of the north as those of the south; for those of the south as those of the north. These remedies, slow working indeed, but sure in their effects, are —the rational training of youth, and, so far as possible, the instructional improvement of the present generation. All other panaceas but these I distinguished clearly for quack nostrums; and determined to forsake all practical experiments for the great work of national regeneration. . . .[2]

In spite, therefore, of a financial loss of over sixteen thou-

[1] *Biography*, pt. i, pp. 32-33.
[2] *Free Enquirer*, October 21, 1829.

sand dollars, she decided to give up Nashoba, and devote her time and attention to the instruction of the present generation in rational principles. The result, she hoped, might be the initiation of public measures looking to the adoption of a system of rational education, for only upon such a wide and firm foundation could a well-ordered society exist. To accomplish her purpose, she joined Robert Dale Owen, a kindred spirit, in publishing and editing the *New Harmony Gazette*. This interesting paper, to which Frances Wright had been an early contributor, had been founded, in 1825, by William Owen and Robert L. Jennings to set forth the social theories of Robert Owen, and meet the news needs of the community. It had already established a reputation for fearless enquiry into the social and religious questions of the day. Under its new editors, as *The New Harmony and Nashoba Gazette or Free Enquirer*, it proposed to devote itself "without fear, without reserve, without pledge to men, parties, sects or systems, to free, unbiassed, and universal enquiry," desiring "to aid in the diffusion of truth, in the spread of liberal principles, and in the dissipation of those prejudices which observation and experience may designate as obstacles in the progressive march of the world from error and suffering toward wisdom and enjoyment." It proposed, moreover, to enquire vigorously into whatever customs or institutions its editors deemed inimical to the rational progress of mankind.[1]

On the Fourth of July, 1828, Frances had the honor of delivering the patriotic address of the day in New Harmony, and the opportunity to dwell again upon what she believed

---

[1] *New Harmony Gazette*, July 30, 1828. The quotation appeared in the published prospectus of the *New Harmony and Nashoba Gazette or Free Enquirer*. The change of name was due to a desire to get away from the social experiments about New Harmony with which the *New Harmony Gazette* had been bound up.

to be the crowning glory of American political institutions, their adaptability to change through amendment. Far more important than the content of her address was the discovery that she possessed no little ability as a public speaker, a discovery opening up unlimited possibilities for the instruction of the public in the principles she advocated. Needless to say, Frances Wright was not the woman to shirk the duty such an opportunity presented, nor did she long wait for an occasion to stand before the public in the rôle of popular lecturer, and spread broadcast with all the eloquence at her command the principles of rationalism. The appearance in Cincinnati of one of those great revivals, not uncommon in that day of highly emotional religion, gave her the opening she desired:

The city of Cincinnati [she tells us] had stood for some time conspicuous for the enterprise and liberal spirit of her citizens, when [in the summer of 1828], by the sudden combination of the clergy of three orthodox sects, a revival, as such scenes of distraction are wont to be styled, was opened in the homes, churches, and even on the Ohio river. The victims of this odious experiment on human credulity and nervous weakness were invariably women. Helpless age was made a public spectacle, youth driven to raving insanity, mothers and daughters carried lifeless from the presence of the ghostly expounders of damnation; all ranks shared the contagion, while the despair of Calvin's hell itself seemed to have fallen upon every heart, and discord to have taken possession of every mansion.

A circumstantial account of the distress and disturbance in the public mind in the Ohio metropolis led me to visit the afflicted city, and since all were dumb, to take up the cause of insulted reason and outraged humanity.[1]

---

[1] *Course of Popular Lectures*, pp. 8-9. This was probably the revival so vividly described by Mrs. Trollope in her *Domestic Manners of the Americans*, vol. i, pp. 102-111.

That Frances Wright should take such a step was not unnatural, for, aside from the opportunity to advance her own cause, she had been an enemy to organized religion from the days of her conversion to Epicureanism. Moreover, in the missionary and revival activities of the evangelical churches she thought she discerned a spirit of intolerance quite hostile to the independence of American thought. With Robert Owen she believed the time had come for a declaration of mental independence:

There is a secret influence at work which all feel and none distinguish. It infects all society, taints every institution in the land, poisoning alike human instruction, human laws, and human recreation. In your schools—it diseases the infant mind with superstitious terrors, and with reason-confounding, heart-distorting creeds. In your colleges—it stifles the breath of your teachers of science, and constrains the entanglement of their simple facts with the dreams of theology. In your books and periodicals—but it matters not to speak of the press. In your courts of law—it tempts to perjury, sitting in judgment on the religious creed of witnesses, and reflecting even on that of the prisoner. In your legislatures—it dictates unconstitutional ordinances, and unconstitutional disposals of money and lands. Nay! at this moment, it is outraging the ear of your national congress with presbyterian Sabbath law petitions. In your amusements—alas! there its influence hath been mortal! Your amusements, which under wise direction and judicious encouragement, should elevate the mind and humanize the heart—your amusements, I say, it has degraded, it has perverted, and so led the mind astray from pleasure to vice, from healthy recreation to mind-debasing, life-destroying licentiousness.[1]

This unfortunate influence, she believed, found complete expression, in the summer of 1828, in what became widely known as the Christian Party in Politics:

[1] *Course of Popular Lectures*, pp. 145-146.

It was in this year, 1828 [she informs us in her autobiography],
that the standard of the 'Christian Party in Politics' was
openly unfurled.  Of this party, which had been long secretly
at work, Frances Wright had previously detected the manoeu-
vers in all sections of the country.  This was an evident
attempt, through the influence of the clergy over the female
mind—until this hour lamentably neglected in the United
States—to affect a union of Church and State, and with it a
lasting union of Bank and State; and thus effectually to pros-
trate the independence of the people, and the institutions of the
country.  Clearly distinguishing the nature of the move, Frances
Wright determined to arouse the whole American people to meet
it, at whatever cost to herself.[1]

If such a menace existed, it was time, indeed, that the
American public be aroused; but that the menace did exist,
it seems difficult for us today to believe.  In 1828, however,
there was just enough back of the idea to cause apprehension upon the part of many good people less radically
minded than Miss Wright.  To understand what the Christian Party in Politics was, and what aid Miss Wright might
expect in her struggle against it, it will be necessary to turn
for a moment to certain aspects of the religious development of the country just prior to, and during, the twenties.

Shortly after the War of 1812 a new feature made itself
felt in the character of the great religious movement, which
was so important a factor in American life during the first
half of the nineteenth century.  Up to that time, the efforts
of the various churches to spread the gospel into the waste
places of the land, and to improve the tone of public morality, had been carried on independently.  Now there appeared
a strong tendency to gain the advantages of cooperative
effort, of mass action, through the organization of great
national societies, with ramifications in all parts of the coun-

[1] *Biography*, pt. i, p. 13.

try. So successful were the earlier efforts of this kind, the American Tract Society, the American Society for Educating Pious Youth for the Gospel Ministry, and the American Bible Society, that many good people concluded that through similar associations almost any desired reforms might be brought about:

In truth [said the Reverend William Ellery Channing in his sermon, "Remarks on Associations"], one of the most remarkable circumstances or features of our age, is the energy with which the principle of combination, or of action by joint forces, by associated numbers, is manifesting itself. It may be said, without much exaggeration, that everything is now done by societies. Men have learned that wonders can be accomplished in certain cases by union, and seem to think that union is competent to every thing.[1]

That the objects and ideals of such societies were generally well worth while, and their leaders good men, was not to be doubted; but coöperative effort in the United States, on such a scale, was something new, and, to many people, seemed to bear within it a spirit at war with the traditional individualism of our earlier history. Hence, the well meant, but often indiscreet and sometimes intolerant, efforts of the great religious societies to attain their ends, aroused, not unnaturally perhaps, a suspicion that back of all this stir in the churches a great conspiracy was afoot; that the evangelical churches led by the Presbyterians planned to effect a union of church and state, and thus dominate the social, political, and religious life of the nation. This suspicion, which seems to have definitely taken form by 1826, was confirmed in the minds of those hostile to the religious movement of the day by the notorious Fourth-of-July sermon, in 1827, of the Reverend Ezra Stiles Ely, pastor of

[1] Channing, William Ellery, *Works*, 6 vols., Boston, 1845, vol. i, p. 282.

the Third Presbyterian Church of Philadelphia. In his zeal for reform through the cooperative efforts of the churches, Dr. Ely quite let his imagination run off with him:

I propose, fellow-citizens [said Dr. Ely], a new sort of union, or, if you please, a Christian party in politics, which I am exceedingly desirous all good men in our country should join; not by subscribing a contribution and the formation of a new society, to be added to the scores that now exist; but by adopting, avowing, and determining to act upon, truly religious principles in all civil matters. I am aware that the true Christians of our country are divided into many different denominations; who have, alas! too many points of jealousy and collision; still, a union to a very great extent is not impracticable. . . . All who profess to be Christians of any denomination ought to agree that they will support no man as a candidate for any office, who is not professedly friendly to Christianity, and a believer in divine Revelation. We do not say that true or even pretended Christianity shall be made a constitutional test of admission to office; but we do affirm that Christians may in their elections lawfully prefer the avowed friends of the Christian religion to Turks, Jews, and Infidels.

For this purpose, urged Dr. Ely, the Christian sects

may accordingly settle it in their minds, that they will never vote for anyone to fill an office in the nation or state, who does not receive the Bible as the rule of his faith. If three or four of the most numerous denominations of Christians in the United States, the Presbyterians, the Baptists, the Methodists, and the Congregationalists for instance should act upon this principle, our country would never be dishonored with an avowed infidel in her national cabinet. The Presbyterians alone could bring half a million electors into the field, in opposition to any known advocate of Deism, Socinianism, or any other species of avowed hostility to the truth of Christianity. If to the denominations above mentioned we add the members of the Protestant Episcopal Church in this country, the electors of these five classes of true Christians, united in the sole requisition of apparent friendship to Christianity in every candidate for office whom they will support, could govern every public election in our country, without infringing in the least upon the character of our civil liberties.[1]

That Dr. Ely's Christian Party in Politics ever existed, outside of the minds of a few overzealous clergymen, there is no conclusive evidence, but by many this sermon was accepted as indicative of dangerous aspirations upon the part of the clergy, if not positive proof of a menacing conspiracy. For circumstantial evidence of such a scheme, the growth, size, and elaborate organization of the great religious societies was pointed out, the interlocking character of their boards of directors, and their apparently huge financial resources. Other traces of the scheme, it was believed, were to be seen in the widespread efforts, through organized petitioning, to induce state and national legislatures to aid in restoring the puritan Sabbath; this to be accomplished by legislation abolishing Sunday travel on post-road, river, and canal, and by putting an end to the Sunday mail service.[2] For more effectively and quickly attaining these ends, there had been formed, in 1828, a General Union for Promoting the Observation of the Christian Sabbath, an organi-

[1] Ely, Ezra Stiles, *The Duty of Christian Freemen to elect Christian Rulers; A Discourse delivered on the 4th of July, 1827, in the Seventh Presbyterian Church, in Philadelphia, by Ezra Stiles Ely, D. D., pastor of the Third Presbyterian Church in that City. With an Appendix, Designed to Vindicate the Liberty of Christians, and the American Sunday School Union*, Philadelphia, 1828.

[2] New York *Observer* (Presbyterian), January 3, 1829; New York *Telescope*, April 4, 1825. The *Observer*, January 17, 1829, boasted that 500 petitions would be presented to Congress in 1829, praying for the abolition of the Sunday mail service. The *Telescope* was a little anticlerical paper published in New York by William Beach. In 1830 it was combined with the *Working Man's Advocate*.

zation much feared and disliked by the liberal-minded.[1] The attempt to introduce religious tracts as text-books into the schools of New York state,[2] the efforts made to secure a charter in Pennsylvania, in 1828, for the American Sunday School Union, in which Dr. Ely was much interested,[3] and the great outburst of revivalism, characterized, particularly in western New York, by an unusual degree of intolerance and fanaticism, were felt to be other evidences of the sinister ambitions of the clergy:[4]

It is seriously believed by the enlightened and liberal of all denominations [said the Unitarian *Christian Intelligencer*]

[1] Tappan, Lewis, *Arthur Tappan*, New York, 1870, pp. 17, 97-98; *Christian Advocate*, June, 1828, p. 282; *New York Journal of Commerce,* June 2, 1828. The *Journal of Commerce* was established by Arthur Tappan, in 1827, to meet the demand for a good financial paper. In accordance with Tappan's belief in the strict observance of the Sabbath, the paper for Monday was not printed on Sunday, as was the general custom of the New York papers.

[2] New York *Telescope*, January 1, 1825, December 30, 1826. Secretary Yates of New York was responsible for the introduction of the tracts into the schools. So much opposition to the plan appeared that Yates soon withdrew his permission.

[3] *Correspondent*, March 15, 1828; Ely, Ezra Stiles, *The Duty of Christian Freemen*; see also article quoted from the *Democratic Press* of Philadelphia in the *Free Enquirer*, August 19, 1829.

[4] Brownson, Orestes Augustus, *The Convert: or, Leaves from my Experience*, New York, 1857, p. 20. In this book Brownson describes the interesting religious experiences which eventually carried him into the Roman Church. He states that about 1827 a movement was started in the Presyterian Church to induce all the members to pledge themselves to non-intercourse with the rest of the community, except in regard to conversion, and to refuse to patronize, or have business dealings, with anyone not of the Church. As the Presbyterians were few in numbers those agitating the matter admitted the other evangelical sects. See also a pamphlet by Perkins, Ephraim, *A Bunker Hill Contest, A. D. 1826, Between the " Holy Alliance" for the Establishment of Hierarchy, and Ecclesiastical Domination Over the Human Mind, on the one side; and the Asserters of Free Enquiry, Bible Religion, Christian Freedom, and Civil Liberty on the other,* Utica, 1826. This was an attack by a Unitarian upon the activities of the evangelical churches in upper New York State.

that the Presbyterian and other " Orthodox " Clergy have been manoeuvring for years to effect an unholy union between Church and state, for the establishment of a " National Religion." They have accordingly, concentrated their forces and resources in these combinations, called " National Societies," have in a clandestine manner recommended the adoption of a " National Creed," a " National Costume," and at length come out boldly in the " Evangelical Witness," in recommending the adoption of a " union of the several Orthodox denominations, for the purpose of forming or selecting for the whole, one Confession of Faith." [1]

While these might be the words of Unitarian alarmists, there were, undoubtedly, many who agreed with the Reverend William Ellery Channing, that in the great national religious societies there was evident an influence growing up, at war with the spirit of our institutions and one that, " unless jealously watched, will gradually but surely encroach on freedom of thought, of speech, and of the press.[2] "

It was not unnatural that the Unitarians should look with some suspicion upon evangelical activities which might threaten their own existence. More important for our study, however, was the reappearance of the anti-christian, deistical, and sceptical movement, which had flourished in the last years of the eighteenth and early years of the nineteenth centuries, under the inspiration of the French Revolutionary doctrines, the pen of Thomas Paine, and the eloquence of Elihu Palmer.[3] Encouraged by the hostility of

[1] *The Telescope,* February 2, 1828. Quoting from the *Christian Intelligencer.* For further information in regard to this plot see the *Correspondent,* May 31, July 19, 1828; *The Telescope,* December 1, 1827; *New York Courier and Enquirer,* July 21, 1830, and May 6, 1831; *Gospel Advocate* (Auburn, N. Y.), July 5, 1828; *New Harmony Gazette,* October 22, 1828; *The Journal of Commerce,* February 6, 1829; Perkins, *A Bunker Hill Contest,* pp. 43-48; Royall, Anne, *The Black Book,* 3 vols., Washington, 1828, vol. i, pp. 163-164, 226-227; vol. iii, pp. 186-187.

[2] Channing, *Works,* vol. i, p. 305.

[3] Elihu Palmer, though blind, was the ablest speaker the American

a part of the public to the religious movement of the day, the latent spirit of infidelity in the country, which had been quiet for fifteen years, again became articulate and aggressive under new and energetic leaders.   On the twenty-ninth of January, 1825, "a few friends in this city [New York] celebrated for the first time the birthday of Mr. Paine. Mr. Young of Harmony Hall, was the only person who had the courage and liberality to provide a dinner on that occasion." [1]   Probably the "few friends" met again in 1826, but of their activities until January, 1827, we know little.   By that time their numbers had increased to such an extent that George Houston of New York City felt justified in establishing a weekly freethought paper, the *Correspondent*.   Houston was an Englishman, a friend and follower of the English freethinker, Richard Carlisle, and had been persecuted, fined, and imprisoned for two years in Newgate on a charge of blasphemy; his offence being the translation and publication of d'Holbach's *Ecce Homo*. [2] Upon leaving Newgate, Houston had sought refuge in the United States, where he had settled in the city of New York. Here for several years he edited the *Minerva,* a literary miscellany which carefully avoided all political and religious disputation. [3]

The first issue of the *Correspondent* appeared on the

deistical movement produced between 1796 and 1806.  He also did much to organize the deistical clubs, and make the movement popular.  For a brief account of his life see, Palmer, Elihu, *Posthumous Pieces, being three chapters of an unfinished work intended to have been entitled "The Political World" to which are prefixed a Memoir of Mr. Palmer by his friend Mr. John Fellowes of New York*, London, 1824.

[1] *Correspondent*, February 2, 1828.  Thomas Paine's birthday first appears to have been celebrated in London, in 1818.

[2] *Ibid.*, April 25, 1829.  Houston was imprisoned in Newgate in 1813.

[3] The *Minerva* first appeared in 1822.  It seems to have been discontinued in 1825.

twentieth of January, 1827, declaring its object to be " a diffusion of correct principles, which alone form the basis of morals and of happiness," and that, " notwithstanding the vast number of publications that are daily issuing from the press, there is still wanting a paper which will fearlessly advocate the paramount importance of the laws of Nature and the dignity of Reason." [1]   From the first the paper was pronouncedly anti-clerical and destructive in its religious criticism.   It received little attention from the secular press, but one or two of the religious papers noted its appearance. The *National Advocate* declared this to be " probably the first periodical work ever published in the United States, that publicly avows and defends deism," while the *Christian Intelligencer* objected strenuously to its attack upon Christianity without offering anything better.[2]

The establishment of a freethought press was followed by the organization on Paine's birthday, January 29, 1827, of the " Free Press Association," the object of which, according to its constitution, was to remedy the evils of error and superstition so prevalent in the books and periodicals of the time.   The funds of the Association were to be appropriated first to the support of a free press, and afterward to the purchase of books for a philosophical library.   The Association apparently grew very rapidly, as it was forced to remove to larger quarters three times within the next eight months.   Eventually this rapid growth led to the organization of a second society, " The Society of Free Enquirers,"

---

[1] *Correspondent*, January 20, 1827.   The *Correspondent* was not the first paper to avow deistic principles in the United States.   Earlier papers of a somewhat similar character were *The Temple of Reason*, published in New York and Philadelphia in 1800-1801, Elihu Palmer's *The Prospect, or View of the Moral World*, which appeared for a brief time in 1804, and the *Theophilanthropist*, of which several numbers came out in New York in 1810.

[2] *Correspondent*, February 10, 17, 1827, respectively.

having its headquarters farther uptown. Interest in the
movement was stimulated and sustained through the pages
of the *Correspondent,* the Sunday lectures of the " Free
Press Association," the establishment of a " Free Debating
Society," and the sale, at low rates, of philosophical works.
In the philosophical library, as advertised in the *Correspondent,* were to be found d'Holbach's *Ecce Homo,* Paine's
*Age of Reason,* Volney's *Ruins,* and the works of Hume,
Gibbon, and Palmer, as well as many others of a deistical or
sceptical character.[1]  To meet the methods of the religious
societies, the advantages of tract distribution were not overlooked, and freethinkers were even sent out to lecture in the
country towns.[2]

If scepticism, or infidelity as the clergy termed it, first
became articulate in New York City, it did not long remain
a local phenomenon.  Societies similar to the " Free Press
Association " soon began to appear in other places.  In
Paterson, New Jersey, it was the " Paterson Free Reading
Association "; in Cincinnati, " The Society of Mutual Instruction in Natural Science," which seems to have anticipated the " Free Press Association " itself; and in Woodstock, Vermont, was founded the " Woodstock Free Reading
Society."  Societies of a like character were quickly established in Boston, Philadelphia, Buffalo, Baltimore, Utica,
and Cincinnati.[3]  Freethought papers were also springing

[1] For a list of these books see the *Correspondent,* August 25, 1827.
There is a note in the issue of September 8, 1827, to the effect that a
supply of infidel books, described by the press as " the dregs of an English
bookstore that had scarcely escaped burning at the hands of the hang-
man," had recently been brought from England.

[2] *Correspondent,* May 31, August 2, 1828.  The distribution of the tracts
was not a joke.  Benjamin Offen's lecture tour through the Mohawk
Valley in the fall of 1828 was at the expense of the *Correspondent.*
*Correspondent,* June 6, November 8, 1828.

[3] *Ibid.*  See the issues of March 31 and April 4, 1827.  Also those of
January 26, February 24, July 4, 12, 1828.

up. In the West, the *New Harmony Gazette* was already
in the field, although up to this time it had devoted itself
largely to community affairs, and the exposition of Owen's
views. Now it was joined by the *Western Tiller* of Cincinnati, and later by the *March of Mind,* when the *Western
Tiller* passed into conservative hands. In the East, until the
early spring of 1829, the *Correspondent* monopolized the field,
although other papers were proposed from time to time.
That the distribution of these papers was extensive, however small their actual subscription lists, is evident from a
glimpse at the list of agencies mentioned in the *Correspondent,* and later in Frances Wright's paper, the *Free Enquirer.*
Agents were to be found all the way from Woodstock, Vermont, to St. Louis, Missouri; and in the south at Memphis,
Tennessee. In view of this rapid and extended growth of
infidelity it is not surprising that the pastoral letter of the
General Assembly of the Presbyterian Church should say,
in 1827; " We also hear that there is, in many parts of the
country, a rising of the spirit of infidelity and in others a
zealous propagation of erroneous and heretical opinion, destructive of the very life of Christianity." [1]

Of the personalities back of this movement we unfortunately know but little. George Houston has already been
mentioned. His chief assistants in New York City appear
to have been Benjamin Offen, a gentleman who ventured to
lecture, with some success apparently, through the Mohawk
Valley in the fall of 1827, William Carver, an old associate
of Paine's, and George H. Evans, who later became better
known as the editor of the *Working Man's Advocate.*
Another interesting figure was that of Robert L. Jennings,
whom we have already met as a trustee of Nashoba. Jennings had trained for the ministry, but had given up his
studies to join Robert Owen in the community scheme at

[1] *Christian Advocate (Presbyterian)*, July, 1827, p. 331.

New Harmony.   Upon the collapse of the community in the
spring of 1827, he had gone to New York to establish a
school, and to join with Houston in the editing of the *Correspondent.*   Early in 1828 he again journeyed west, hoping
to establish a freethought paper in Cincinnati, but, finding
the ground already pretty well occupied by the *New Harmony Gazette* under the guidance of Robert Dale Owen and
Frances Wright, he decided to organize a school at New
Harmony.   This he gave up to aid in editing the *Gazette,*
and to lecture throughout the country with Miss Wright.[1]

Thus, by the summer of 1828, it is clear that organized
scepticism was again becoming a force to be reckoned with
in the religious life of America.   All that was needed to
make its menace more generally felt was a leader whose personality and eloquence would appeal to the popular imagination.   Such a leader Frances Wright proved to be.

Of Frances Wright's first appearance in Cincinnati, as a
popular lecturer in the cause of free enquiry, we shall let
her friend Mrs. Frances Milton Trollope tell the story.   No
sooner, says Mrs. Trollope, was it known that Miss Wright
proposed publicly to address the people " than the most violent sensation was excited " :

That a lady of fortune, family, and education, whose youth had
been passed in the most refined circles of private life, should present herself to the people as a public lecturer, would naturally
excite surprise any where, and the *nil admirari* of the old world
itself would hardly be sustained before such a spectacle; but
in America, where women are guarded by a seven-fold shield
of habitual insignificance, it has caused an effect which can
scarcely be described.   " Miss Wright, of Nashoba, is going
to lecture at the court house," sounded from street to street,
and from house to house.   I shared in the surprise, but not in
the wonder; I knew her extraordinary gift of eloquence, her

[1] *New Harmony Gazette*, July 30, 1828.

almost unequalled command of words, and the wonderful power of her rich and thrilling voice; and I doubted not that if it was her will to do it, she had the power of commanding the attention, and enchanting the ear of any audience before whom it was her pleasure to appear. I was most anxious to hear her, but was almost deterred from attempting it, by the reports of the immense crowd that was expected. After many consultations, and hearing that many other ladies intended going, my friend Mrs. P——, and myself, decided upon making the attempt, accompanied by a party of gentlemen, and found the difficulty less than we anticipated, though the building was crowded in every part. We congratulated ourselves that we had had the courage to be among the number, for all my expectations fell far short of the splendor, the brilliance, the overwhelming eloquence of this extraordinary orator. . . . It is impossible to imagine anything more striking than her appearance. Her tall and majestic figure, the deep and almost solemn expression of her eyes, the simple contour of her finely formed head, unadorned, excepting by its own natural ringlets; her garment of plain white muslin, which hung about her in folds that recalled the drapery of a Grecian statue, all contributed to produce an effect, unlike any thing I had ever seen before, or ever expect to see again.[1]

For three consecutive Sundays in July, Frances Wright lectured to crowded audiences in the Cincinnati Court House, and so popular were her lectures, or, perhaps, so novel the appearance of a woman upon the public lecture platform, that late in August the series was successfully repeated in the Opera House.

The three lectures delivered in Cincinnati contained the gist of Miss Wright's philosophy, as well as her criticism of those social institutions which she felt to be detrimental to the progress of reason. It was in this manner that she chose to combat the revival spirit in Cincinnati, and arouse

---

[1] *Domestic Manners of the Americans*, vol. i, pp. 94-98.

the American people to the menace of the Christian Party in Politics. Somewhat modified, and expanded eventually to six in number, these discourses made up the Course of Popular Lectures which she delivered in the principal cities of the Union from Boston to New Orleans. In 1829, and again in 1831, the series was published for the benefit of those unable to hear her speak.[1]

That the reader may better understand the excitement caused by Frances Wright during the next two years, it seems advisable, at this point in our story, to discuss in some detail the principles and opinions which she advanced as lecturer and editor. The basis of her philosophy was materialistic, and the principles set forth were essentially those of *A Few Days in Athens,* modified in some measure, perhaps, by the influence of Robert Owen and her own more mature reflections. The true foundation of human happiness, she pointed out to her auditors, must depend upon rational practice, that is, upon practice based on just knowledge. Just knowledge, she defined as knowledge gained through the medium of " our senses; and our faculties, as awakened and improved in by the exercise of our senses." [2] "All knowledge," she declared, " is compounded of the accurately observed, accumulated, and agreeing sensations of mankind," [2] and upon such knowledge alone should men venture to establish their opinions and their practice. The trouble with America, as indeed with all mankind, was its failure to accommodate its life to rational principles, and to accept for real knowledge, what in truth was but uncertain authority. The result, as might be expected, was a veritable riot of intellectual confusion, prejudices, and irrational practices, which everywhere set men at loggerheads with one

---

[1] *Course of Popular Lectures,* New York, 1829. A second edition containing several additional lectures was published in New York in 1831. The following citations are to the edition of 1829.

another. "Everywhere about us we see varying opinions and authorities—men breaking up into innumerable sects in consequence of opinion until we are forced to cry 'Where, then, is right or wrong, but in the human imagination, and what is truth more than blind opinion?'"[1] To escape from this unfortunate situation, to rid mankind of its unhappy prejudices, we must appreciate the character of just knowledge, and accord our practice with it. For this purpose a judicious system of education was needed, and a free spirit of enquiry, the latter alone possible in the present generation.

As to our present institutions, said Miss Wright, let us subject them to a free unbiased investigation, and if their character, and the foundations upon which they are based, prove irrational, let us revise them in the interest of all mankind. America alone, of the nations, she believed, was prepared for such an experiment, for in America the will of the people through legislation was supreme, and once aroused to the importance of harmonizing its practice with just principles, might so mould its educational and instructional system as to secure the desired result. To the attainment of this happy outcome Frances Wright declared herself ready to devote body and soul:

I have wedded the cause of human improvement; staked on it my reputation, my fortune, and my life; and as, for it, I threw behind me in earliest youth the follies of my age, the luxuries of ease and European aristocracy, so do I, and so will I, persevere, even as I began; and devote what remains to me of talent, strength, fortune, and existence, to the same sacred cause—the promotion of just knowledge, the establishing of just practice, the increase of human happiness.[2]

Such was the spirit with which Frances Wright coura-

[1] *Ibid.*, p. 29.
[2] *Ibid.*, p. 18.
[3] *Ibid.*, pp. 71-72.

geously set forth to effect the moral regeneration of America
and of the race. And it needed courage, for not only were
the doctrines set forth anathema to the religious sentiment
of the nation, but the very fact of a woman taking the public
lecture platform was felt to be an outrage upon American
convention, in the eighteen-twenties; woman's place was in
the home.

Having pointed out to her auditors the true nature of
knowledge, and the desirability of guiding our practice in
sympathy with just principles, she boldly launched her enquiry into existing institutions. Religion came first, for it
was the insidious menace of the religious movement, as evidenced in the Christian Party in Politics and the Cincinnati
revival, that had brought her to that city to lecture. Religion she considered as one of the greatest evils afflicting
men, for it turned their attention from a life guided by
rational principles to one based upon speculation and conflicting opinion. Just practice could not be based on " a
belief in, and homage rendered to, existences unseen and unknown," and that was what religion was.[1] Religion, indeed, was not a fit subject for discussion, for of the things
with which it dealt we could know nothing. Her own personal attitude toward the subject was one of hostility, and
toward the existence of God, indifference. She neither
affirmed nor denied Him, believing the whole subject beyond
the ken of man:

If beyond the horizon of things seen—without the range of
our earthly planet, and apart from the nature of our human
race, any speculations should force themselves upon my fancy,
I keep them to myself, even as I do the dreams of my nightly
sleep, well satisfied that my neighbor will have his speculations
and his dreams also, and that his, whatever they may be, will not
coincide precisely with mine.[2]

[1] *Ibid.*, pp. 111-112.
[2] *Ibid.*, pp. 102-103.

As she felt that all ecclesiastical practice was but an imposition upon the credulity of men, she had no sympathy for any particular creed or belief:

My friends, I am no Christian, in the sense usually attached to the word. I am neither Jew nor Gentile, Mohammedan nor Theist; I am but a member of the human family, and would accept truth by whomsoever offered—that truth which we can all find, if we will but seek it—in things, not in words; in nature, not in human imagination; in our hearts, not in temples made with human hands.[1]

Examine our present religious system. Calculate what is spent in multiplying churches and ministers, " in clothing, and feeding travelling preachers, who fill your streets and highways with trembling fanatics, and your very forests with frantic men and hysterical women." Estimate the fruits of honest industry engulfed in the treasuries of bible societies, tract associations, and christian missions, in sending men forth, " to preach of things unseen to nations unknown; compassing the earth to add error to ignorance, and the frenzy of fanaticism to the ferocity of savage existence." Twenty millions of dollars, it is estimated, are devoted to religion yearly. " Twenty millions! For teaching what? Things unseen and causes unknown! Why, here is more than enough to purchase the extract of all just knowledge— that is, of things seen and causes known, gathered by patient philosophy through all past time up to the present hour." Let us enquire:

Take for your teachers experimental philosophers, not spiritual dreamers! Turn your churches into halls of science, and devote your leisure day to the study of your own bodies, the analysis of your own minds, and the examination of the fair material world which extends around you!

[1] *Ibid.*, p. 148.

Receive no man's assertion. Believe no conviction but your own; and *respect not your own* until ye *know* that ye have examined both sides of every question; collected all the evidence, weighed, compared, and digested it; sought it at the fountain head; received it never through suspicious channels— altered, mutilated, or defaced; but pure, genuine, from the authorities themselves. Examine ye things? look to the fact. Examine ye books? to the text. And, when ye look, and when ye read, *be sure that ye see, and be sure that ye understand.* Ask *why* of every teacher. Ask *why* of every book. While there is a doubt, suspend judgment; while one evidence is wanting withhold assent.[1]

Religion, argued Miss Wright, is not a code of morals, and has no place in moral practice, for religion is " a belief in, and homage rendered to, existences unseen and causes un- known "; while morals comprise a mode of just practice, deduced " from the consequences of actions as ascertained through our sensations, and our observations of the sensa- tions of others." [2] Moral actions are those actions which produce good; immoral actions are those producing evil; and what is good and what is evil must depend upon the ac- cumulated experiences of the race. To base moral practice upon any other ground must inevitably lead to error and con- fusion.

Toward the existing educational system of the nation Miss Wright was almost as hostile as toward religion. Here again she noted a dependence upon irrational author- ity and opinion, rather than on actual investigation of the facts involved. To her, it appeared, that the student stuffed his head full of fallacies, theories, and hypotheses, his reason prostrated by the " dogmatism of teachers, the sophism of words, and the false principles engrafted by means of pre-

[1] *Ibid.*, pp. 74-77.
[2] *Ibid.*, p. 110.

tended science, ostentatiously inculcated, of real science, erroneously imparted." [1] The proper aim of our schools should be the search for just knowledge by means of experimental investigation, and in this connection she called attention to the work of Pestalozzi, which she much admired. Educational systems ought to acquaint the student, through experimental instruction, in so far as possible, first of all with himself, his body and mind, and second with the world about him. The first would include a study of anatomy, physiology, and the natural history of man. The second would include physics in its three great branches of chemistry, natural philosophy, and natural history, all of which were extremely important, for "the best road to correct reasoning is physical science; the way to trace effects to causes is through physical science; the only corrective, therefore, of superstition, is physical science." [2] History, as handed down by tradition, oral or written, should be studied and carefully compared with our own knowledge of men and things that its credibility might be the better judged. Travel accounts should be treated in a like manner. In teaching it must ever be the first duty of the instructor to encourage in the child a spirit of enquiry. As to the teacher:

He is never to advance an opinion without showing the facts upon which it is grounded; he is never to assert a fact, without proving it to be a fact. He is not to teach a code of morals, any more than a creed of doctrines; but he is to direct his young charge to observe the consequences of actions on himself and on others; and to judge of the propriety of those actions by their ascertained consequences. He is not to command his feelings any more than his opinions or his actions; but he is to assist him in the analysis of his feelings, in the

[1] *Ibid.*, pp. 24-25.
[2] *Ibid.*, p. 96.

examination of their nature, their tendencies, their effects. Let him do this, and have no anxiety for the result. In the free exercise of his senses, in the fair development of his faculties, in a course of simple and unrestrained enquiry, he will discover truth, for he will ascertain facts; he will seize upon virtue, for he will have distinguished beneficial from injurious actions; he will cultivate kind, generous, just, and honorable feelings, for he will have proved them to contribute to his own happiness and to shed happiness around him.[1]

Thus education would become rational and constructive, bettering the condition of mankind, rather than inculcating error and conflicting opinion. Such education must be equal, general, and open to all. It was not consistent with the republican practice of which America boasted that there should exist " endowed colleges for the rich, and barely common schools for the poor." [2] The real equality, for which in theory America stood, meant equal educational opportunities for all. Of Frances Wright's own solution of this most important of problems—" National, Rational, Republican Education; Free For All At The Expense Of All; Conducted Under The Guardianship Of The State, And For The Honor, The Happiness, The Virtue, The Salvation Of The State "—we shall have more to say in another place.[3]

Another important matter to which Miss Wright called the attention of her audiences, and in which she felt American practice to be irrational, was the position and treatment

---

[1] *Ibid.*, pp. 51-52. There is a strong hint of Rousseau in Miss Wright's educational ideas, but whether this came directly through her own reading or through her contact with the educational theorists at New Harmony she has left no indication.

[2] *Ibid.*, p. 46.

Owen, Robert Dale, and Wright, Frances, *Tracts on Republican Government and National Education*, London, 1840. The plan offered in Miss Wright's tract on education is the same as that proposed in her *Course of Popular Lectures*, pp. 166-170.

accorded to women. She had much admired American women on her first visit to the country, although feeling, even then, that their education was too much neglected for the best interests of the nation. She now felt much more strongly on the subject, believing that the failure to provide for their mental needs left them at the mercy of all who would prey upon their ignorance and credulity, a condition of affairs which the clergy had not been slow to take advantage of in the furtherance of their missionary, reform, and political schemes. General female education, equal to that received by the opposite sex, was the only remedy:

Until women assume the place in society which good sense and good feeling alike assign to them, human improvement must advance but feebly. It is in vain that we would circumscribe the power of one half of our race, and that by far the most important and influential. If they exert it not for good, they will for evil; if they advance not knowledge, they will perpetuate ignorance. Let women stand where they may in the scale of improvement, their position decides that of the race. Are they cultivated?—so is society polished and enlightened. Are they ignorant?—so is it gross and insipid. Are they wise?—so is the human condition prosperous. Are they foolish?—so is it unstable and uncompromising. Are they free?—so is the human character elevated. Are they enslaved?—so is the whole human race degraded. Oh! that we could learn the advantage of just practice and consistent principles! [1]

Equal education was not the only right demanded by Frances Wright for her sex. With Robert Dale Owen, she protested bitterly in lecture and editorial against a system of law which deprived a woman upon marriage of what property she possessed, and merged her legal identity with that of her husband; a system which inflicted " absolute spoliation, and allows of absolute robbery, and all but murder,

---

[1] *Course of Popular Lectures*, pp. 44-45.

against the unhappy female who swears away, at one and the same moment, her person and her property, and as it but too often is, her peace, her honor, and her life ":

I would ask every father not absolutely dead to all human feeling how he can permit his daughters blindly to immolate all their rights, liberties, and property by the simple utterance of a word, and thus place themselves, in their tender, ignorant, and unsuspecting youth, as completely at the disposal and mercy of an individual, as is the negro slave who is bought for gold in the slave market of Kingston or New Orleans.[1]

Nothing does Frances Wright more credit than this demand, one of the first to be voiced in the cause of women's rights, that upon marriage the rights and property of the wife be recognized and protected by law.   She lived to see many of the states put through the legislation she desired.

If Miss Wright startled her auditors, by attacking as irrational the religious and educational institutions of the country, and by advancing radical ideas as to the rights of women, she alarmed them still more by her open advocacy of birth control, and her hostility, theoretically at least, to the marriage tie.   Her interest in the question of birth control was aroused by a feeling that the bounteous plenty which America had long offered its people was slowly but surely giving way before the increase of population, and that the traditional large-sized American family, especially among the poorer working classes of the rapidly growing cities, was becoming a real calamity.   Big families among the laboring class meant overburdened parents, poverty from which escape was difficult, and neglected children, and to Frances Wright there seemed no greater evil possible than bringing into the world children who could not be properly provided for.   The remedy lay in restricting the size of the

[1] *Free Enquirer*, April 29, 1829.

family to the number of children the parents could adequately care for—in other words intelligent birth control.[1]
All this seems less astonishing today, and, no doubt, birth control was extensively practiced by the upper classes in the twenties, but to have such ideas aired in public, and openly advocated by a woman on the public lecture platform, that was something that the conservative could never forgive. Frances Wright had fallen hopelessly from grace. Almost anything might be believed of such a traitor to the modesty of her sex.

Probably no charge was more often brought against Miss Wright, during the years of her public activity, than that of being an advocate of free love, a charge originating in the published account of occurrences at Nashoba sent out by James Richardson, and in her own sentiments upon the marriage relation, as expressed in the " Explanatory Notes." Time and again the "Explanatory Notes" were dragged before the public, with the hope of discrediting their author and her cause. Her defense upon these occasions was that the theories of sex relationship, there set forth, were meant only for an advanced state of society, and could scarcely be appreciated by the present generation. It was Miss Wright's belief that the marriage tie, as a legal obligation, was mischievous, inefficient, and hypocritical. As a legal obligation binding people together it put a premium on neglect, brutality, slovenliness, and all kinds of domestic misery, and weakened the moral inducement to retain through the affections what it was attempted to retain through compulsion. Robert Dale Owen, in answering the request of a correspondent for Frances Wright's views on marriage, replied

[1] *Free Enquirer*, July 22, 1829. In the *Free Enquirer*, March 5, 1831, Miss Wright expressed her approval of Robert Dale Owen's *Moral Physiology*, New York, 1830, which dealt with the subject of birth control in the most outspoken manner.

that " the legal obligations of marriage she considers to be
sometimes mischievous and always inefficient, and she would
gradually substitute therefore moral obligations." [1]   Both
Miss Wright and Owen believed this to be possible:

We believe that children may be trained so that moral obligation shall gradually supercede legal obligation, both as regards
the marriage law, and perhaps every other, and we believe
that when this is done, a prolific source of vice and dissention
will be removed.   So far from proposing to remove moral
obligation, we propose to render it all-powerful.[2]

Realizing the hopelessness of substituting the moral obligation for the legal in the present state of society, Miss Wright
urged the passing of more liberal divorce laws which would
allow those unhappily wed to go their separate ways.

Frances Wright's public advocacy of her philosophy of
rationalism, and the freedom with which she expressed her
opinions on existing institutions and conventions, made her
at once the foremost American freethinker, and to the support of so courageous and brilliant a leader the infidels and
sceptics of the country rallied almost as a unit.   More radical, more persuasive, and more constructive in her criticisms
than Houston, she quickly usurped the position of that
gentleman in the movement, as shortly after, did her paper,
the *Free Enquirer*, that of the *Correspondent*.

[1] *Ibid.*, October 14, 1829.  For Miss Wright's views on marriage see
the *Free Enquirer* of March 4, and May 13, 1829.  She lectured once
on the subject in Cincinnati, at the request of her audience, but unfortunately the lecture seems to be no longer in existence.

[2] *Ibid.*, October 14, 1829.

# CHAPTER VII

## The Free Enquirer

The Cincinnati lectures proved so successful in arousing popular interest in rational principles that the Free Enquirers next decided upon an extensive lecture tour through the towns and cities of the Ohio Valley. Leaving Owen to carry on the *Gazette,* Miss Wright and Jennings journeyed west to St. Louis and thence down the Mississippi to Memphis. Everywhere their lectures were warmly received by the liberals. In St. Louis, wrote Frances to Camilla, " My last discourse there produced an effect beyond any I have yet delivered and the intelligent enthusiasm and pure feeling which sparkled in the eyes and burnt on the cheeks of many young and old hearers in the crowd who stood as if still listening when I had ceased, will, I think, never leave my memory." [1] Jennings, too, was all enthusiasm over their reception, writing to his friend Houston in New York that Miss Wright's lectures were producing an excitement hardly to be imagined. Already liberal principles had been openly avowed by hundreds.[2]

But the Free Enquirers soon found that they could hope for little encouragement from the conservative element in the community. The clergy urged their people " not to listen to that woman who was teaching foolishness," and the public press remained silent, evasive, or definitely hostile, confirming Miss Wright's opinion of its gross ignorance and

[1] Wright MSS. Frances to Camilla, November 24, 1828.
[2] *Correspondent,* December 6,. 1828.

shameless servility.[1]  But perhaps Frances Wright herself failed to appreciate quite the shock to American convention her appearance on the lecture platform caused.  One hundred years ago that sort of thing was not done by American women.  Except for a few choice spirits the emancipated woman of today was not even a dream.  The very idea that women should publicly interest themselves in business or politics was considered not only highly immodest and presumptuous but even unnatural.  Physically and intellectually they were deemed unsuited for such activities:

Miss Wright, considered as a lady, agreeable to the conventional proprieties of civilized society [said " Fidelis " in the *Louisville Focus*], has with ruthless violence, broken loose from the restraints of decorum, which draw a circle round the life of women; and with a contemptuous disregard for the rule of society, she has leaped over the boundary of feminine modesty, and laid hold upon the avocations of man, claiming a participation in them for herself and her sex.

Miss Wright stands condemned of a violation of the unalterable laws of nature, which have created a barrier between the man and the woman, over which neither can pass without unhinging the beneficent adjustments of society, and doing wanton injury to the happiness of each other.[2]

Such criticism as this bothered Miss Wright not a whit, for she knew something of the reception which a radical reformer might expect, and had schooled herself to meet it in a philosophical spirit.  Only rarely in the years that followed did she lose her self-control, even though press and pulpit descended to the most outrageous slander and calumny.  Principles, not men, was her motto, and to it she adhered with splendid courage and determination.  To

[1] *New Harmony Gazette*, September 3, 1828.

[2] *New Harmony and Nashoba Gazette or Free Enquirer*, December 10, 1828.  Quotation taken from the *Louisville Focus*.

her, hostile criticism and comment were but further evidences of the irrational and hide-bound prejudices of her generation; prejudices the foundations of which it was her duty to undermine.

The success of the Western venture encouraged the Free Enquirers to believe that they were now ready to invade the larger field open to them in the East, and to establish their paper in one of the Eastern cities.[1] Such a move would bring them directly in contact with the bulk of liberal sentiment in the country, and carry them into the very stronghold of clerical and conservative opposition.

Late in November, 1828, therefore, Miss Wright and Jennings set out from Cincinnati for Baltimore, again leaving Owen to carry on the *Gazette* with occasional help in the form of letters. At Wheeling, where they stopped for a short time before crossing the mountains, Miss Wright's lectures were well received.[2] Upon their arrival in Baltimore they were met by Dr. Haslam, a Baltimore liberal, and by Lovegrove, the local agent of the *New Harmony and Nashoba Gazette or Free Enquirer*. In a letter to Camilla, Frances describes her reception and success:

We found them both [Dr. Haslam and Mr. Lovegrove] in waiting at the door of the stage office from whence the good Doctor carried us to his house which he insisted should be our home. The smaller theater was thrown open by its owner (a warm liberal) for the lectures. I gave five on successive nights to an audience whose pressure seemed to endanger the building and whose enthusiasm seemed to portend danger to the old system and its servants. I can give you no conception of the state of the public mind during the past week. Baltimore has been the stronghold of priestcraft for some years past and

[1] Wright MSS. Frances to Camilla, November 24, December 7, 1828.

[2] *New Harmony and Nashoba Gazette or Free Enquirer*, January 7, 1829.

the churches are more spacious and costly than in any city of the union. The reaction seems likely to be in proportion, that is if we should settle there but we are earnestly called for in Philadelphia and New York, and must see all before we can determine. We assisted at a meeting of the Liberals last night when it was proposed to take measures for the erection of a Hall of Science and a school of industry on the plan suggested in my discourses. An ingenious mechanic (who has erected several of the public buildings in the city) proposes to raise the Hall (worth $20,000) for the sum of $4,000, the mechanics to receive shares entitling so many children [to] free gratis instruction for the work given. A committee has been appointed of a few popular and influential citizens who are to attempt raising the necessary contributions privately as many it is thought will aid the measure secretly who could not publicly. On the last week of January they are to report progress, when I have pledged myself, if necessary, to return and assist by a repetition of the course.[1]

Although warned of possible disturbances, the lectures in Baltimore went off smoothly, with no more precautions needed than the placing of a few members of the committee through the room and at the door to apprehend possible trouble makers.[2] Rarely in her lectures throughout the country did Miss Wright find it necessary to plan against disturbing interruptions, although she did not lack many trying moments and experiences. From these she was saved more than once by her splendid poise and ready wit, and by her refusal to deal in personalities. In Louisville her coolness in the face of a spurious cry of "fire" had prevented a serious catastrophe, and it was probably during this first visit to Baltimore that she met a hostile audience

[1] Wright MSS. Frances to Camilla, December, 1828. No specific date given.

[2] *Biography*, pt. i, p. 41.

by assuring it at the outset that, as being composed of American gentlemen, she had every confidence in its attention and courtesy.[1]   Frances Wright lacked neither courage nor a quick wit.

To many of the good ladies of Baltimore Miss Wright's conduct must have seemed scandalous.   At least Miss Wright conceived that such must be their state of mind.   " I write on my knee, my sweet love," she wrote Camilla, as she journeyed toward Philadelphia, " in a cabin crowded with ladies who perhaps feel in my company as in the presence of a new importation from the south seas, and I most certainly in theirs as some such unfortunate antipodean to whom the surrounding minds and manners are as uncongenial as the bonnets." [2]

In Philadelphia she addressed a great crowd in the old State House,[3] and then started north for New York, " the head seat at once of popular energy, sectarian and clerical wealth and power, and financial and political corruption." [4] It was a very sober Enquirer who, on the evening of December thirty-first, boarded the ferry on the Jersey shore :

She passed an hour or two on the deck, gazing on that which was to be the chief seat of her exertions, and, as she foresaw, of painful and complicated sacrifices and persecution.   In that city were some heart affections, which dated from her first landing in the country.   These, the course prescribed to her by duty, was perhaps about to sever.   Friends in official situations or political standing, whom considerations of propriety would oblige her in appearance to forget.   Houses in which she

---

[1] *New Harmony Gazette*, October 15, 1828; Gilbert, *A Memoir of Frances Wright*.

[2] Wright MSS. Frances to Camilla, December, 1828.   No specific date given.

[3] *Biography*, pt. i, p. 43.

[4] *Ibid*.

had been as a daughter, and which she must now pass with the regardless eye of a stranger. Some she knew would understand her course, and in silence appreciate her motives. Others might feel embarrassed.[1]

In New York were the Wilkes and Colden families, Dr. Mitchill, Dr. Macneven, and others whose friendship and interest dated from her first visit to the city in the fall of 1818, a young woman full of enthusiasm for America. How would they receive her in this new rôle, the editor of a freethought paper, and a popular lecturer in the cause of rationalism and free enquiry? To Charles Wilkes, now the dignified president of the Bank of New York, she wrote at once, explaining her object in visiting the city and leaving with him the decision as to their future relations. Wilkes felt it wise to give up what might prove an embarrassing friendship, and resigned also the charge of her financial affairs, a step which caused her some financial loss later on as she found no one quite capable of taking his place.[2]

Except among the liberals Frances Wright's arrival in New York seems to have been quite unheralded. Temporarily she took up her residence with " an amiable unfortunate widow in Murray Street whom others shunning on account of the change in her circumstances from wealth to poverty we see reasons for preferring." [3] Jennings opened up an office nearby where he gave out such information as was desired, and received subscriptions to the *Gazette*. Arrangements were quickly made for a series of six lectures to be delivered alternately in Masonic Hall and the City Hotel, and on the morning of Saturday, January third, the *Correspondent* announced that Frances Wright would give

[1] *Ibid.*

[2] *Ibid.*, pp. 43-44.

[3] Wright MSS. Frances to Camilla, January 5, 1829.

her first lecture on Knowledge that evening in the Masonic Hall at seven o'clock, admission free.[1]

A little before seven o'clock on that eventful evening Frances Wright ascended the lecture platform in Masonic Hall to face an audience of some fifteen hundred curious and interested New-Yorkers, a number of whom were women.[2] She wore, we are told, a Queen Mary ruff and a dark-colored spencer. Jennings, "a thick-set and well-constituted little Scotsman," and four or five female companions accompanied her onto the platform, where the former took charge of her cloak and hat.[3] The lecture went splendidly, and first impressions seemed to be favorable to Miss Wright. "Her person," said the *Commercial Advertiser,* "is striking and commanding, and her carriage as a declaimer graceful. Her features are strong and expressive; nor did they lose any of their expression for want of exercise." At times the writer of this article found her inclined to be rather painfully intense, when the words and thoughts scarcely seemed to demand it:

Her voice, which filled the room without apparent effort on the part of the speaker, is both strong and sweet. We recollect no female whose recitations in this city have been celebrated, at all comparable to this lady, in this particular. Her enunciation is perfect, and she has complete command over it. Her emphasis and pauses, and the whole of her delivery are excellent, and her gestures appropriate and graceful. So far as these qualifications constitute an orator, we believe she is unrivaled by any of the public speakers, of any description in this city. For an hour and a half she held the attention of her audience enchained, excepting that attempts made to applaud

[1] *Correspondent,* January 3, 1829.

[2] *New York Commercial Advertiser,* January 5, 1829.

[3] *New York American,* January 5, 1829. Frances Wright was often accompanied upon the lecture platform by a group of Quaker ladies who sympathized with her views.

which were frequently suppressed by the majority, from a
wish not to interrupt her, at length succeeded, and towards the
conclusion she received several distinct and thunderous rounds
of approval.   Nor would it be doing justice to the lady, if we
did not add, that her language was singularly well chosen and
accurate; that there was much of the eloquence of style, added
to that of manner; and the keeping of the whole performance
was so good that the sensation of the ludicrous, naturally suggested by its novelty, was entirely suppressed.[1]

As to the substance of her discourse the writer was not
so favorably impressed.   Her ideas of knowledge he thought
rather simple, and he could see no sense in her references to
priestcraft, although these were greatly applauded by the
members of the Infidel Club present.

In a letter written to Camilla two days after her first lecture Miss Wright gives us her own impressions of her success :

Dearest Love,—We are about to pitch our tent here.  All
things considered this is the most central spot both with respect to Europe and this country.   The excitement produced
by my opening discourse (delivered the night before last in
the Masonic Hall, supposed to contain when well packed,
which it most undoubtedly was, from 1,500 to 2,000 people)
has been very great though I will not say greater than elsewhere since the same spirit of enquiry and reformation seems
to exist throughout the land and to require only the match to
burst into flame.   To-night, Monday, I shall resume and complete the course with the week.   Good McNeven found me this
morning and seems to grow young again at the thought of
our settling here.   C. Colden was among the audience on
Saturday which convinces me I had not misconceived respecting the secret liberality of his opinions.   I was amused at the
fervor of Dr. Mitchill who stood during the lecture at the foot

[1] *New York Commercial Advertiser*, January 5, 1829.

of the [illegible] and who running up the steps as I closed, greeted me with all the enthusiasm he could have bestowed upon the sea serpent itself. My time has of course been much broken by visitors as my letters will bespeak. The poor libs are so happy to get their breath out and look so cheerful— it does my heart good to see them and to feel the warm shake of their hands.[1]

It was not until after her third lecture, in which she turned upon the clergy and declared her intention of establishing her freethought paper in New York, that the press became abusive, and serious efforts were made to create disturbances when she spoke. To the *Commercial Advertiser* she now became "a bold blasphemer and a voluptuous preacher of licentiousness," eager to break down the barriers of virtue and reduce the world to one grand theater of vice and sensuality in its most loathsome form. No rebuff could palsy her, no insult agitate. "It is iron equally in her head and heart; impervious to the voice of virtue and case-hardened against shame."[2] The columns of the *New York American* were even more offensive in their comment. One scathing article closed as follows:

It may be thought that these remarks are harsh, and that there is a degree of generous courtesy which should never be withheld from woman. But when one thus shamefully obtrudes herself upon the public waiving alike modesty, gentleness, and every amiable attribute of her sex, she also waives all claims to its privileges; she ceases to be a woman, and is no longer aught else than what we have taken the liberty of calling her— a female monster.[3]

The *Evening Post* declared that "female expounders of any kind of doctrine are not to our taste," and that the sex

[1] Wright MSS. Frances to Camilla, January 5, 1829.
[2] *New York Commercial Advertiser*, January 12, 1829.
[3] *New York American*, January 8, 1829.

ought not to engage in such pursuits.[1] The *Journal of
Commerce* was shocked to learn of ladies among Miss
Wright's auditors, and proceeded to print extracts from her
" Explanatory Notes," wherewith to frighten them away.[2]
In the New York *Observer,* a well-known religious weekly,
Miss Wright was described as " Infidelity in an Angel's
garb ";[3] concealing " her infidel principles under a false
species of morality, liberty, equality and the like, aiming at
the ridicule of vital religion, and reproaching the pious, faith-
ful preachers of the Gospel."[4]

But, when the *Evening Post* discovered that the Park
Theater had been leased to Miss Wright for a second series
of lectures, it lost its head completely, and came very near
inciting riot and bloodshed:

We perceive with utter astonishment, and no less alarm than
astonishment, that the lessees of this theater have agreed to let
it for six nights to Frances Wright, as a place to deliver her
lectures in. Have they considered what may be the consequences of the displeasure of the people? Suppose the singular spectacle of a female, publicly and ostentatiously proclaiming
doctrines of atheistical fanaticism, and even the most abandoned lewdness, should draw a crowd from a prurient curiosity, and that a riot should ensue, which should end in the
demolition of the interior of the building, or even in burning
it down, on whom would the loss fall? Would the policy of
insurance against fire, which describes it as a building devoted
to theatrical exhibitions of a very different description, and
which must attract a very different order of people, cover the
loss? This is a question for the insurance offices seriously to
consider, as well as the proprietors and lessees. It is also a

[1] *New York Evening Post,* January 10, 1829.
[2] *New York Journal of Commerce,* January 16, 1829.
[3] *The Observer,* January 17, 1829.
[4] *Ibid.,* January 10, 1829.

question for the public authorities to reflect upon. Is there no danger of collecting an unruly mob, which nothing perhaps can restrain short of public force and bloodshed itself? We shall merely put these bare questions for the present, and let those answer them on whom the awful responsibility would devolve if any frightful consequences should happen to the city or its inhabitants. Remember the good old homely proverb. "A pennyworth of prevention is worth a pound of remedy."[1]

It is not surprising that these fulminations were followed by active efforts to break up Miss Wright's meetings. During one lecture in Masonic Hall an attempt was made to smoke the meeting out by placing a barrel full of combustible matter covered with turpentine in the doorway and setting it ablaze. Dense clouds of smoke rolled up through the Hall, but Miss Wright's presence of mind did not desert her and her coolness prevented the dangers of a panic. A few days later in the same Hall the gas was suddenly turned off, leaving some 2,000 people in complete darkness. It was probably as the result of these activities that her liberal admirers organized a personal guard to protect her from possible molestation on her way to and from the meetings. It is hardly to be wondered at that Miss Wright should have been somewhat provoked at this outburst of scurrility and mob violence:

When Frances Wright explained the nature of knowledge, " She would repeal the marriage act," cried the clergy; and when she developed the first principles of moral science, " She denies the existence of a God," exclaimed the press; when she denounced the assumptions of orthodoxy and the arts of an aspiring priesthood, " The destruction of the Bible would involve the ruin of us all," shouted both. Now Frances Wright, all this time, had said nothing about marriage; never meddled with the Bible, and questioned no man's belief in his God.

[1] *New York Evening Post*, January 26, 1829.

But it was necessary to distract the attention, to disturb the public mind, to break the order of Frances Wright's investigations, and therefore must her place of meeting be involved in alternate fire and darkness, and her audience distracted with shouts about marriage while she was discoursing upon knowledge.[1]

Such hostility and violence naturally only increased the interest and curiosity of the public.[2]   So great was the crush at the door of the lecture hall that a small fee was deemed advisable, the proceeds being set aside for the erection of a Hall of Science.[3]   Newspaper offices were thronged with people seeking copies of the papers which discussed the lectures.[4]   The managers of the Park Theater took advantage of the popular excitement to reproduce Miss Wright's *Altorf,* and the play met with a very good reception from a large audience.[5]   One good lady was so thrilled at Frances Wright's defense of her sex that she simply had to express her emotions in rhyme:

### THE PANIC

What a panic has seized all the men!
    How scared, that we women should know
Something more about handling a pen,
    That our grandams, some ages ago!

They say that we authors are turning;
    (Alas! how they grieve at the times!)
And our knowledge of housewifery spurning,
    To eke out a few paltry rhymes.

[1] *Free Enquirer,* March 4, 1829.

[2] The *Telescope,* January 31, 1829. A writer in the *Telescope* thus described the effects of the campaign of low ridicule and scurrility carried on by the *Commercial Advertiser* and the *Evening Post.*

[3] *Free Enquirer,* February 25, 1829.

[4] *New York Commercial Advertiser,* January 17, 1829.

[5] *New York Courier and Enquirer,* January 24, 1829. *Altorf* was given on the evenings of January 22, and 24, 1829.

> The dear fellows have taken a fright;
>     And forsooth not without a good cause;
> For the lectures of Miss Frances Wright
>     Are received with unbounded applause.
>
> What a fuss among bigots and priests,
>     What a running and groaning and praying,
> And proclaiming of fasts and of feasts,
>     To disprove all that Fanny is saying.
>
> She tells us we women possess
>     An intellect equal with them;
> But this the poor souls won't confess,
>     And that part of her doctrine condemn.[1]

Even William Cullen Bryant, then editor of the *Evening Post,* was moved to write a somewhat sarcastic ode to Miss Wright:

> Thou wonder of the age, from whom
> Religion waits her final doom,
> Her quiet death, her euthanasia,
> Thou in whose eloquence and bloom
> The age beholds a new Aspasia!
> \*   \*   \*   \*   \*   \*   \*   \*
> O 'tis a glorious sight for us,
> The gaping throng, to see thee thus
> The light of dawning truth dispense,
> While Colonel Stone, the learn'd and brave,
> The press's Atlas, mild but grave,
> Hangs on the words that leave thy mouth,
> Slaking his intellectual drouth,
> In that rich stream of eloquence,
> And notes thy teachings, to repeat
> Their wisdom in his classic sheet . . .[2]

By the time that the second series of lectures closed, the New York press had apparently come to the conclusion that it would be wiser to ignore Miss Wright and her works

---

[1] *Free Enquirer,* February 8, 1829, " The Panic," by Ada.

[2] Nevins, Allen, *The Evening Post,* New York, 1922, pp. 126-127. This poem appeared in the *Evening Post* of January 29, 1829. Colonel Stone was the editor of the *Commercial Advertiser.*

altogether, and such, with occasional flare-ups, was the policy
pursued, until the free enquiry movement became entangled
with the workingman's cause late in the fall of the year.
That Miss Wright and her principles had been advertised to
good effect is evident from Frances' letter of February
twenty-first to Camilla:

The whole country is waking up—invitations pour in from
every town and county round and about and afar off. Last
week I went to Paterson, Pasaic Falls, under escort of the
libs—a carriage being sent for me. On coming home nothing
would satisfy them but a carriage and four from New York,
which when applied for by the Paterson libs of the mail conductor here, he sent what he calls Gen. J—'s four grays—saying
he would not have sent them for money for anyone else, but
for F. W. he would send them for nothing, and so he did—
refusing all compensation from the citizens. The Free Enquirer goes on well—the cause well, and all well. I have to
postpone all distant visits until Robert arrives. The business
of editor not allowing me longer absences than may embrace
the nearby towns.[1]

Miss Wright was now convinced that she had located the
Eastern city in which the Free Enquirers might to advantage
establish their paper and their headquarters. Without
waiting for the coming of young Owen she and Jennings
transferred the activities of the *New Harmony and Nashoba Gazette or Free Enquirer* to New York, where it first
appeared on January twenty-eighth, as the *Free Enquirer,*
a name more expressive of its real character.[2] This interesting and ably edited little paper of which a few files still
exist devoted itself to fearless and unbiased enquiry on all
subjects.[3] Although for the first two years of its life the

[1] Wright MSS. Frances to Camilla, February 21, 1829.

[2] Owen seems to have carried on the New Harmony edition until shortly
before his departure for New York.

[3] *Course of Popular Lectures*, p. 12.

chief topic of discussion was theology, time was found to advocate the abolition of capital punishment and of imprisonment for debt, social, pecuniary, and political equality for women, equal civil rights for all, and the right of every man to testify in court without enquiry being made as to his religious creed. The paper also urged the adoption of a national system of education " free from sectarian teachings, with industrial schools where the children of the poor might be taught farming or a trade, and obtain, without charge, support as well as education." [1]   Of this system of education we shall have more to say in a later chapter.

The appearance of the *Free Enquirer* delighted the liberals, who were fascinated " with the charm of style, beauty of diction, and boldness of invective " which characterized the paper.[2]  Moreover, its appearance was timely, for George Houston's *Correspondent* was on its last legs, due to the financial difficulties of its editor.[3]  Left with an open field the *Free Enquirer* rapidly increased its subscription circulation to one thousand copies, and soon had its agencies distributed from Vermont to Louisiana.[4]

In the excitement over Miss Wright's lectures few of the metropolitan papers noticed the appearance of the *Free Enquirer*. The *Commercial Advertiser*, however, took occasion to denounce the paper as " empty, insignificant, and tedious." As " inaccurate as the ' Tour in America '— fabulous as ' The Days in Athens,' and chimerical as the ' Institutions of New Harmony,' its imbecile dullness renders it harmlessly wicked." Frances Wright it called a mere imitator of Mary Wollstonecraft without the loveliness of the latter.[5]  The editor of the *Boston Manufacturer*,

---

[1] "An Earnest Sowing of Wild Oats."

[2] A correspondent in the *Free Enquirer*, February 8, 1829.

[3] Wright MSS. Frances to Camilla, January 5, 1829.

[4] *Free Enquirer*, June 10, November 7, 1829.

[5] *New York Commercial Advertiser*, January 31, 1829.

after seeking an exchange with the wicked paper, declared that he hoped " the good sense and sound principles of the people of the United States, will confine its influence to a narrow sphere of activities." [1]

Miss Wright's next task was to locate a lecture hall, for after the disturbances in Masonic Hall the proprietors and lessees of that, and other large halls in the city, refused to rent.[2]   The problem was happily solved by the purchase at auction of the old Ebenezer Church in Broome Street near the Bowery for seven thousand dollars.[3]   After some re-modeling, the church became the Hall of Science with a seating capacity of about twelve hundred.[4]   In the base-ment were located the offices of the *Free Enquirer*.   The management of the Hall of Science Miss Wright placed in the hands of five trustees, who were to secure competent lecturers on scientific and moral subjects, arrange for the sale and distribution of tickets, and organize the day and Sunday schools which it was proposed to establish.   Later in the history of the Hall the trustees provided a dispensary with an attending physician.   When not otherwise engaged, the Hall might be rented to outside lecturers, and this was occasionally done.   On the twenty-sixth of April Miss Wright delivered the opening address before a crowded house.   Freethought odes composed by the lecturer, we are told, preceded and followed the lecture, to the edification of the faithful.[5]

Even while busy with her editorial and lecture work Miss

[1] *Free Enquirer*, March 18, 1829.

[2] *Ibid.*, April 22, 1829.

[3] Wright MSS. Frances to Camilla, March 11, 1829.

[4] Ferral, S. A., *A Ramble of Six-Thousand Miles through the United States of America*, London, 1832, p. 14.

[5] *Free Enquirer*, March 29, April 29, September 24, 1829.   See also *Introductory Address, delivered by Frances Wright, at the opening of the Hall of Science*, New York, 1829.   This pamphlet contains the odes.

Wright was seeking to secure a home for her little family of Free Enquirers. After some searching, she leased from the city recorder, Richard Riker, a commodious mansion on the bank of the East River about a half-mile southeast of Yorkville. It afforded, she wrote Camilla, " convenience, comfort, retirement and beauty of situation—a garden, 10 Acres of land, stables, cow house, poultry yard,— good water."[1]   All for four hundred and forty dollars a year. To this little arcadia came Robert Dale Owen to aid in the editing of the *Free Enquirer,* and Camilla with her baby— having left the unhealthy surroundings of Nashoba for all time:

There we lived [says Robert Dale Owen] and there our paper was handsomely printed by three lads who had been trained in the New Harmony printing-office. They boarded with us, and we paid them a dollar a week each. . . .

We lived in the most frugal manner, giving up tea and coffee, and using little animal food; were supplied with milk from a couple of good cows, and vegetables from our garden. We kept two horses and a light city carriage: had two female servants, and a stout boy who attended to the stable and garden. I have now before me a minute account which I kept of our expenses. Including paper (upwards of five hundred a year), printing, expenses of house, stables, and office, rent, etc., our total expenditure was but three thousand one hundred a year when Miss Wright and her sister were with us, and after they went, twenty-seven hundred dollars only.[2]

The summer of 1829 was a busy one for the Free Enquirers. Jennings looked after the business end of the *Free Enquirer* and Miss Wright's lecture tours, and took general charge of the Hall of Science. Robert Dale Owen, who finally reached the city late in June, assumed the bulk of the editorial work, thus enabling Miss Wright to undertake

[1] Wright MSS. Frances to Camilla, March 11, 1829.
[2] "An Earnest Sowing of Wild Oats."

more extended tours.   The nearby towns had already been
visited, and her lectures received by quiet and attentive
audiences.   A second visit to Philadelphia was also well received.[1]   While lecturing in Wilmington, Delaware, in a
slave state, Miss Wright attacked the institution of slavery
and gave her own experiences in emancipation.[2]

She now set forth to carry the light into New England.
Upon learning of the approaching visit, the *Boston Gazette*
advised that Miss Wright be undisturbed unless she questioned the marriage laws.   Not that the editor of the
*Gazette* sympathized with the lady, " we confess we do not
feel predisposed to relish the masculine eloquence of this
bold and forcible female.   We shall not be gratified by her
visit to the city.   We get on very well as we are.   Innovations and new lights are sometimes as uncomfortable as they
are at other times necessary.   Let her come and we will
listen or not as we desire." [3]   On her arrival, however, a
" good deal of pious artifice " seems to have been employed
to prevent her appearance.   The public halls of the city
were refused her, and recourse was finally had to the Federal Theater.[4]   Unable to stop her speaking, a petition,
signed by a number of prominent individuals, several of
whom represented Boston business firms, was circulated
about among the Boston newspaper editors, asking them to
preserve a policy of silence toward Miss Wright while she
remained in the city.   This was not wholly a success as
there existed far too much curiosity regarding the lady and
her lectures.[5]   From sundry editorials and correspondence

---

[1] *Free Enquirer*, August 5, 1829.

[2] *Ibid.*, June 10, 1829.

[3] *Ibid.*, July 22, 1829.   Quoting from the *Boston Gazette*.

[4] *Ibid.*, August 5, 12, 1829.

[5] *Ibid.*   In the *Free Enquirer* of May 8, 1830, Miss Wright published
this petition, stating that it had been sent to her in a blank cover from
Boston.

in the papers we learn that the lectures went off pretty well, and that Boston had not been treated to as much intellectual excitement since the lectures of Joseph Lancaster on education. The editor of the *Boston Courier*, however, found little original in the lectures of Miss Wright. In fact, he thought that her lecture on knowledge might have been a good introduction to a course in chemistry. Her digs at the clergy were no worse than those they gave each other in the pulpit. There was, he felt, no occasion for anathemas or hallelujahs, for Miss Wright was not going to upset religion or bring on a moral millennium. His chief objection to the lady was that she was doing what only a man should attempt. Women must not assume the prerogatives of men. They had their own place in society and that place was in the home.[1]

The Boston clergy, however, were not so sure of Miss Wright's harmlessness:

About this time [said the Reverend Lyman Beecher in one of his sermons on Political Atheism] the female apostle of atheistic liberty visited the city, and her lectures were thronged, not only by men, but even by females of respectable standing. And the effect of these lectures on such listeners was not the mere gratification of curiosity. She made her converts, and, that, too, not among the low and vicious alone. Females of education and refinement—females of respectable standing in society—those who had been the friends and associates of my own children—were numbered among her votaries, and advocated her sentiments.[2]

One curious bit of human interest turned up in Boston, for two of the Boston editors were much interested in the

---

[1] *Free Enquirer*, August 12, 1829. From the *Boston Courier*, July 30, 1829.

[2] Beecher, Lyman, *Works*, 3 vols., Boston, 1852, vol. i, pp. 92-93.

manner in which Miss Wright did up her hair. This she always wore short and curled, probably for the sake of comfort and convenience:

Her hair is worn short, close curled in her neck and around her forehead. This arrangement has something of singularity in it, yet it forms a pleasing contrast with the perched up head-dresses of our young ladies, who in their rage for wrought India combs, pile up about their brows a tower of tortoise-shell and tresses newly purchased from the frizeurs which converts those of dwarfish statures into giantesses, and the tall ones into something very like a Chinese pagoda looming aloft in the air.[1]

In the fall of 1829 Miss Wright found it necessary, temporarily, to give up her lectures and editorial work that she might bring to a close her Nashoba experiment by colonizing her slaves. She left New York for New Orleans on the twenty-first of October, Owen and Jennings remaining in the city to carry on the free enquiry agitation during her absence.[2] Her plan was to proceed overland by way of Albany, Buffalo, and Pittsburg, and thence down the Ohio and Mississippi to New Orleans, which she hoped to reach about Christmas time. There she would meet her slaves and embark with them for Haiti, where President Boyer had already provided for their coming.

Naturally Miss Wright did not neglect the opportunities her long journey gave her for lecturing in the more important towns and cities along her route. She appears, indeed, to have been deluged with invitations to stop at every little village through which she passed. At Albany she lectured twice. In Utica, which she found strongly clerical, she was

---

[1] *Free Enquirer*, August 12, 1829. Quoting from the *Boston Mercury*. The *Boston Statesman* also remarked upon the manner in which Miss Wright did up her hair.

[2] *Ibid.*, October 31, 1829.

obliged to deliver her lecture in a dirty old circus, though arrangements had originally been made for the use of the Court House. Syracuse was more liberal in its views, and there her lectures were well received.[1] In Auburn, New York, she first met Orestes Augustus Brownson, then editing a little Universalist paper, the *Gospel Advocate*. Brownson is best remembered today as an editor and philosopher, and as one of the foremost of American converts to Roman Catholicism. His religious experience was a curious one. Born in Stockbridge, Vermont, of puritan stock, he became in turn Presbyterian, Universalist, Freethinker, Unitarian, and Roman Catholic.[2] When Frances Wright met him in the autumn of 1829 he inclined toward scepticism, and the rationalism of Miss Wright naturally made a strong appeal. Years later he could still describe with enthusiasm the power of her eloquence:

Her free, flowing, and ornate style,—French rather than English,—her fine, rich, musical voice, highly cultivated and possessing great power, her graceful manner, her tall commanding figure, her wit and sarcasm, her apparent honesty of purpose, and deep and glowing enthusiasm, made her one of the most pleasing and effective orators, man or woman, that I have ever heard.[3]

Brownson was so impressed with Miss Wright, her philosophy, and ambitions, that he became the corresponding editor of the *Free Enquirer*, a position which he held until the spring of 1830.[4]

[1] *Ibid.*, October 31, November 14, 21, 1829.

[2] *Appleton's Cyclopedia of American Biography*, edited by James Grant Wilson and John Fiske, 6 vols., New York, 1887-1889. See under Brownson, Orestes Augustus.

[3] Brownson, Orestes Augustus, *The Convert: or Leaves from my Experience*, New York, 1857, p. 124.

[4] *Free Enquirer*, November 7, 1829; May 8, 1831.

After lecturing in Rochester and Buffalo, Miss Wright passed on to Pittsburg, where she seems to have met with considerable opposition from the orthodox element in the community.[1] Cincinnati and Louisville were next visited, and then she hastened on to New Orleans which she reached the last of December. Here, while awaiting the arrival of her slaves, she lectured in the American and French theaters.[2]

With her slaves she left New Orleans for Port au Prince, Haiti, on the eighteenth of January, 1830.[3] In the *Free Enquirer* of May first she announced her return to New York after six months' absence from the city, during which she had seen her people " advantageously and happily settled under the immediate protection of the Haitian President."[4]

Upon her return from Haiti Miss Wright at once took up her lecture and editorial work again, devoting much of her time and energy to the forwarding of her educational schemes through the medium of the Working Men's Party, of which we shall have more to say. The Wright-Owen-Jennings partnership, however, was now broken up by the retirement of Jennings, who had received and accepted an offer from the free enquirers of Boston to settle in that city for the following year as their lecturer.[5] Why he should have left Miss Wright and Owen is not wholly clear. It may be that Miss Wright's announcement of her engage-

[1] *Ibid.*, November 28, 1829; H. B. Stanton, in his *Random Recollections*, New York, 1886, p. 21, mentions hearing Miss Wright speak in Rochester. She spoke, he says, with grace and ability, but was hardly so beautiful as the engraving of her in the first volume of the *History of Woman Suffrage*. See Susan B. Anthony and others, *The History of Woman Suffrage*, 4 vols., New York, 1881-1902, vol. i, the frontispiece.

[2] *Free Enquirer*, January 30, February 13, 1830.

[3] *Ibid.*, February 20, 1830.

[4] *Ibid.*, May 1, 1830.

[5] *Ibid.*, April 17, May 8, June 12, 1830.

ment to William Phiquepal, a gentleman whom she had first met in New Harmony, had something to do with it.[1] Phiquepal would naturally expect to have an important voice in the management of the *Free Enquirer* and the Hall of Science, and it seems probable that Jennings resented this. Phiquepal, indeed, does not appear to have been very heartily welcomed by Miss Wright's associates. Brownson did not care for him, and Owen says that though he was "gifted with a certain enthusiasm which had its attraction" he was from the first an "unwise, hasty, fanciful counselor, and ultimately a suspicious and headstrong man."[2] It is only fair to Phiquepal, however, to say that Owen's feeling may in part have been due to a conflict over money matters, for his finances and those of Miss Wright were badly confused.

Two months later Frances Wright brought her first two years of lecturing in the United States to an end. On the first of July, 1830, she left with Camilla for France after delivering a series of farewell lectures in New York and Philadelphia.

It is now time for us to consider what Frances Wright had accomplished in her two years of lecture and editorial work. She had started out in the summer of 1828 to educate the present generation in rational principles, with the hope that she might thereby weaken the influence of the clergy over the female mind, and shake the foundations of those hide-bound prejudices and irrational conventions which she believed hindered the progress of the race. Further than this she had dreamed of establishing a system of education which would result in the next generation in the

[1] "An Earnest Sowing of Wild Oats." Owen says that Miss Wright first told him of her engagement to Phiquepal upon her return from Haiti.

[2] *Ibid.* Brownson expresses his opinion of Phiquepal in *The Convert*, p. 134.

founding of a rational society. Leaving for the following chapter our discussion of her efforts to secure such a system of education, what had been her success in arousing the nation to an appreciation of rational principles? Not inconsiderable if we may believe Miss Wright herself:

We have done what in us lay, to awaken and to inform the public mind on subjects connected with the people's vital interests; and it has been our reward to perceive, that our words fell not unheeded to the ground. It has been our reward to know that we have encouraged many to throw off the shackles of misguided prejudice; that we have led even the fearful to think for themselves; and, at times, won the ear and half persuaded the heart, even of some among the strictest of religion's professors. It has been our reward to feel, that we have often supported the gentle and the faint hearted, and strengthened the hands of freedom's champions.[1]

And not inconsiderable had been her success if we may believe the testimony of clergy and press. To the Reverend Ashbel Green, one time president of Princeton, and now the editor of the *Christian Advocate*, a leading Presbyterian organ, the state of the country seemed deplorable. " Fearful efforts," he wrote, " are now making to change the character of our nation, and to render us an infidel instead of a Christian people. If these efforts should succeed, our ruin would be sealed." [2] And in a later editorial he declared that:

Never since the hey-day of infidelity, in the time of the French revolution, have we witnessed a spirit like that which is now abroad. We greatly fear that our national sins will be followed by national judgments, and the everlasting ruin of many of our citizens, and especially of our precious youth.[3]

[1] *Free Enquirer*, October 21, 1829.
[2] *Christian Advocate*, February, 1830.
[3] *Ibid.*, April, 1830.

In Boston the operations of the free enquirers led the
Reverend Lyman Beecher to deliver a series of sermons on
Political Atheism, so entitled because the theories of in-
fidelity in France and America

extend to the modification of the religious, civil, and social
state of man—contemplating nothing less than the abolition
of marriage and the family state, separate property, civil government, and all sense of accountability, and all religious wor-
ship;—an effort to turn the world upside down, and empty it
of every institution, thought, feeling, and action, which has
emanated from Christianity, to unite mankind under the auspices of atheism.[1]

That associations with such objects in view existed, said
Doctor Beecher, was a matter of notoriety. In Boston,
New York, Philadelphia, and Baltimore, and, indeed,
throughout New England and the middle states such or-
ganizations were " as open and as well known as that of
Christian Churches." [2]   In Boston it was openly boasted
that " there were six hundred men on their side, ready to
pledge their property for the propagation of their principles.
And they actually petitioned the legislature for the charter
of a college, to be established under their auspices."   Indeed,
said Beecher:

It it the testimony of the female champion of atheistic liberty,
whose opportunity to feel the pulse of moral evil in the nation
was unequalled, and whose spirit-stirring eloquence was well
calculated to apply the torch to the concealed train, that atheistical education must and will come, either by public suffrage
or by revolution.[3]

To Doctor Beecher the growth and success of the infidel
movement was due to our increasing contact with European

[1] Beecher, Lymann, vol. i, p. 20.
[2] Ibid., pp. 92-93.
[3] Ibid., p. 94.

thought through the channel of trade, to " the streams of dissipation which pour from our cities," and to the growing disregard of business, national and private, for the sanctity of the holy Sabbath. The remedy was an exposure of the principles and horrors of infidelity, and a return by the nation to the religion of the fathers.[1]

The press, however, believed Miss Wright's success due to quite a different cause :

How is it that Fanny Wright, with her infidel doctrines, has thousands of admiring listeners [asked the *New York Courier and Enquirer*] ? How comes it that on all sides we have communities springing up who deride religion and its attributes? It is because men like Arthur Tappan are constantly employed in engrafting what they call religion upon every act and every incident in human affairs.[2]

Perhaps the real secret of the stir caused by Miss Wright and the Free Enquirers lies between these points of view. In part the movement undoubtedly was a reaction against those activities of the evangelical churches which suggested an attempt to restore the puritan tradition in religious matters, and hinted at a union of Church and State. In part it was no doubt due to such exotic influences as that of Miss Wright, the Owens, and George Houston. But more profoundly the growth and success of infidelity in the United States at this time was the outcome of the clash between the restlessly expanding social, political, and economic life of the nation and outworn colonial practices and institutions. Where the latter restricted the development of the former, there dissent arose, a dissent which often took the form of infidelity, because the chief conservative influence was that of religion. It was Miss Wright's fortune to appear at the moment when that dissent was ripe for leadership, and her singular ability enabled her to mould it to her own purposes.

[1] *Ibid.,* p. 123.

[2] *New York Courier and Enquirer,* June 11, 1830.

# CHAPTER VIII

## THE REFORMER

FRANCES WRIGHT and Robert Dale Owen hoped that the free enquiry agitation begun in the summer of 1828 would eventually lead to the adoption of a "rational system of education." Thus the principles they advocated so earnestly would be institutionalized, and future generations might enjoy the blessings of a well-ordered society. That there was any immediate prospect of initiating so desirable a reform, however, does not seem to have seriously occurred to them until they reached the Eastern cities. There the free enquiry movement came in contact with the awakening of American labor; and in the rather pathetic faith of the workers in education as a panacea for their many ills the Free Enquirers saw the possibility of securing a hearing for their own educational program.

The awakening of American labor in the late twenties was not the work of Robert Dale Owen and Frances Wright, although some of their contemporaries would have it so. Fundamentally the awakening was due to important economic changes in the life of the country. More immediately it was the outcome of hard times, and the attempt of the workers to seek redress for certain irritating and oppressive grievances—grievances which appeared to them to widen the gap between the rich and the poor, and threaten the position of the workingman as a free citizen in a democratic state.

Economically, the background of this earliest of American labor movements lay in the changing character of

American business and methods of production. The rapid extension of markets, which followed hard upon the development of turnpike, canal, and river steamboat, brought to the merchant and capitalist of the twenties new worlds of commerce to conquer. To meet the increased demand for goods, wholesale methods of production as well as distribution were necessary, and the old domestic system of production for a local market gradually gave way to machine production and the factory system. It was a period of transition in which the position of the workers was not a happy one. In the keen competitive struggle for markets profits were all too often sought in the exploitation of the unorganized and helpless workingmen, and, to add to the distress occasioned by such practices, there were frequent and disastrous periods of financial and industrial depression, the result of an inadequate banking and credit system, and of overproduction. Moreover, the utter inability of the domestic system to meet the challenge of large scale industry made the lot of the worker under the older system most unfortunate. Unemployment and privation among the working classes were common and widespread.[1]

To the worker, however, the underlying economic causes of his distress were not wholly apparent. More immediately grievous seemed those evils which tended to set apart the rich as a privileged class and thereby menaced the very existence of the American democracy. Chief among these, and the evils about which most of the trouble centered, were the unconscionably long hours of labor, from

[1] The best account of the labor movement in the late twenties, and early thirties, is to be found in John R. Commons's cooperative *History of Labor in the United States*, 2 vols., New York, 1918. See particularly the section by Miss Helen Sumner in volume i. A good short account of the political efforts of the workingmen in New York City is given in Carleton, F. T., "The Workingmen's Party of New York City," *Political Science Quarterly*, vol. 22, pp. 401-415.

" sun to sun," and the lack of anything like universal democratic education.[1]  The former gave to the worker no leisure time for effective participation in the social and political life of his country.  The latter left him without the education intelligently to assume the duties of citizenship, even had he possessed the necessary leisure.  Both tended to throw the control of government and society in democratic America into the hands of the rich, and threatened to leave the working classes an ignorant, discontented, easily exploited mob.  Little thought was required to perceive the danger to American institutions in such a situation.

In the redress of these grievances the workingman saw his salvation.  More leisure would enable him to take a larger part in the life of the community.  Education, he fondly hoped, would narrow the gap between the rich and the poor by giving to all an equal intellectual preparation for the work of the world.  And an educated laboring class, possessed of the franchise, would make but short work of its other grievances.  It was, indeed, through the exercise of their recently acquired franchise rights that the workers sought to attain their ends.  Given the right to vote in a country ruled by majorities, it was not unnatural that the labor movement which started with the demand for a ten-hour day in Philadelphia in 1827, and for the defense of that day in New York in 1829, should develop into a strong political movement, to the dismay of the conservative and the consternation of the politician.

The workingmen's movement in New York, with which Frances Wright and the Free Enquirers became most closely associated, began on the evening of the twenty-third of April, 1829, when a public meeting of " Mechanics and

[1] Other evils which the workingmen found particularly burdensome for their class were imprisonment for debt, the auction and banking monopolies, the lack of an adequate lien law, and the existing militia system.

Others, opposed to all attempts to compel them to work more than ten hours a day" was called "to take such measures as they may deem expedient."[1]  These measures proved to be the adoption of resolutions upholding the principle of the ten-hour day, "by long practice established, and found to be consistent with the best interests of the employer and the employed," and calling upon the workers to boycott those employers who violated the existing rule.[2]  A subsequent meeting five days later placed upon the employers the responsibility for any trouble which might arise, and authorized the appointment of a Committee of Fifty, to assist those who might need aid during the expected struggle, and to call another meeting when it thought advisable.[3]  This businesslike attitude of the workers seems to have intimidated their employers, for the spring and summer passed without the anticipated trouble.  Not until the nineteenth of October did the workers again come together.  It was then decided, if possible, to take advantage of the approaching November elections to send to the legislature at Albany men pledged to support the true interests of the workingmen.  In order to understand the part played by the Free Enquirers in the forthcoming venture of the New York workingmen into politics it is necessary to turn for a moment to certain of their activities after reaching the city.

The interest of Miss Wright and her associates in the unfortunate condition of the working classes had begun shortly after their arrival in New York:

It makes the heart bleed [said the *Free Enquirer* of March 11, 1829] to look at the hundreds and thousands of shivering,

[1] *New York Morning Courier*, April 23, 1829.
[2] *Free Enquirer*, April 29, 1829.
[3] *New York Morning Courier*, April 30, 1829.

hungry applicants for charity who have thronged the old Alms House in the Park this forenoon, pleading their cause in the most woeful and supplicating terms.[1]

A few days later Frances Wright began a series of articles in the *Free Enquirer* on " The Causes of Existing Evils " in which she set forth her theories as to the prevailing unhappiness and discontent, and suggested what she believed the only possible remedy.[2]

The causes of existing evils Miss Wright found not in changing economic conditions, but in the unfortunate character of present governments, and in the unhappy organization of existing society. In all countries, she argued, we find the same evils, differing only in degree, and that degree bearing an exact proportion to two circumstances: " the pressure of constraining power, whether administered in the form of despotic executive authority, coercive law, or terrifying superstition; and the unequal distribution of wealth, with all the other inequalities, instructional and occupational, therein involved."

The first circumstance, or cause of evil, she called " government by violence." In countries " styled civilized " this took the forms of religion and law. " Its motive principles are fear and coercion; its proposed objects—obedience, restraint, and constraint." At base it presupposed man " a vicious animal; in need of control." Such government, wherever it existed, pampered the few at the expense of the many. Under it the priest and the lawyer prospered, and hypocrisy and fraud were rampant. The professions tended to become the bloodsuckers of the producing many,

---

[1] The winter was a very hard one for the poor. "It is almost impossible to imagine," said the *Morning Courier*, February 26, 1829, " and consequently beyond the reach of our pen to describe the sufferings under which the poor of our city are at this moment laboring, by reason of Cold and Hunger."

[2] *Free Enquirer*, March 18–April 22, 1829.

and "not only monopolize worldly respect and bodily
ease (this must be understood comparatively) for themselves of the present generation, but entail the same monopoly to their descendants." Labor under such a system was
rewarded in inverse ratio to its usefulness, and worth while
occupations were in disgrace.

That previously man had possessed much of the tiger in
his make-up Miss Wright did not deny. But, she urged,
much as he may be in need of control, the principle of coercion was fundamentally wrong, for, under proper guidance, the tendency of man " to resist power from without "
was the source of all moral excellence; while the attempt by
violence or *ipse dixit* command to subject the mind was the
source of all moral evil.

The second circumstance, or cause of evil, inequality of
condition, Miss Wright believed due to the "adventitious
circumstances of artificial wealth or artificial employment."
Certainly it was not superiority of intellect, or our organization at birth, that determined who was "to ride or be
ridden." Existing inequalities of condition were evil because they divided "the community into classes—distinct
from, and hostile to each other," and because they created
a "monopoly of that species of instruction which secures to
the class possessing it all the offices of government, together
with the administration of the laws of the land and the disposal of the public funds."

The remedy for inequality of condition, as for "government by violence," lay, according to the belief of Miss
Wright, in the reform of education. "What has been partial in its distribution, imperfect, irrational, and unconstitutional in its nature, must be liberalized, equalized, ration-
alized, and nationalized ";

I would simply point out one measure—against which the
boldest enemy of improvement in this country *dare* not *openly*

object. I would call on the people to bestir themselves—to enquire and examine how they may best be fitted to exercise the rights secured to them by their political institutions. I would call on them, in my writings as in my popular discourses, to prepare their minds for a judicious exercise of the elective franchise. I would exhort them to study, until they discover, their real interests, and then to send men to their legislative assemblies who will represent those interests, men who shall be interested to devote the people's funds to the people's benefit; men, who, instead of sanctifying facts, protecting sabbaths, chartering theological seminaries, and endowing exclusive colleges, shall organize a system of equal and universal education, supported by the public money, and protected by the public care.

By such a measure

a revolution would indeed be effected; the present order of things completely subverted; distinctions of sect annihilated; distinctions of class despoiled of their worst features; and the whole population, then, in very truth, fellow citizens and fellow creatures, would consult rationally and sincerely, to promote their common interests and arrange all things in unison with the public weal. I see no other mode than this of removing vice, preventing pauperism, correcting the whole system of legislation, and gradually applying a remedy to every evil, whether in our private usages or public measures.[1]

A few weeks later while lecturing in Philadelphia on " Existing Evils, and Their Remedy " she undertook to show her auditors how " the present cumbrous, expensive, useless, or rather pernicious, system of partial, opinionative, and dogmatical instruction " might be changed to " one at once national, rational, and republican." [2]

This happy reform was to be effected by the adoption of a

[1] *Ibid.*, April 22, 1829.

[2] *Course of Popular Lectures*, p. 151.

system of " National, Rational, Republican Education; Free
For All At The Expense Of All; Conducted Under The
Guardianship Of The State, And For The Honor, The Happiness, The Virtue, The Salvation Of The State "; a plan
evolved apparently from the theories of Miss Wright, the
educational experiments of Jennings and Phiquepal, and
from Owen's recollections of Emmanuel Fellenberg's school
at Hofwyl, and of the schools established by his father at
New Lanark, Scotland.

Under this plan the state was first to be laid off into
townships or hundreds.  The legislature would then organize, at suitable distances and in convenient and healthful
locations, establishments for the permanent reception of all
the children resident within the school district.  These establishments, furnished with the necessary instructors and
apparatus, would be devoted severally to the reception of
children between certain ages.  In the first would be the
infants from two to four, or two to six years of age; in
the second children from four to eight, or six to twelve;
and in the third children from twelve to sixteen years or
even older.  Progress would be made by the child from one
establishment to the other in regular succession.  To ob-
viate trouble, at the start children with bad habits would be
separated from those with good habits.  Parents might
visit at suitable hours, but in no way would they be allowed
to interfere with the schools.  From the age of two, on
through childhood and early youth, the guardianship of the
state was to be complete:

In these nurseries of a free nation, no inequality must be allowed to enter.  Fed at a common board; clothed in a common garb, uniting neatness with simplicity and convenience;
raised in the exercise of common duties, in the acquirement of
the same knowledge and practice of the same industry, varied
only according to individual tastes and capabilities; in the ex-

ercise of the same virtues, in the enjoyment of the same pleasures; in the study of the same nature; in pursuit of the same
object—their own and each others happiness—say! would not
such a race, when arrived at manhood and womanhood, work out
the reform of society—perfect the free institutions of America.[1]

The upper schools it was thought would soon be more
than self-supporting through the well directed and protected
labor of the students, but until the system was able to main-
tain itself a double tax would probably be necessary. This
was to be derived in the first place from a moderate tax on
every child—to be levied on the parents conjointly. To
provide for this, all children were to be registered at birth
by the state. At two years of age the parental tax would
fall due and the juvenile schools would be opened for the
child's admission. The second tax was to be on property,
increasing in percentage with the wealth of the individual.
Thus the entire community would be rallied to the support
of the system.

Such were the details of the famous " state guardianship "
plan of education whereby the Free Enquirers hoped to
effect the regeneration of American society. To the conservative a plan so radical in character naturally made but
little appeal; to those who sympathized with the ideals of
Miss Wright, and to many a workingman, it appeared a
scheme both desirable and feasible. In its adoption the
Free Enquirers saw the ultimate triumph of rational principles, and the workingman the disappearance of the evils
of poverty and inequality.

Throughout the summer of 1829 the Free Enquirers
strove earnestly to convince the working classes that national,
rational, republican education under the guardianship of the
state was the only solution of their troubles, and that to

[1] *Ibid.*, pp. 168-169. See also *Tracts on Republican Government and
National Education*, p. 21.

secure the desired reform they must send to their legislative
assemblies men pledged to its support.[1]  To facilitate the
discussion, and, eventually, the execution of their plan, the
Free Enquirers proposed the organization of popular associations.  In behalf of this suggestion Miss Wright spoke
in New York, Philadelphia, and other Eastern cities:

I would suggest the propriety [she said] of organizing in each
city, town and district of influence, popular associations for
the single object of discovering and promoting the true interests of the American people, distinct from all class, all sect, all
party, and all speculative opinions.  That the better to impart
energy and unity of plan to the whole, a central point be chosen,
say Philadelphia, that city appearing the best prepared to take
the lead; and that, by means of standing committees, a correspondence between that center and all other parts of the country be opened.

In this manner the attention of the American nation may
rapidly be awakened, the spirit of popular union fostered, useful enquiry set afloat, the plots of orthodoxy and priestcraft
exposed and defeated, pledges interchanged for carrying, at
the elections, friends of human liberty, or rather, men pledged
to the support of upright measures; and first and chief to the
carrying the one great measure of a system of equal universal
republican education.[2]

[1] *Free Enquirer,* June 10, August 12, 26, September 2, 1829.

[2] *Course of Popular Lectures.* "On the State of the Public Mind,"
p. 19.  This address was given in New York and Philadelphia, in the
fall of 1829.  Brownson in *The Convert,* p. 134, states that to get their
plan adopted, it was proposed to organize the whole Union secretly much
after the plan followed by the Carbonari in Europe.  How far the
organization went, he did not know, "but I do know that a considerable
part of the state of New York was organized, for I was myself, one of
the agents for organizing it."

Brownson has the following to say of the motives that led the Free
Enquirers to take up the cause of the workingmen.  "We hoped by
linking our cause with the ultra-Democratic sentiment of the country.
which had had from the time of Jefferson and Tom Paine something of an

The result was the organization in New York City of an "Association for the Protection of Industry and for the Promotion of National Education." Associations of a similar character soon appeared elsewhere, becoming familiarly known as " Fanny Wright Societies." Into these societies all were welcomed who signified their intention " to assist in defending the rights and promoting the interests of the people, and in carrying through the State Legislatures a system of Equal Republican Education," but it was expected that the true friends of equal rights and popular instruction would be found chiefly among the " industrious " classes.[1] The creed of the association as drawn up by Robert Dale Owen ran as follows:

I believe in a National System of Equal, Republican, Protective, Practical Education, the sole regenerator of a profligate age, and the only redeemer of our suffering country from the

anti-Christian character, by professing ourselves the bold and uncompromising champions of equality, by expressing a great love for the people, and a deep sympathy with the laborer whom we represented as defrauded and oppressed by his employer, by denouncing all proprietors as aristocrats, and keeping the more unpopular features of our plan in the background as far as possible, to enlist the majority of the American people under the banner of the Working Men's Party; nothing doubting that if we could once raise that party to power, we could use it to secure the adoption of our educational system." *The Convert*, p. 135. But Brownson wrote this comment after having become a Catholic in religion, and an ultra-conservative in politics, and it seems not quite fair to either Miss Wright, or to Owen, both of whom, it appears to the writer, were sincere in their sympathy for the workingmen, and honestly hoped through their system of education to better the condition of the working classes. Owen's contact with the evils of the Industrial Revolution in England, and with the efforts of his father to ameliorate the position of the workers, naturally accounts for his interest, while the humanitarian instincts of Miss Wright were aroused by the sufferings of the poor she had witnessed in New York and other large Eastern cities.

[1] *Free Enquirer*, September 23, 1829. Quotation from the constitution of the "Association for the Protection of Industry and for the Promotion of National Education.

equal curses of chilling poverty and corrupting riches, of
gnawing want and destroying debauchery, of blind ignorance
and unprincipled intrigue.

By this creed, I will live.   By my consistency or inconsistency with this, my professed belief, I claim to be judged.   By
it I will stand or fall.[1]

Through these associations Miss Wright and her fellow
reformers seem to have organized very effectively the sentiment among the people, particularly of New York City, for
radical social reform through education, and the machinery
thus created enabled them to play a not inconsiderable part
in directing the fortunes of the workingmen's adventure
into politics.

The first step in the organization of the New York Working Men's Party, however, was not taken by the Free Enquirers but by the Committee of Fifty.   This Committee,
it will be recalled, had been appointed by the workers in
April to handle the then impending strike in behalf of the
ten-hour day.   The strike had failed to come, but the committee, under the leadership of one Thomas Skidmore, concluded, apparently, that the time was ripe for the New York
workingmen to follow the example of their Philadelphia
brethren, and seek redress for their numerous grievances
through political organization.   Accordingly, having matured
their plans, the Committee called a great public meeting of
the workers on the evening of October nineteenth in the
Wooster Street Military Hall.[2]   Just how much of a part

---

[1] *Ibid.*, November 7, 1829.   One of the first acts of the New York Association was to send a memorial to the New York State Legislature, urging
the adoption of a state guardianship system of education, and asking that
$100,000 be appropriated for the establishment of a model school some-
where near the center of the state.

[2] *New York Courier and Enquirer,* October 23, 1829; *Free Enquirer,*
October 31, 1829; *New York Evening Journal,* November 11, 1829.   An
offer of the free use of the Hall of Science was rejected.

the propaganda and activities of the Free Enquirers played in influencing the Committee of Fifty to take this action, or in encouraging the workingmen to consider the possibilities of political organization, it is hard to say. Undoubtedly, however, their influence was considerable, for, in the preliminary report offered by the Committee at the meeting, the desirability of a communal system of education was stressed.[1]

This report and the resolutions presented to the workers for adoption were in large measure the work of Thomas Skidmore, a radical with an economic philosophy of an agrarian character, whose thought seems to have dominated the Committee. It was Skidmore's contention that man's right to property was one of those rights of nature which could never be alienated except through ignorance or force, and which might be reclaimed whenever ignorance and force disappeared. Without going too deeply into his ideas, it may be said that he favored the frequent redistribution of all property by the state, and the abolition of the right of inheritance. Thus existing inequalities would be done away with, and with each new division of property all would start again upon an equal footing.[2] In view of Skidmore's ascendency in the Committee the resolutions presented to the meeting were unfortunately very radical in character. It was resolved, for instance, that " the first appropriation of the soil of the state to private and exclusive possession was eminently barbarous and unjust "; that the hereditary transmission of wealth was the prime source of evil; that chartered banking and auction monopolies were the result of legislation which tended " to create and sustain exclusive privilege " and represented " a rapacious and cruel plunder

[1] *Working Man's Advocate*, October 31, 1829.

[2] For the exposition of Skidmore's ideas, see his book, *The Rights of Man to Property*, New York, 1829.

of the people"; that the partial exemption of the churches
and clergy from taxation was direct robbery of the public;
and that the lack of a lien law enabled unfortunate or un-
scrupulous employers to take from the workers three or four
hundred thousand dollars annually. " Just experience," it
was declared, " teaches that we have nothing to hope from
the aristocratic orders of society; and that our only course to
pursue is, to send men of our own description, if we can, to
the Legislature at Albany." This it was resolved to attempt at the ensuing election in November.[1]

These resolutions, according to Robert Dale Owen, who
was present at the meeting and acted as one of the secretaries, were passed " en masse " without discussion, after an
effort to have them taken up one by one had been defeated
by Skidmore and the leaders of the meeting. For their
agrarian tendencies Owen and the Free Enquirers had little
use; Owen pointing out to the workingmen, through the
columns of the *Free Enquirer,* " that inequality is often of
mind as well as of property; and that the only security
for the enjoyment of equal rights is, not agrarian laws or
any laws whatever, but equal, national, republican education." [2]

A few days after the Wooster Street meeting the workingmen met again at the call of the Committee of Fifty to
draw up a party ticket of *bona fide* workingmen, and to prepare for the coming election.[3] In these measures the Free
Enquirers seem to have played no active part. Not that
they were uninterested, however. Miss Wright, it is true,
had left the city for Haiti, but Owen and Jennings, backed

[1] These resolutions are given in the *New York Courier and Enquirer,*
October 23, 1829. They may also be found in the *Working Man's
Advocate,* October 31, 1829.

[2] *Free Enquirer,* October 31, 1829; see also Owen's account of the
origin of the party in the *Free Enquirer,* March 20, 1830.

[3] *Working Man's Advocate,* October 31, 1829.

by the Association for the Protection of Industry and for
the Promotion of National Education, eagerly pressed upon
the workingmen the desirability of sending to the legislature men who would advocate reform through education.
To further their efforts, and aid the cause of the workingmen, the *Working Man's Advocate* was established; the
reputation of the *Free Enquirer* for infidelity and radicalism rendering it of doubtful value to the cause.[1]   The new
paper, the second labor paper to be published in the United
States, was " edited by a mechanic," George H. Evans, and
was published weekly.[2]   For a motto it took the following:
" All children are entitled to equal education; all adults, to
equal property; and all mankind to equal privileges."   The
aims and purposes of the paper the editor stated in his prospectus :

We shall oppose the establishment of all exclusive privileges,
all monopolies, and all exemptions of one class more than another from an equal share of the burdens of society; all of
which, to whatever class or order of men they are extended,
we consider highly anti-republican, oppressive and unjust.
We consider it an exclusive privilege for one portion of the
community to have the means of education in colleges, while
another is restricted to common schools, or, perhaps, by extreme poverty, even deprived of the limited education to be
acquired in those establishments.  Our voice therefore shall
be raised in favor of a system of education which shall be
open to *all,* as in a real republic it should be.[3]

[1] The first issue of the *Working Man's Advocate* appeared October 31,
1829.  The editor, George H. Evans, was one of the Free Enquirers, and
a devoted follower of Miss Wright.

[2] The first paper was the *Mechanics' Free Press* of Philadelphia, which
appeared in 1828.

[3] *Working Man's Advocate,* October 31, 1829.  The motto was changed
in the issue of November 21, 1829, to read as follows: " All children are
entitled to equal education; all adults to equal privileges."  The change
represents the declining influence of Skidmore, and the growing importance of the Free Enquirers in the labor movement.

On the evening of October thirtieth the Association for
the Protection of Industry and for the Promotion of National
al Education invited "the Mechanics and Working Men
of this city, and those favorable to their interests" to assemble in the Wooster Street Military Hall.[1] Here the
usual resolutions were adopted denouncing existing inequalities of wealth, power, and privilege, and the workingmen
were urged, before attempting any minor reforms, to unite
in carrying through the legislature the great regenerating
measure of state guardianship education, compared to which
all other modes of reform were "partial, inefficient, temporary, or trifling." Some concession was made to the Committee of Fifty and its followers in the second resolution
which declared "that any peaceful and effectual measures
which shall tend permanently to equalize the possession of
landed property and of all other property, will prove eminently useful to society."[2] To this particular resolution
Miss Wright objected, as she felt that the popular mind was
not yet ready for it. "Let us not now tax our ingenuity," she
wrote to the *Free Enquirer,* "to imagine what future measures a generation trained up equal in knowledge, and similar in habits, tastes, and occupations may propose, to secure
equality in all their rights and enjoyments. Let us train
that generation as they ought to be, and let us leave them to
decide . . . how their property shall be inherited and
divided."[3]

Upon the adjournment of the Wooster Street meeting,
those present, accompanied by Owen and Jennings, proceeded to Masonic Hall where they interrupted, and made
their own, a gathering "unfriendly to the proceedings at

---

[1] *New York Courier and Enquirer,* October 29, 1829.

[2] *Free Enquirer,* November 7, 1829.

[3] *Ibid.,* November 21, 1829. The letter was dated Auburn, New York,
November 7, 1829.

Tammany Hall, without reference to party," a meeting
which seems to have been made up largely of men who had
voted for Adams for the presidency in 1828, and now opposed the Democratic administration in city and state.
Scarcely had the original meeting drawn up and adopted its
electoral ticket than the " Agrarian Party," as the *Journal of
Commerce* called the invaders, took command and adopted
resolutions approving the workingmen's ticket, as well as
the measures just taken in Wooster Street by the Association for the Protection of Industry and for the Promotion
of National Education.[1] By this rather high-handed performance the Free Enquirers linked up their own program
with the cause of the workingmen in the coming election.
No doubt many of the workingmen were present and approved, but it may be noted in passing that on the same
evening the Committee of Fifty was holding a meeting of
workingmen in a hall on Ludlow Street.[2]

These proceedings attracted the attention of the city press
which hitherto had paid but little heed to the activities of
the workingmen.   The Free Enquirers were promptly ac-
cused of organizing and guiding the new party, which the
*Evening Post* dubbed the " Fanny Wright Party," declaring
that it knew of " no other name so proper to designate the
crew of which Robert Dale Owen and Robert L. Jennings
are leaders."   It was a party, said the *Post,* " favorable to
the abolition of all social relations," and one which would
gladly " sunder the ligaments which held the community together, and reduce everything to pristine chaos and confusion."   But the *Post* had too much confidence in the
general intelligence of the mechanics and laboring classes

---

[1] *New York Courier and Enquirer,* October 30, 31, November 3, 1829;
*New York Evening Post,* October 31, 1829, *New York Journal of Commerce,* October 31, 1829.

[2] *New York Courier and Enquirer,* October 30, 1829.

to believe that they would seriously lend their aid in promoting the wild schemes and dark designs of the Free Enquirers.[1]

Three days later the tone of the press had become almost panicky, for, to the dismay of the conservative, the Working Men's Party had carried all before it on the first day of the three-day election, a success due in part to the distribution of the vote polled among no less than five tickets, and in part to the failure of the press to estimate correctly the strength of the workingmen's movement, and to warn the voters that with a vote so widely scattered there was some chance of its success.[2]  This last mistake the press now endeavored to rectify.  At the same time it strove to discredit the new party by denouncing it as the " Fanny Wright," " Agrarian," or " Infidel " Party:[3]

We understand with astonishment and alarm [said the *Courier and Enquirer*] that the " Infidel Ticket," miscalled the " Working Men's Ticket," is far ahead of every other assembly ticket in the city—not excepting even the regular Tammany Hall Ticket.  What a state of things have we reached!  A ticket got up openly and avowedly in opposition to all banks—in opposition to social order—in opposition to the rights of property—running ahead of every other!  Is not this sufficient to startle men who have regard for the fundamental laws of society?  Look to it, bank gentlemen—look to it you who oppose regular nominations.  On whom does the responsibility rest of a state of anarchy and confusion?

Mechanics and Working Men, you are deluded, deceived, be-

[1] *New York Evening Post*, October 31, 1829.

[2] There were five tickets in the field: the Working Men's Ticket; the Tammany Hall Ticket; the " Pewter Mug " Ticket which represented a split in the Tammany ranks; the Masonic Ticket; and the Anti-Masonic Ticket.

[3] *New York Evening Post, New York Journal of Commerce, New York Courier and Enquirer*, November 3, 1829.

trayed!—We call upon you to examine the nature of the original resolutions passed at the Military Hall in Wooster Street, and then go and vote any ticket you can find, rather than lend yourselves to the support of a ticket got up by Fanny Wright, Robert Dale Owen, and R. L. Jennings.[1]

With the close of the polls on November fourth it was found that the workingmen had polled over six thousand of the twenty thousand votes cast, and had elected one of their candidates to the state legislature at Albany. The concern of the press was great. *The Evening Post* feared that in view of the apparent strength of the new party and the character of the principles upon which it was based people would hesitate to make investments in, or become residents of, the city. The *Post* found some consolation, however, in the thought that probably many had voted the ticket through ignorance, or because it was called the Mechanics' Ticket, or because they hoped through it to secure a lien law.[2] The *Commercial Advertiser* became positively hysterical, referring to Miss Wright as the " priestess of Beelzebub," and to the workingmen as " poor deluded followers of a crazy atheistical woman ":

Lost to society, to earth and to heaven, godless and hopeless, clothed and fed by stealing and blasphemy . . . such are the apostles who are trying to induce a number of able bodied men in this city to follow in their own course . . . to disturb the peace of the community for a time; go to prison and have the mark of Cain impressed upon them; betake themselves to incest, robbery, and murder; die like ravenous wild beasts, hunted down without pity; and go to render their account before God, whose existence they believed in their miserable

[1] *New York Courier and Enquirer*, November 3, 1829.

[2] *New York Evening Post*, November 5, 9, 18, 1829; *New York Courier and Enquirer*, November 5, 9, 1829.

hearts, even while they were blaspheming him in their ignorant, snivelling, and puerile speculations. Such is too true a
picture in *all* its parts of some of the leaders of the new political party, which is emerging from the slime of this community,
and which is more beastly and terrible than the Egyptian
Typhon.[1]

It is interesting to note, as showing a practical result of
this apprehension, that shortly after the election the *Courier
and Enquirer* was hoping that at the coming session of the
legislature something might be done about a lien law.[2]
Something was done.

On the whole the workingmen themselves were not ill-
pleased with the outcome of the election. That they had
not attained complete success the *Evening Journal* believed
due to a poor choice of candidates, and to the hasty adoption
of measures of an agrarian character which had antagonized
many in the community.[3]   In this, Robert Dale Owen
agreed, adding that the appearance of his own name as
secretary of the Wooster Street meeting of October nineteenth may also have injured the cause. He denied em-
phatically, however, that he and Jennings had had anything
to do with getting up the workingmen's ticket, and declared
that the cry of atheism and irreligion raised with respect to
the character of the new party was but a stratagem of the
press:

They contrived to identify the cause of the Mechanics and
that of scepticism for reasons best known to themselves; and
employed the simple circumstances of my having assisted the

[1] *New York Commercial Advertiser*, November 7, 1829.

[2] *New York Courier and Enquirer*, November 9, 1829.

[3] *New York Evening Journal*, November 9, 1829. This paper had a
circulation in the upper wards of the city, where the workingmen's movement was strongest. It had become an organ of the Working Men's
Party shortly after the Wooster Street meeting.

Mechanics at their first meeting as secretary, for a pretext whereupon to build their assertion, that this was not the " Mechanics," but the " Fanny Wright Ticket," by which name it passed current at last among friends and foes. An infidel ticket could, of course, augur nothing but anarchy; and Tammany was too old in the trade of politics to neglect so convenient a handle. He worked it with his utmost skill, yet scarcely with success enough to prevent the Mechanics ticket from going in, as it stood. Poor prospects enough has he for next year.[1]

Owen also took occasion to point out that the editors of the *Free Enquirer* had " never directly or indirectly advocated or approved anything approaching to an agrarian law," or " any proposal to make a division of lands or property." They had merely proposed and advocated the earnest consideration of equal education under the guardianship of the state. What measures a generation brought up under such a system might adopt in respect to their property " we conceive it neither possible for us now to decide, nor useful for us now to imagine." [2] Miss Wright, herself, felt that the use of her name by those hostile to the workingmen had been a mistake. It simply indicated the lack of all good grounds of opposition.[3]

The success of the workingmen in polling so respectable a vote naturally led the Free Enquirers to feel that through the new party their own program might still be carried out. Encouraged by Owen and Miss Wright, another paper now appeared to support the cause of the workingmen, as well as that of the Free Enquirers. This was the *New York Daily Sentinel,* a paper started by several young men from

[1] *Free Enquirer,* November 14, 1829.

[2] *Ibid.,* November 28, 1829.

[3] *Ibid.,* November 21, 1829.

the office of the *Courier and Enquirer*.[1]　The efforts of the Association for the Protection of Industry and for the Promotion of National Education were redoubled, and circulars describing the character and aims of the Association were addressed by Owen, as corresponding secretary, to the various mechanics' societies of the city.　These seem to have been fairly well received, although the Typographical Society, in a scathing reply to the request for its position on state guardianship education, denounced the scheme as unnecessary and impugned the motives of Owen in forwarding it.[2]

This post-election campaign of the Free Enquirers in behalf of state guardianship education had its reward in the great reorganization meeting of the new party on the evening of December twenty-ninth, when a report prepared by the Conference Committee of the several wards, and adopted by the meeting, called for a system of education which should " unite under the same roof the children of the poor man and the rich, the widow's charge and the orphan, where the road to distinction shall be superior industry, virtue, and acquirements, without reference to descent." [3]　The rise of the Free Enquirers in the party councils was marked by the downfall of Skidmore and the agrarians.　This, Owen tells us, was due to the fact that the workingmen

began more clearly to distinguish the errors into which they had been drawn ; first, in countenancing crude and impractical propositions, such as a proposal to divide property among the adults of the present generation, and then by running a ticket which was in itself objectionable.　They called to mind, too,

[1] *Ibid.*, December 12, 1829.　Miss Wright appears to have loaned the young men back of the *Sentinel* $1,000, to get the paper established. Wright MSS. Robert Dale Owen to Frances Wright, April 19, 1832.

[2] *Free Enquirer*, December 12, 1829.

[3] *Ibid.*, March 20, 1830.

Thomas Skidmore's management, and his somewhat overbearing and dictatorial manner throughout the whole proceeding; and the remembrance did not operate favorably to his views or to his popularity.[1]

Skidmore's actual downfall was accomplished by simply replacing the Committee of Fifty with a General Executive Committee made up of five delegates from each of the several wards of the city. In spite of the efforts of Jennings, Skidmore was not even given an opportunity to defend his position, being howled down by the meeting. The result was the first serious split in the ranks of the party, for Skidmore and his followers, fortunately few in number, promptly withdrew to organize a small but noisy party of their own.[2] To Owen, Skidmore appeared as "an ambitious, head-strong, and imprudent schemer, honest, perhaps, in his first intentions, but very careless what harm he does in striding to his object."[3]

The victory of the Free Enquirers, however, was not quite complete, for, although their educational ideas had been accepted in theory by the meeting of the twenty-ninth, the development in detail of the system of education to be supported by the workingmen had been placed in the hands of a subcommittee on education of the General Executive Committee.[4]

The deliberations of this subcommittee lasted more than four months. During this interval the Free Enquirers did all that lay within their power to advocate and clarify their ideas, and to strengthen the element in the party favorable to their cause. In this work the *Daily Sentinel* seems to

[1] *Ibid.*

[2] *Ibid.* This party they called the "Poor Man's Party." It was supported by Skidmore's paper, *The Friend of Equal Rights.*

[3] *Ibid.*, March 30, 1830.

[4] *Ibid.*, March 20, 1830.

have taken the lead by publishing a series of articles on education, probably from the pen of Robert Dale Owen.   These articles on " Public Education" were republished in the *Free Enquirer* and *Working Man's Advocate,* and were approved at first by the *Evening Journal.*   In them sundry questions in regard to the proposed scheme were asked and answered, and various objections discussed.   It was made clear, for instance, that although the parental tax would be levied on all, parents might send their children to the state schools, or not, as they saw fit.[1]   Outside of New York City the campaign for state guardianship education attracted attention wherever Miss Wright had lectured in the fall of 1829, and established, perhaps, a " Fanny Wright Society," or wherever workingmen's parties had been organized.   The greatest interest appears to have been felt in Philadelphia and in upper New York state.   The propaganda of the Free Enquirers was tremendously aided, of course, by the fact that two of the three prominent workingmen's papers in New York City were quite in sympathy with their educational ideals, the *Working Man's Advocate,* and the *Daily Sentinel.*   Even the *Evening Journal,* although not inclined to be very favorably disposed toward the influence of Owen and Jennings in the affairs of the party, was not unfriendly to state guardianship education at this time.

Unfortunately for the cause of the Free Enquirers, however, there were those within the party who were none too eager for their success.   Among these were certain politicians who had joined the party for reasons of their own shortly after the fall elections.   There was also a group of conservatives who feared the radical ideas of Owen, Jennings, and Miss Wright, as being detrimental to party progress, and tending unduly to alarm the community.

[1] They were republished in the *Free Enquirer,* beginning with the issue of May 1, 1830.

This last group may have been influenced by the irritating campaign carried on in the columns of the *Courier and Enquirer* to discredit and make ridiculous the new party. Typical of the methods used by the *Courier and Enquirer*, and illustrative of its deliberate attempt to confuse the principles of Skidmore with those of the Free Enquirers, is the following satirical sketch of a meeting of the mechanics:

At a numerous and highly respectable meeting of the friends of *Wright Reason,* held at the sign of " the World turned upside down " in the Five Points, last evening, Mr. Ichabod Ragamuffin was called to the Bench and Messrs. Rag, Tag, and Bobtail appointed secretaries. The meeting being properly disorganized the following preamble and resolutions were passed unanimously:

Whereas all men are born free and equal, and bring nothing with them into this world, it stands to reason they ought to remain so, and take nothing with them out of it. It is therefore contrary to Wright reason, and the laws of nature for talent, industry, economy, enterprise, and honesty to raise one man above another, in reputation or property. Therefore:

Resolved unanimously, That the social state as it exists at present is contrary to Wright reason—and a great evil.

That it is against the laws of nature and the principles of Wright reason, that because one man chooses to work and another do nothing, the former should get rich and the latter remain poor.

That it is bad enough for a man to have the exclusive enjoyment of the fruits of his labor during his life; but that he should be permitted to leave them to his own children instead of ours, is a crying sin against law and Wright reason.[1]

That those hostile to the influence of the Free Enquirers in the party were in active opposition became evident about

[1] *New York Courier and Enquirer*, February 18, 1830. There were more resolutions of a similar character.

the middle of May when without warning the *Evening
Journal* intimated that it by no means agreed with all of
Owen's "peculiar notions on the subject of education."[1]
This seemed a rather startling change of front, as the
*Journal* had approved and accepted the remarks on educa-
tion made at the great meeting of December twenty-ninth,
had indirectly defended Owen as the secretary of the
Wooster Street meeting of October nineteenth, and had but
just published a series of articles on education, so strikingly
similar to those in the *Sentinel* that the *Working Man's
Advocate* had felt it almost unnecessary to republish the
*Sentinel* articles.[2]  The grounds of opposition offered by
the *Journal*, that it would be unjust to tax those parents
desiring to educate their own children and that the proposed
system would tear the children away from their parents,
the *Working Man's Advocate* considered ridiculous.  No
general system of education could be supported without a
general tax, and no paper or individual, asserted the *Advocate*, had ever urged that parents be forced to send their
children to the state schools.  To the *Working Man's Advocate* it appeared that there must be "treason in the camp
of the workingmen."[3]

The trouble came to a head when the subcommittee on
education rendered its report to the General Executive Committee on the twenty-first of May.  The deliberations of
the subcommittee, it appears, had resulted in the production of majority and minority reports.  These reports had
been offered to the General Executive Committee for consideration and final action, but, after the reading of the
majority report, both were referred back to the subcom-

[1] *New York Evening Journal*, May 14, 1830.

[2] *New York Courier and Enquirer*, May 29, 1830; *New York Evening
Journal*, April 29, 1830; *Working Man's Advocate*, May 15, 1830.

[3] *Working Man's Advocate*, May 22, 1830.

mittee, with additional documents, for further consideration. According to the story of a minority member of the sub-committee, several meetings were then held, and it was agreed to withdraw the reports and submit one on general educational principles, without attempting to enter into detail on any particular scheme. Such action, it was felt, would tend to prevent a possible split in the party over the question. This decision, however, was suddenly altered by the majority of the committee, and a new report introduced and adopted despite the protests of the minority, a report which, while offering nothing of a constructive nature, denounced the original report drawn up by the minority, as being based upon the educational ideas of Robert Dale Owen.[1] Attached to the report were resolutions to the effect that; "the Report on the subject of education, submitted to your committee by a minority, embracing a system of guardianship and support, is unwise in its details, impolitic in its operations—at variance with the best feelings of our nature, and based upon the doctrines of infidelity"; that "the Report alluded to be rejected"; and that "we utterly disapprove of the course pursued by those journals which have endeavored to palm upon the public this system as one that is approved by the great body of Working Men."[2] On the evening of May twenty-first the above report and resolutions were submitted to the General Executive Committee, and after a heated debate were adopted by a vote of twenty-five to twenty.[3]

This was a direct attack upon the state guardianship element of the party, and the influence of the Free Enquirers,

---

[1] *Ibid.* Also the issue of June 16, 1830, for the statement of Paul Grout, a minority member of the sub committee. The actual minority report is given in the issue of June 19, 1830.

[2] *Free Enquirer*, June 5, 1830.

[3] *Ibid.*, *Working Man's Advocate*, May 29, 1830.

and was promptly recognized as such. To the leaders of
the state guardianship group it seemed that the action of the
majority of the subcommittee in submitting to the General
Executive Committee a report upon a minority report, which
the larger committee had never read, was uncalled for and
unfair. Moreover, it had been railroaded through the General Executive Committee on an evening when the attend-
ance was small, and the anti-guardianship forces had made
sure of their majority.[1] Twenty-nine members of the
General Executive Committee who favored state guardianship education, but who actually represented only a minority
of the Committee, now proceeded to issue a call for a great
public meeting of the workingmen, to be held in the North
American Hotel on the evening of May twenty-sixth.[2] To
this, the "political workingmen," as the *Daily Sentinel*
dubbed the anti-guardianship members of the General Executive Committee, replied with a communication, signed by
some thirty-seven members of the Committee, in which the
action of the twenty-nine guardianship members was denounced as unconstitutional.[3] Furthermore, on the evening
of the twenty-fifth the following hand bill was posted
throughout the city:

Liberty! Principle!! Mechanics and other Working Men, to
your posts! Another base attempt is making to palm upon us
INFIDELITY and AGRARIANISM!
You, then, who love your country, your children, and the
cause of Liberty and Principle—You who wish to preserve
the civil institutions of your country free from the baneful
levelling system of a fanatical set of Foreigners, attend; rally
round the standard of Liberty, at the North American Hotel,

[1] *Free Enquirer*, June 5, 1830. The account in the *Free Enquirer* is
taken from the *Daily Sentinel*.

[2] *Working Man's Advocate*, May 29, 1830.

[3] *New York Evening Journal*, May 25, 1830.

this (Wednesday) evening, May 26, at 7 o'clock, and put down forever, these infuriated individuals, who wish to ruin the Working Men's cause.[1]

The meeting on the evening of the twenty-sixth was described by the *Courier and Enquirer* as "probably without exception, one of the wildest, most singular scenes—short of personal violence and bloodshed—which ever took place in this country."[2] The crowd which gathered not only filled the room hired for the occasion but the lobby and stairs of the Hotel and even the neighboring streets.[3] Efforts on the part of anti-guardianship men to effect an early adjournment of the meeting, and, failing in that, to prevent the passage of resolutions by clamor and uproar proved futile. Several such disturbers were ejected bodily from the hall. The meeting then expressed its disapproval of the action of the General Executive Committee on the twenty-first by an overwhelming vote, and resolved that while expressly disclaiming any idea of advocating a system of education which should force the children from their parents against the latter's desire " we are not to be intimidated, by having such a sentiment falsely charged upon us, from contending for a system which shall afford the means of education equally to all—the poorest man's child as well as the richest—who choose to avail themselves of their right."[4]

Of the twenty-five members of the General Executive Committee who accepted the report of the subcommittee, the majority, it was pointed out, had opposed the workingmen in the election of the preceding November. Such leadership it behooved the workingmen to avoid.[5]

[1] *Working Man's Advocate*, May 29, 1830.
[2] *New York Courier and Enquirer*, May 28, 1830.
[3] *Free Enquirer*, June 5, 1830.
[4] *Ibid.* See the article by Frances Wright, on " Plots and Plotters."
[5] *Ibid.*

The outcome of this row in the General Executive Committee, and of the subsequent struggle of guardianship and anti-guardianship men for the control of the several wards, was a second serious schism in the ranks of the party. Whether this disaster was due wholly to the question of state guardianship education, or in part to the machinations of politicians within and without the party, is not wholly clear. To Owen and the *Working Man's Advocate* it was the work of shrewd men of the latter kind, who had joined the party after the November elections had shown its potential strength.[1] Miss Wright seems to have believed it the result of Tammany plottings.[2] There is little doubt, however, that many workingmen mistrusted the motives of the Free Enquirers, and looked upon the system of state guardianship education with considerable suspicion. These were probably not sorry to see the downfall of the Wright-Owen faction in the party. Whatever the cause of the schism it could not but prove fatal to the future of the party and to the hopes of the Free Enquirers.

In the midst of all this excitement Miss Wright announced her early departure for Europe. She had returned to the city from Haiti about the first of May, and had plunged at once into the campaign for state guardianship education. Whether her return had greatly benefited the cause is doubtful, for the city press lost little time in renewing its attack upon her principles and her character. Some of these attacks attempted to be facetious, as the following, which appeared in the *Courier and Enquirer* shortly after her return:

There is a scandalous report about town, that Miss Epicene Wright has abstracted, or rather Agrarianized, a pair of Mr.

---

[1] *Working Man's Advocate*, June 16, 1830.
[2] *Free Enquirer*, June 19, 1830.

Jennings' inexpressibles, and means to appear in them at her
next lecture, which report says is to be delivered at the sign of
" All Things in Common," Five Points.[1]

But more often the remarks of the press were bitterly hostile and even slanderous. Colonel Stone, the editor of the
*Commercial Advertiser,* went so far as to impugn the motives
of her trip to Haiti, declaring that twenty-seven of her thirty
slaves were already free when she left New Orleans, and
that she had not only received a rebate of the duties paid on
certain merchandise carried to Haiti, but had received lavish
presents from President Boyer. The whole scheme, the
*Commercial Advertiser* hinted, was nothing but a money-
making venture.[2]   To this Miss Wright answered by ex-
hibiting the original bills of sale of her negroes and the
account of the duties regularly paid into the Haitian treasury. The gift of one hundred dubloons from President
Boyer she explained as money given her to cover the cost
of colonization. Colonel Stone was forced to apologize,
which he did in a rather unsportsmanlike manner.[3]   The
*Courier and Enquirer* thought Colonel Stone's remarks un-
gentlemanly, but did not hesitate, itself, to drag again before
the public the " Explanatory Notes," as well as certain
letters which had been written to Robert L. Jennings by
Camilla and Frances in the spring of 1828, asking him to
come to Nashoba and start a school. In these letters financial arrangements were suggested which would enable Mrs.
Jennings to remain temporarily in the East. The letters
had been directed to Jennings in care of George Houston,
the editor of the *Correspondent,* but had never been de-

[1] *New York Courier and Enquirer,* May 8, 1830.

[2] *New York Commercial Advertiser,* May 28, 1830; *Free Enquirer,*
June 12, 1830.

[3] *New York Commercial Advertiser,* June 2, 1830.

livered. Houston now turned them over to the *Courier and Enquirer* which promptly published them together with sundry outrageous and wholly unwarrantable insinuations. These Miss Wright met with an explanation of the origin of the letters and their meaning.[1]

These incidents seem to have convinced Miss Wright that her continued presence in the country might prove injurious to the cause of the workingmen. It may be, too, that after the latest troubles of the Working Men's Party she despaired of the success of state guardianship education. Whatever her reasons for going, she left New York for France on the first of July, after giving a series of parting lectures both in New York and Philadelphia in which she encouraged the workingmen to persist in their efforts for reform, and denied that the state guardianship element of the party was tainted with agrarianism or infidelity. Her departure was not made without a few parting shots from the press, some of which were rather amusing. The following verses appeared in the *New York Courier and Enquirer:*

A doleful Ditty made upon the departure of that " mother of the Gracchii " Frances Wright, the " petticoated politician "— from free America, after a brilliant career of regeneration, concluded by three distinct farewell addresses. To be sung in the most melancholy strain imaginable by Robert Dale Owen, Doct. Baxter, and every American Mechanic and Working Man who cannot think or act without the aid of English radicals and Jacobins and American Tories.

[1] *New York Courier and Enquirer,* June 3, 17, 19, 1830; *Free Enquirer,* June 19, 1830.

TUNE "OH! PUT THE ONION TO YOUR EYE"

I

Oh Fanny Wright—sweet Fanny Wright
    We ne'er shall hear her more:
She's gone to take another freight
    To Hayti's happy shore.
She used to speak so parrot-like,
    With gesture small and staid;
So pretty in her vehemence—
    Alas! departed maid.
Tho' we are men of age mature
    How can we rule ourselves?
Unless we all wear petticoats,
    We're laid upon the shelves!

II

She beat Jemima Wilkinson
    Joana Southcote quite,
E'en mother Lee was nothing to
    Our little Fanny Wright.
For she had gold within her purse,
    And brass upon her face;
And talent indescribable,
    To give old thoughts new grace.
And if you want to raise the wind,
    Or breed a moral storm
You must have one bold lady-man
    To prate about reform.

III

But now she's gone—alack—alas!
    Och hone and ullaloo!
She's ta'en old Spence for Boyer—
    And we have nothing new.
How can we raise the " ready "—
    Our Owen's face too small,
Our Kneeland a chameleon—
    Our Baxter lank and tall!
Farewell ye young mechanics
    Ye lusty men and true;
All—one and all—both great and small,
    My heart is warm for you.

IV

Thus cried she on that Tuesday night
    When in her whitest gloves,
Her grey eyes, at the Bowery,
    Looked on her hundred loves,
Her Owen was forgotten,
    And Baxter looked an ass;
Tho' one hung up her Leghorn
    The other filled her glass!
Those dignified Philosophers,
    Those Platos of the west,
Were nothing to the jacket-boys
    Who fired her virgin breast.

V

Ye are the bone and sinew
    The marrow of this land;
And yet ye are but blockheads
    Who cannot understand:
So I have come to teach you
    What Spence has taught before,
That—if mankind were all made rich
    They would—be poor no more!
Tom Skidmore—he came out too soon—
    And now we tread him down,
Because we find his monstrous plans
    But horrify the Town.

            *    *    *    *

XV

Thus spake this gentle maiden,
    Not more than six feet high.
How beautiful her curly wig!
    How restless clear her eye!
She had a very little book
    She seemed to look upon;
But buxom lads with peachy cheeks
    Much more her notice won.[1]

With the departure of Miss Wright for Europe, and the removal of Robert L. Jennings to Boston, Owen was left in New York to carry on the state guardian agitation as best he could with the aid of George H. Evans, the editor of

[1] *Ibid.*, June 14, 1830.

the *Working Man's Advocate*. But the cause was doomed, for the schism in the ranks of the Working Men's Party, produced in part at least by the education question, proved impossible to heal, and, in consequence, whatever chance for political success the workingmen had possessed was lost. Instead of one Working Man's Party three now appeared in the field: the " Agrarian," or " Poor Man's Party," led by Skidmore, the " Anti-Guardianship Party," or " political " workingmen backed by the *Evening Journal*, and the " Guardianship Party," or " original " workingmen, supported by the *Daily Sentinel* and the *Working Man's Advocate*. Under the leadership of Evans, the *Daily Sentinel* and the " original " workingmen kept their organization intact throughout the summer and fall, and finally, as the " Liberal Working Men's Party," polled some two thousand votes in the November elections.[1] Skidmore, too, managed to keep his few supporters together until the election, but the fate of the *Evening Journal* faction, the " political " workingmen, justified in part the belief of Owen and Miss Wright that politics had done much to disrupt the party in May. This group indicated its future course by joining the Adams-Clay party in carrying a fifth-ward aldermanic election in July, a coalition which became permanent in the fall under the name of " National Republicans," " Clay Working Men," or the " North American, Clay, Anti-Masonic, Working Men." [2] A great number of the workingmen, however, seem to have returned at this time to the ranks of the Democratic Party whence they had originally come, placated no doubt by the passage of a mechanics' lien law in the spring of 1830.[3]

[1] *New York Journal of Commerce*, November 9, 1830.

[2] *Ibid.; New York Evening Post*, November 1, 1830.

[3] Myers, Gustavus, *History of Tammany Hall*, New York, 1901, p. 99. The law that was passed applied only to New York City. See also Commons, John R., *History of Labor in the United States*, vol. i, p. 329.

With the election of 1830 the story of the first organized venture of the New York workingmen into politics comes to an end. Politically the workingmen's movement had been a failure, wrecked by internal dissensions, ultra-radical leadership, and the machinations of designing politicians. Practically, however, the movement had gained for the workers the redress of several of their more pressing grievances, for the Democratic Party, alarmed by their potential political power, hustled a mechanics' lien law through the legislature at Albany in the spring of 1830, and followed this up in the next year with the abolition of imprisonment for debt, and the reform of the existing burdensome militia system.[1] The movement to abolish the detested auction and banking monopolies developed more slowly, but the ultimate disappearance of the chartered monopoly was hastened without doubt by the activities of the workingmen in 1829 and 1830.

The collapse of the Working Men's Party brought to an end the agitation for state guardianship education, for it was clear that the American public was not prepared to accept any such radical method of regeneration. Nor were the bulk of the workingmen convinced that it was exactly the panacea they were looking for. If the vote polled by the workers in 1829 be compared with that polled by the Liberal Working Men's Party in 1830 it would appear that about one-third of the workers had actually supported the scheme. That so considerable a number accepted the plan does credit to the eloquence and clever propaganda of the Free Enquirers. Although it caused dissension in the ranks of the workers, state guardianship education probably played its part in bringing about an increase in the appropriations

[1] Carleton, F. T., "The Workingmen's Party of New York City." See also Fox, Dixon R., *Decline of Aristocracy in the Politics of New York*, New York, 1921, p. 359.

for education in New York City, and perhaps sped the adoption of a more democratic system of education.[1]

The campaign for state guardianship education was never renewed, for the little band of Free Enquirers had dispersed even before the fall elections had shown the futility of their dreams. Miss Wright had gone to Europe, and was not to return for five years. Jennings had severed his connection with Owen and Miss Wright to join the society of free enquirers in Boston. Owen alone remained in New York to carry on the *Free Enquirer* with occasional assistance in the form of letters from Miss Wright. A little more than a year later he too sought Europe, leaving the paper in the hands of Amos Gilbert, a Quaker of liberal principles. Another year and the *Free Enquirer* came to an end, and with it ended the story of the effort made by Frances Wright and Robert Dale Owen to effect the regeneration of the American people.

[1] Bourne, W. O., *History of the Public School Society of the City of New York*, New York, 1873, p. xxxii.

# CHAPTER IX

## MARRIAGE

ON the first day of July, 1830, the little home of the Free Enquirers on the banks of the East River at York-ville was broken up by the departure of Miss Wright and her sister Camilla for Europe.[1] A number of reasons induced Frances Wright to go abroad at so critical a moment in the fortunes of the Working Men's Party and of state guardianship education. The unwarrantable use of her name in connection with the origin and activities of the Working Men's Party in the fall of 1829 convinced her, as we have seen, that her presence in New York City during the forthcoming political campaign of 1830 would be more of a hindrance than a help to the workingmen.[2] Then, too, she was tired out. Two years and a half of strenuous effort in behalf of free enquiry and educational reform, carried on despite much hostile criticism and some scurrilous abuse, had left her sadly in need of " mental repose." [3] Camilla also needed a change, for the death of her baby had left her ill and despondent.

A more personal reason for leaving the United States at this time may have been the thought of her approach-

[1] *Free Enquirer*, July 10, 1830. They probably sailed on the " Edward Quesnal", which cleared for Havre on the first.

[2] Wright, Frances. *Parting Address, as delivered in the Bowery Theater to the People of New York in June, 1830*. New York, 1830.

[3] *Free Enquirer*, January 1, 1831. Letter from Frances Wright to the editor of the *Free Enquirer*.

ing marriage to William Phiquepal.  In view of all she
had said and written in criticism of the marriage tie, to
have contracted a conventional marriage upon this side
of the Atlantic would have subjected her to charges of
inconsistency, and made her the laughingstock of the
American press.  On the other hand, to have remained
in the country and to have accepted the more unconven-
tional relation, of which in theory she approved, would
have brought down upon her head much personal abuse,
and greatly weakened her popular influence.  A quiet
marriage in France, followed by a short residence abroad,
probably seemed the best solution of the problem.

But if the sisters expected to secure quiet and "mental
repose" in France in the summer and fall of 1830, they
were doomed to disappointment, for the good ship "Edward Quesnal" could hardly have reached Havre before
the dramatic events of the "July Days" drove the last
of the Bourbons from his throne.  To Frances it must
have been an interesting and exciting moment, for at
last it seemed that the liberal cause in France was about
to triumph.  And in the downfall of Charles X lay the
vindication of those unfortunate conspiracies of the early
twenties in which she had aided and abetted the efforts
of the liberals to overturn the government of Louis
XVIII.  That her hero, Lafayette, was again the man of
the hour, and apparently held within his hands the
political future of France, naturally increased her enthusiasm.  Settling down in Paris, she studied the course of
the revolution with keen attention.

The success of the July Revolution was in large measure due to the efforts of the republican element among
the workingmen and students of Paris, "*ma chère population des barricades*," as Lafayette called them, who
hoped for the establishment of a republic based upon an

extensive suffrage.[1]  This, Miss Wright, with her pre-
dilection for the republican form of government, and her
sympathy for republicanism in France, believed should
have been the outcome of the revolution.   Unfortunately
for the republicans, however, republican sentiment in
France, outside of Paris, was almost nil, and the middle
class had little trouble in imposing upon the nation the
bourgeois monarchy of Louis Philippe, a constitutional
monarchy to be sure, but one not inaptly characterized
by Miss Wright as "a government of patronage for the
wealthy classes."[2]

From the first she had little confidence in the professed
republicanism of the July Monarchy, or in its promises
of liberal reform.   Indeed, her opinion of constitutional
monarchy was low.   " I have never had faith in *constitutional monarchy*," she wrote Lafayette shortly after
Louis Philippe had become the ruler of France, "and
for as I think, an all sufficient reason—its *constitutional
pledges* are *oaths* and *paper* while its *monarchical force*
is *plenty of money* and *plenty of patronage.*"   As no
effort had been made to control the "*monarchical force*"
of the new government, she was less surprised than
grieved, she informed her friend in the same long and
interesting letter, to find the course of the government
not so very different from that of its predecessors.   The
hesitation in carrying out the promised liberal reforms,
the failure actively to support revolution elsewhere in
Europe, and the bid for the friendship of the Tory government in Great Britain convinced her that the people
had been hoodwinked.   Their efforts had resulted only

---

[1] Wright MSS. Lafayette to Frances Wright, October 13, 1830.

[2] *Free Enquirer*, January 1, 1831.   In her letter to the editor of the
*Free Enquirer*.

in the establishment of a government of patronage catering to the middle classes.[1]

But in Lafayette's control of the National Guard she still saw hope for the republican cause. Throughout the country, she wrote the General, the people were shaking their heads at the conduct of the government, and were questioning—" *Que pense et que dit L[afayett]e* " while " the national guard, everywhere ready to protect *public order* forget not that they have also to protect liberty and equality. They see the discontent of the people and they *themselves are the people.*"[2] To this hint that he use his position as commander of the National Guard to effect a republican revolution Lafayette remained deaf, still believing in the good intentions of the monarchy. Not until it was too late did he bring himself to the point of action, and then the government found itself strong enough to abolish the office which he held and deprive him of his power. Republicanism in France had still to bide its time. To Frances Wright the collapse of republican hopes and the triumph of the monarchy were great disappointments.

The first interest of Miss Wright in the July Revolution had been in the possible success of republican principles, but, as the revolution spread from France to other parts of Europe, it occurred to her that back of it was something far more significant than the desire to establish republics or to overthrow sundry incompetent and vicious restoration monarchies. In Europe, as in America, she believed that she was now witnessing the rise of the people against privilege, that the present struggle was a war of class against class:

[1] Wright MSS. Frances Wright to Lafayette, October 26, 1830.
[2] *Ibid.*

What distinguishes the present from every other struggle in which the human race has been engaged, is, that the present is, evidently, openly, and acknowledgedly, *a war of class,* and that *this war is universal.* It is no longer nation pitched against nation for the good pleasure and ,sport of Kings and great Captains, nor sect cutting the throats and roasting the carcasses of sect for the glory of God and the satisfaction of priests, nor is it one army butchering another to promote the fortunes of their leaders—to pass from a James to a George or a Charles to a Louis Philippe, the privilege of coining laws, money, and peers, and dividing the good things of the land among his followers. No; it is now everywhere the oppressed millions who are making common cause against their oppressors; it is the ridden people of the earth who are struggling to throw from their backs the " booted and spurred " riders whose legitimate title to starve as well as to work them to death will no longer pass current; it is labor rising up against idleness, industry against money, justice against law and privilege.[1]

That the " ridden people of the earth" deserved to succeed in the struggle with their " booted and spurred" riders Miss Wright firmly believed, for, she said, " It has long been clear to me that in every country the best feelings and the best sense are found with the laboring and useful classes, and the worst feelings and worst sense with the idle and useless." That their victory would be an easy one, however, she doubted. " It is to be feared," she wrote, " that the people will win no redress but what they carry by force. Yet has it ever been otherwise! or can it ever be otherwise until *all* are the people and the people are everything."[2]

This conception of the revolutionary movement of 1830 as the beginning of the class struggle was undoubt-

[1] *Free Enquirer,* November 27, 1830.
[2] *Ibid.*

edly due to Miss Wright's recent experience with the
workingmen in New York City, and to her residence in
Paris during the excitement following the " July Days."
In Paris, as in New York, radical leaders among the
workingmen hinted at a war of class, but in ascribing
any great degree of class consciousness to revolutionists
elsewhere in Europe Miss Wright quite let her imagination run away with her.  She wrote of what she hoped
to see rather than of what in truth existed.  Perhaps
the chief interest in her statement lies in the fact that
she envisaged the class struggle so clearly many years
before the conception was made popular by the Marxian
socialists.

But not all of her time in the fall and winter of 1830–
1831 was devoted to the study of Europe in revolution.
Not long after her arrival in France she renewed her
correspondence and friendship with General Lafayette:

I say not how I long to reach you [she said in closing her first
letter], and yet perhaps it is as well that I should not be seen
at your side just at this crisis.  The more so as I feel it must
soon be decided.  I have done what I could to make myself
forgotten at this moment in America and the public motives
which decided me to this have made me less regret that private
ones should have led me just now into retirement.  I could
wish however that these had been unconnected with the health
and spirits of our Camilla.  These are, as I have assured you,
reviving, and will authorize me I trust ere long to embrace
you. [1]

But there could have been few opportunities for Frances and Camilla to meet their old friend, or to visit La
Grange, for Camilla's health grew steadily worse until
on the eighth of February, 1831, that dear sister and

[1] Wright MSS. Frances Wright to Lafayette, October, 1830.

comrade passed away.[1] To Frances it was a blow hard
to bear, for the sisters had been inseparable from childhood.

Of Camilla we unhappily know but little, for her personality and her interests seem to have been dominated
almost wholly by the stronger willed and more energetic
Frances. According to Robert Dale Owen who seems
to have been very fond of her, and to whom she left a
small annuity, she was "inferior in talent to Frances,
but unassuming, amiable, and temperate in her views."[2]
Her few remaining letters would indicate a quiet, intelligent woman, whose greatest interest was in her sister.
Her marriage to Richeson Whitby was unfortunate and
probably the product of loneliness. Whitby was a good
man, and his letters show him to have been a devoted
husband, but intellectually and socially he could offer
little of real companionship to his wife. In the end, the
Nashoba wilderness and the absence of Frances proved
too much for Camilla, and shortly after the birth of her
baby she left Whitby to join Frances in New York.
Whether she planned to return to her husband is not
clear. The baby might have held them together; its
death separated them forever. For a number of years
Whitby remained in charge of Nashoba, and, until her
own death, in 1852, Frances paid him the annuity left
him in Camilla's will. He died in 1853, leaving a second
wife and a daughter.

Whatever plans Miss Wright may have had for returning to the United States in the spring of 1831 were upset by the shock of Camilla's death. She wrote Owen
that she would need several more months of rest, but

[1] *Ibid.* Extract from the registry of deaths, first *arrondissement*,
Paris, 1831.

[2] "An Earnest Sowing of Wild Oats."

the months stretched into years before Frances Wright again took up her work in the United States.[1]

A little more than five months after the death of Camilla, Frances married William Phiquepal, who at this time resumed the family name, D'Arusmont, at Miss Wright's desire. The ceremony was performed in the office of the mayor of the tenth *arrondissement* in Paris, and witnessed by several friends, among whom was Lafayette.[2] In contracting this marriage Miss Wright was hardly so inconsistent as some of her contemporaries would have us believe. She was perfectly aware that the ideal relation of the sexes, which she had outlined in her Nashoba address, was quite impracticable, as society was then constituted, and that marriage was a necessity. But she did believe that the marriage tie might be made less onerous for the wife by allowing her to retain control of her own property, and by providing for the relief of unhappy marriages through liberal divorce laws. In marrying D'Arusmont she retained control of her property, though her husband took care of most business matters for her.

Guillaume Sylvan Casimir Phiquepal D'Arusmont, the eldest son of Guillaume Phiquepal D'Arusmont and Frances Lacombe D'Arusmont, was born in the commune of Monsant, in the Department of Lot-et-Garonne, March 9, 1779.[3] He was, therefore, at the time of his marriage, fifty-two years old, and sixteen years his wife's senior. Of the early years of his life we know almost nothing, although it may be inferred from the interests of his later life that his education was the best the times

---

[1] *Free Enquirer*, May 28, 1831.

[2] Wright MSS. Extract from the registry of marriages, tenth *arrondissement*, Paris, Friday, July 22, 1831.

[3] *Ibid.*

afforded. In 1814, at the mature age of thirty-five, he went to Paris to take up the study of medicine. There, according to his daughter Sylva, his devotion to the famous French alienist, Doctor Pinel, led him to pro-long, by half, the usual four-year medical course. He was finally offered the opportunity to succeed Doctor Pinel at the Salpêtrière, the asylum for women, but re-fused—just why is not clear.[1]

From medicine D'Arusmont's interest seems to have turned to educational theory and practice. He became a disciple of Pestalozzi, and, being of an inventive turn of mind, worked out several devices for speeding up the Pestalozzian process of education. His ideas finally came to the attention of William Maclure, a wealthy, retired Philadelphia merchant with scientific leanings. Maclure had become much interested in educational matters, and had already started near Philadelphia what he called a "School of Industry," based upon Pestalozzian princi-ples. His enthusiasm for D'Arusmont's improvements on the Pestalozzian method induced him to establish a small school, under the direction of the latter, in his own home in Paris, an experiment which attracted consider-able attention from such prominent scientists as Francois Magendie, the celebrated physiologist, and Doctor Pinel. Unfortunately, however, educational innovations were not wholly to the liking of the Bourbon government, particularly when the school equipment included a print-ing press, and "this interesting private institution— although conducted with the greatest prudence, and visited with the utmost caution by the enlightened indi-viduals above quoted—could not escape a domiciliary

[1] Wright MSS. From a brief sketch by Mrs. Guthrie (Sylva D'Arusmont) of the life of her father.

visit from the police of the Bourbon Government."[1] Following this event Maclure hastily transferred the school to Philadelphia, where it would be free from the interference of stupid reactionary governments.

D'Arusmont's particular contribution to the general Pestalozzian method appears to have been in its application to the teaching of the trades. Of his ability as a teacher Miss Wright tells us in her autobiography that

she had seen him master himself—by watching, analyzing, and simplifying the operations of different workmen—and then communicate to his pupils, the process peculiar to almost all the leading trades—such as carpentering, turning, coopering, blacksmithing, tinning, weaving, tailoring, shoemaking, hatmaking, broom and brushmaking. All of these she had seen going on under his direction at one time, and all of these were studied and practiced by the same youths who changed their occupations in rotation.[2]

He also contributed several devices for enabling the student to master mathematical subjects more easily. For the study of arithmetic there was the arithmometer. geometry and trigonometry were taught with the aid of mathmometers and trigonometers " by which the most useful properties of Euclid are reduced to the comprehension of, a child of five or six years old." Music he taught by means of a sonometer, and for the languages he invented a system of phonetics.[3] Just what these devices were is not clear, for their inventor unfortunately left no written account of them.

When, in the fall of 1825, Maclure decided to become the partner of Robert Owen in the community venture

[1] *Biography*, part i, p. 35.
[2] *Ibid.*, part i, p. 41.
[3] *New Harmony Gazette*, February 15, 1826.

at New Harmony, D'Arusmont followed his patron, making the journey down the Ohio in Owen's famous "boatload of knowledge." At New Harmony he started anew his School of Industry, using for a nucleus three young French boys, whose education had been entrusted to his care before leaving France. If we may believe the testimony of Robert Dale Owen, the school was not altogether a success because of the personal idiosyncrasies of its master:

In the educational department [wrote Owen in his autobiography] we had considerable talent, mixed with a good deal of eccentricity. We had a Frenchman, patronized by Mr. Maclure, a M. Phiquepal d'Arusmont, who became afterwards the husband of Frances Wright; a man well informed on many points, full of original ideas, some of practical value, but, withal, a wrong-headed genius, whose extravagance and wilful and inordinate self-conceit destroyed his usefulness. He had a small school, but it was a failure; he gained neither the good-will nor the respect of his pupils.[1]

It would be somewhat unfair to D'Arusmont, however, to accept Owen's statement quite at its face value. Writing his autobiography nearly fifty years later, Owen's memory of community days at New Harmony may not have been of the best. Furthermore there had been considerable personal feeling between D'Arusmont and himself over the question of his financial indebtedness to Miss Wright. Indeed, Owen's carelessness in regard to money matters seems to have been the principal cause of the break in his friendship with Miss Wright.

Miss Wright, who visited New Harmony in the summer of 1826, gives us a more favorable impression of the school. "She experienced," she tells us in her autobiography, "true delight upon inspecting the school of

[1] Owen, *Threading My Way*, p. 283.

industry there in full operation, and fully adequate to its
own support at the expiration of the first Six months.
This really wonderful creation was the only successful
experiment, and, indeed, the only real experiment of any
kind, made in New Harmony."[1]   If this picture seems a
bit rosy, it must be remembered that Miss Wright wrote
her autobiography after her marriage with D'Arusmont
and after her break with Robert Dale Owen.   Probably
the truth lies somewhere between her statement and that
of Owen.

That the school was not altogether a success, however, we may gather from the fact that it did not survive
the life of the cooperative community.   Returning to
New Harmony in the summer of 1828, from the wreck
of her own experiment at Nashoba, Miss Wright says she
found that "the talented and energetic conductor of the
School of Industry was struggling with the depression
of his disappointment, and applying himself in retirement
to the instruction of three youths who had accompanied
him from France."[2]   According to her autobiography,
D'Arusmont now agreed so completely with her views as
to the necessity of educating the public in liberal principles before attempting practical experiments of a reform character that he agreed to learn the printing business, teach it to his pupils, and undertake the printing of
the *Gazette.*[3]   He was as good as his word, and the first
issue of the *New Harmony and Nashoba Gazette or
Free Enquirer* in the fall of 1828 bore on its final page
the statement "Printed by William Phiquepal and His
Pupils."

When the Free Enquirers moved their headquarters to

[1] *Biography*, part i, p. 37.
[2] *Ibid.*, pp. 39-41.
[3] *Ibid.*, pp. 40-41.

New York City, in the spring of 1829, D'Arusmont and his three French boys accompanied them. There they set up their printing press in the home at Yorkville, and there the *Free Enquirer* was printed until the fall of 1830.

It was probably in the intimate associations of the little home on the banks of the East River that Phiquepal's interest in Frances Wright ripened into love. That this should have been the case was not altogether surprising, for they had much in common. Her knowledge of French and her enthusiasm for France must have meant many a congenial hour together. Then, too, they were both absorbed heart and soul in the progress of liberal reform, and to both the salvation of the race lay in the adoption of a system of rational education. In the *Free Enquirer* they had another bond of common interest. Thrown together in their work and in their home life, it is not to be wondered at that the impressionable Frenchman should have fallen in love with a woman of such brilliant intellect and interesting personality as Frances Wright. Moreover, she was a woman of no little personal charm:

She had various personal advantages [says Robert Dale Owen],—a tall, commanding figure, somewhat slender and graceful, though the shoulders were a little bit too high; a face the outline of which in profile, though delicately chiselled, was masculine rather than feminine, like that of an Antinous, or perhaps more nearly typifying a Mercury; the forehead broad but not high; the short chestnut hair curling naturally all over a classic head; the large, blue eyes not soft, but clear and earnest.[1]

Upon her part Miss Wright probably found in Phique-

[1] Owen, p. 297.

pal an enthusiastic follower and a most devoted admirer, one who no doubt made himself indispensable to her comfort. In person he was rather below middle height, but strongly and compactly built. The head was large and well-modeled; the profile of the face strong and clean cut. At fifty-one his hair and eyebrows were gray-black, but his eyes were as keen and black as ever.[1]

When Miss Wright found it necessary to interrupt her editorial work and her lecturing in the fall of 1829 in order to attend to the colonization of her thirty slaves, Phiquepal was sent on ahead to make the arrangements for their embarkation at New Orleans. Here she met him, and together they sailed for Haiti, where President Boyer had made provision for the reception of her slaves. During this interesting voyage Phiquepal must have urged his suit with ability and success, for it was upon returning to New York City in the following spring that Frances Wright announced to Robert Dale Owen her engagement to the brilliant but rather eccentric Frenchman.[2]

Whether Phiquepal returned to France on the "Edward Quesnal" with the sisters in early July is not clear. If not, he must have followed soon after, for in October we find him personally delivering Frances' letters to General Lafayette. His three pupils, however, seem to have remained in New York City until late October, for he last issue of the *Free Enquirer* to carry the statement "Printed by the Pupils of William Phiquepal" is dated October twenty-third.

During the winter following their arrival in France Phiquepal lived with the sisters in the Rue de Montaigne. After Camilla's death he made a brief visit to the United

[1] *Ibid.*
[2] "An Earnest Sowing of Wild Oats."

States upon business connected with Miss Wright's property, during which he took out his naturalization papers.
This was probably done in order that he might the better look after his future wife's property in America. He
was back in Paris in time to be married on the twenty-
second of July.

Following her marriage Frances appears to have had
every intention of giving up her public life. She planned
apparently to settle down in France and devote herself
to the career of her husband. With this in view she
transferred some of her property to France, and aided by
Lafayette, secured for her husband an appointment as
director of a pattern agricultural school, a school in
which he had become much interested.

Of the next three or four years we know very little.
They continued to reside in Paris, Phiquepal probably
busy with his educational projects and his scientific
friends, and Frances with her household duties and the
cares of motherhood—for on the sixteenth of April, 1832,
a daughter, Frances Sylva D'Arusmont, was born.[1] The
old friendship with Lafayette seems to have waned, perhaps because of her disappointment at his conduct during the July Revolution, perhaps because of the new
home interests. These years also saw a break in the
friendship with Robert Dale Owen. This seems to have
been due in large measure to Phiquepal's impatience with
Owen's carelessness in regard to money matters. The
latter not only owed Frances a considerable sum of
money, the interest upon which he was inclined to let
run, but he had sold the Hall of Science in a manner
which did not meet with Phiquepal's approval. Furthermore he offended Frances by publishing, for commercial

[1] Wright MSS. "Manuel de nos affaires." This was a little record
of events and business kept by Phiquepal.

reasons, and against her express orders, an unabridged edition of her little philosophical treatise, *A Few Days in Athens*, which she had been upon the point of revising.[1] This seems to have been the last straw, for when she returned to the United States in 1835 she and Owen were no longer on speaking terms.

In the spring of 1834, Madame D'Arusmont, as she now became known publicly, made a brief visit to England. Here, possibly at the request of Robert Owen, she again went upon the lecture platform in behalf of a system of rational education. This action does not seem to have altogether pleased her husband, for in a long letter complaining of her failure to write he ends by threatening to come after her if her negligence continues.[2] Phiquepal, indeed, while admiring his wife's intellectual ability does not seem to have looked with favor upon her returning to public life. He probably felt that if her interest again became centered in her lecture work her family life might suffer. It was her insistence, a few years later, upon returning to the lecture platform that seems to have caused the first serious rift in the happiness of their married life.

[1] *Biography*, part ii, Political Letters I.
[2] Wright MSS. Phiquepal to Frances, June 1, 1834.

# CHAPTER X

## The Last Years

LATE in the fall of 1835 the D'Arusmonts returned to the United States after an absence, on the part of Frances, of more than five years.[1]  It is probable that the long voyage across the Atlantic was undertaken primarily in connection with Madame D'Arusmont's property interests in the West. That it was to be only a brief visit would seem to be indicated by the fact that Sylva, now three years of age, was left in Paris in the home of one of Phiquepal's friends.[2] After reaching New Orleans they journeyed slowly northward to Cincinnati, stopping for a few days, no doubt, at Memphis that Madame D'Arusmont might meet her old friend Marcus Winchester, and inspect the condition of Nashoba, which was still in charge of Camilla's husband, Richeson Whitby.  In February they reached Cincinnati, where Phiquepal turned his attention to business, while Frances considered the changes which five years had brought about in the problems and needs of the American people.[3]

That she had had any deliberate intention of renewing her public life in America when she left France is very doubtful, but the outcome of her present observation and reflection was the conviction that her presence upon the lecture platform was again called for.  The considerations

---

[1] Wright MSS. " Manuel de nos affaires."

[2] *Ibid.*  Extract from the brief of Madame D'Arusmont in her suit for divorce.

[3] *Ibid.*  Frances Wright D'Arusmont to her daughter, Sylva D'Arusmont, July, 1836.

which led her to this conviction seem to have been the
popular excitement then prevailing over the bank and
slavery questions, and a feeling that the moment was pro-
pitious for putting before the American people her interpretation of human history, past and present, with a sketch of
that ideal society which the future should bring forth.
She also desired to correct an error which mature thought
convinced her had crept into her little book, *A Few Days in
Athens.* It may be, too, that once again upon the scene of
her earlier labors the lure and excitement of the platform
proved too strong for her. In May, 1836, therefore, after
a brief preparation, she began her second experience as a
public lecturer in the United States, and for the next three
years spent much of her speaking time upon Chartered Monopolies, Slavery, and the " Nature and History of Human
Civilization, considered in the Past, the Present, and the
Future." [1] Nor was her activity confined solely to her
lecture work. She contributed articles to the *Boston In-
vestigator,* a liberal paper established by Abner Kneeland,
and herself edited a little paper in Philadelphia called the
*Manual of American Principles.* [2]

In her earlier course of lectures Frances Wright had expressed her disapproval of the practice of chartering auction,
banking, and other monopolies, on the ground that such
monopolies benefited the rich at the expense of the poor.
She had also plainly indicated her hostility to the Second
Bank of the United States, the greatest monopoly of all.
In 1836, therefore, she was quite ready to sympathize with
the attitude of President Jackson and the Democratic Party
toward the continued existence of this great national banking monopoly, and for the first and only time in her life she

---

[1] *Course of Popular Lectures,* vol. ii, Philadelphia, 1836, the preface.

[2] Bradlaugh, Charles, *Biographies of Ancient and Modern Celebrated
Freethinkers,* Boston, 1877, " Frances W. D'Arusmont."

lent her support to one of the prominent political parties of
the country.   With Jackson she not only believed the Bank
of the United States to be a burden to the people, but a
positive menace to the safety of the Republic, because of its
tendency to concentrate the wealth and power of the nation
in the hands of a moneyed aristocracy.   Moreover, she believed, as did many other people at the time, that the Bank
of the United States was part of a vicious financial system,
which bound the economic, as well as the political life of
the American people, ever more closely to the money power
of England:

It was in the cotton field, and while watching the extraordinary fluctuations in the cotton market, and the fearful catas-
trophes in the mercantile and industrial world consequent
thereupon [she says in her autobiography], that she seized the
clue of the banking system, which she gradually followed up,
through its ramifications of State Banks, and United States
Bank, and commercial credits, and commercial failures, until it
landed her in the Bank of England, and the omnipotent Parliament of Great Britain, as the source of that financial power,
stronger than thrones or republics, which convulsed the world
at pleasure, and robbed all the fortunes and industry of the
earth under the pretense of aiding them.[1]

In supporting the opposition of the Democratic Party to
the rechartering of the United States Bank, in applauding
Jackson's Specie Circular which struck at the paper money
evil in the West, and later, in urging the adoption of the
Independent Treasury scheme which she believed would
not only divorce the government from the private business
of the country, but would also prevent the British money
power from gaining an ascendency in American political
life, Madame D'Arusmont brought down upon her head the
wrath of the Whigs.   And they certainly made it hot for

[1] *Biography*, pt. i, p. 33.

her. In Cincinnati where she began her lecture course in the spring of 1836 she seems to have been heard with respect, though there was some little newspaper hostility.[1] Upon attempting to repeat her course in Philadelphia, however, she was in hot water almost from the start. After her first lecture, a " Geographical, Political, and Historical Sketch of the American United States," she was absolutely forbidden by the mayor of the city to speak again in Philadelphia, and the various public halls of the city were denied her. Nothing daunted by this harsh treatment, she sought to lecture in the open fields on the outskirts of the city, only to have the meeting broken up and the platform torn from under her by what she calls the " bank rioters." Eventually she completed her lectures, though not without threats of further trouble, in the Court House at York, Pennsylvania.[2] Two years later, when lecturing in New York, her defense of the Independent Treasury led to similar disturbances which for a time broke up her meetings and even threatened her with personal violence.[3] Only a strong escort seems to have averted bodily harm on at least one occasion :

She has been seen [says her friend Amos Gilbert in his brief account of her life] descending from the second story of a building after she had finished a lecture, with thousands of grim faces peering upon her, giving savage indications of murderous intent, so soon as their masters should give the word " go." But her calm intrepidity awed them, and she was permitted to pass through the formidable crowd to the carriage unscathed. When she was ensconced out of sight in the vehicle—when her tranquil firmness was invisible to them— they several times lifted and leaned the carriage, trying them-

[1] *Course of Popular Lectures*, vol. ii, appendix to the preface.
[2] *Ibid.*
[3] D'Arusmont, Frances Wright, *What is the Matter?* New York, 1838.

selves, whether they had the audacious courage to overthrow it. Prudent, resolute men walked slowly before the coach horses, repeating " steady, steady." The noble animals, as if proud of their office, moved gracefully on, as if cognizant of the contemptible bipeds around them. Meantime Frances sat gently fanning herself, and in easy conversation with her friends.[1]

Nor did her lectures upon slavery enhance her popularity. In the tremendous national problem presented by the existence of human slavery in the South she had been interested since her first visit to the United States, and at Nashoba she had done her best to convince the South of the possibility of gradual self-emancipation, but without success. The failure of Nashoba had convinced her, not that her theory was wrong, but that a degree of public education was necessary before it could be successfully worked out, and it was in part to provide the background of liberal opinion requisite for the ultimate solution of the problem that she had gone on the lecture platform in 1828. At that time she had found public interest in the question somewhat apathetic, but by 1836 the attitude of the nation had changed materially, for the growth of the abolition movement in the North, with its denunciation of slavery as a great moral evil, and the consequent alarm of the South for the safety of its " peculiar institution," had focussed attention on the subject as never before. To Madame D'Arusmont it probably seemed a most auspicious moment to place before the people in more definite form her mature thoughts on the subject. Above all, she told her audiences, the problem must be treated constitutionally and in a spirit of fairness to the Southern planters. For the Garrisonian abolitionists she had no use. Abolition, as now presented, " that is, *the turning adrift on the wide world three millions of benighted*

[1] Gilbert, *Memoir of Frances Wright*, pp. 49-50.

*beings, to collect their living like the fowls of the air,"*
was no solution of the problem for an enlightened mind.[1]

To the mind of Madame D'Arusmont the solution of the
problem was perfectly clear, if only the public could be made
to see it. First would come the general adoption of a
scheme of gradual emancipation, a scheme which would
provide for the intellectual improvement of the slave population as well as its ultimate enfranchisement. Upon securing their freedom the former slaves would be removed
bodily from the United States and colonized in some desirable quarter of the world, where they might work out a
civilization of their own unmolested. The gap created in
the South by their disappearance, Madame D'Arusmont
believed, would be rapidly filled by a great influx of white
labor from the North.[2] As to the free negroes of the South,
whose position differed somewhat from that of the slave
population, these she thought would be gradually assimilated
by the whites. This idea which she had already set forth
in her famous " Explanatory Notes," while at Nashoba,
she again mentions in a letter to her friend Marcus B.
Winchester of Memphis, written sometime in 1838. Winchester, it may be remarked in explanation of the letter, had
married a negress, and was much concerned over the future
of his children.

I have always thought that if the slave question could once be
settled our free colored population would, more especially in
our extreme South—Louisiana for instance—become gradually
and easily incorporated with the white. At the present time,
the least said on the subject the better. The progress of
liberal opinion, if silent, is neither slow nor doubtful, and to
this we must look for the ultimate removal of every prejudice
as of every injustice.[3]

[1] *Course of Popular Lectures,* vol. ii, p. 90.

[2] *Ibid.* " On the Sectional Question—Southern Slavery."

[3] Wright MSS. Frances Wright D'Arusmont to Marcus B. Winchester,
1838.

The suspicion of possessing views so advanced in respect to the free negro probably accounts for the peculiar hostility with which her lectures on slavery were greeted. Although she may have avoided the subject of amalgamation, as she intimated in her letter to Winchester, the contents of the " Explanatory Notes " were public property, and the nation in 1836 was by no means ready to listen to any such suggestion. Even today the amalgamation of the races as a possible solution of the race problem is quite unacceptable to the vast majority of the American people.

The third consideration which led her to renew her public life was the desire to correct an error which she believed had crept into her little treatise on the Epicurean philosophy, *A Few Days in Athens*. In regard to this interesting work it had been her intention to prevent further publication until the book was revised and complete, when she hoped to present in it " a beau ideal sketch of society in an advanced stage of civilization, and as we may rather expect it to be in the future, than conceive it to have been in the past." But the unwarranted publication of an unrevised edition of the book while she was absent in France led her to give up this plan, and to correct the error through a series of lectures upon " The Nature and History of Human Civilization, considered in the Past, the Present, and the Future." [1] These lectures she would never publish, as she was desirous of even further maturing her views, but fortunately they still exist, beautifully written out in longhand, and conveniently bound in neat little booklets that their author might the more readily handle them on the platform.

In these interesting but rather philosophical lectures she first corrected the error which she believed had crept into her earlier works. This error was the confounding of the-

[1] *Biography*, pt. ii, Political Letters I.

ology with religion, "a very fundamental and a very dangerous error, because a most demoralizing, and a socially and politically disorganizing error":

Theology, from the Greek *theos, logos,* renders distinctly the meaning of the subject it attempts to treat. *Theos,* God, or Gods, unseen beings and unknown causes. *Logos,* word, talk, or—if we like to employ yet more familiar and expressive terms—prattle or chatter. *Talk or prattle, about unseen brings or unknown causes.*

Religion, from the Latin *religo, religio,* renders with equal distinctness the thing signified. *Religo,* to tie over again, to bind fast; *religio,* a binding together, a bond of union.[1]

Theology, therefore, was but idle unfortunate speculation quite unworthy the attention of civilized man. Religion, on the other hand, correctly interpreted, was the binding, cohesive principle of society. It was the common bond of union. Theology, not religion, had been the thing attacked in *A Few Days in Athens* and in her *Course of Popular Lectures.*

Having pointed out the distinction between theology and religion she then gave to her auditors a philosophical interpretation of history, to which she must have devoted much time and thought. According to this interpretation the history of human civilization had fallen into four great epochs, each of which had been characterized by a distinctive religion or bond of union. Throughout these four epochs, moreover, "two great Principles and two alone, although disguised under various names, forms, and modifications have struggled for mastery in the minds of men and on the

---

[1] *Ibid.* Political Letters II. In her so-called Political Letters Madame D'Arusmont summarizes the content of her lectures on "The Nature and History of Human Civilization, considered in the Past, the Present, and the Future." In the following discussion I have drawn upon both the Letters and the History.

bosom of this globe. The one has been the enslavement of human labor for the advantage of the Few,—the other has been the enfranchisement of human labor for the good of the Many." [1]

As the first civilization emerged from the dim remoteness of the past it took form under the control of the priest. Of this early civilization which had its centers in India and in Egypt "the binding principle [was] undoubtedly adherence to, and devoted veneration for, all that had been established in the past by the will of Heaven, as expounded by the priest." This bond of union she termed the Religion of the Priest. In this epoch of civilization the political organization of society was "that of the feudal system in its most perfect state." At the head was the priest-king, and under him were hereditary castes and classes, a landed aristocracy, and at the base a vast mass of servile laborers. Such a civilization benefited the few at the expense of the many. It was during the development of this first civilization, Madame D'Arusmont told her auditors, that the subjugation of woman took place, as "the first master measure employed for the more certain enslavement of the species."[2]

While in the countries of the East this earliest phase of civilization had survived, with some modifications, to the present day, a new epoch of human civilization had gradually dawned about the Mediterranean basin. This second epoch was marked by the brilliant civilizations of Greece, and of Rome in the days of the Republic. Its bond of union was patriotism, or love of country; its political theory, government by the greatest number of influential citizens; its political practice, struggle and confusion. This last was due to the imperfection of the binding tie, which looked to false greatness of country rather than to the happiness of the

---

[1] "The Nature and History of Human Civilization."

[2] *Biography*, pt. ii, Political Letters III.

citizenry. It was also due to the lawless passion for war and robbery as national occupations, to the lack of respect for useful industry, to the monopolistic tendencies in land and capital, and, in the Roman Republic, to the vicious trend toward governmental centralization at the expense of personal liberty. In this epoch of civilization, as in the first, the few benefited at the expense of the many for the social organization of both Greece and Rome rested upon a basis of human slavery.

As the binding tie of this second epoch of civilization began to fail in corruption and vice, the civilization of the Graeco-Roman world again fell under the sway of the first idea, the bond of union which had held together the first civilization.[1] But gradually from the wreckage of the Graeco-Roman world arose the third epoch of human civilization. Its binding principle was Christianity. To Madame D'Arusmont Christian theology was a delusion, but as a bond of union in the years which witnessed the tragic downfall of Rome, Christianity was necessary, for a religion of servitude alone could bind a degraded people together. At first, therefore, this new epoch was dominated by the Christian priest. In time, however, the priest found himself forced to share his power with temporal rulers, who, with the consent and ultimately the support of the priest, soon assumed for themselves the position of God's temporal representatives on earth. It was this growing ascendency of the divine-right king that led Madame D'Arusmont to term the binding principle of the epoch, Christianity, the religion of Kings. " Christianity has been, and is, that religion which, considering it in its origin, purpose and history, may be denominated *the religion of Kings.*" [2]

Throughout the greater part of this third epoch of human

[1] *Ibid.* Political Letters IV.
[2] *Ibid.*

civilization the political and social organization of society was that of the feudal system, in which the common people were " bound to-gether by a common belief in their own helplessness and innate depravity, and bound also to their feudal lords and to the throne of kings, under the protection of the priest, by a common belief in their divine right to rule over them." [1]

With the decline of the feudal system in Western Europe it seemed for a moment as if the people would usurp the power and position of these temporal rulers. This desirable outcome, however, was thwarted by the rise of what Madame D'Arusmont called the Banking and Funding System, whereby the personal servitude of the feudal regime became the economic bondage of the modern commercial and industrial world. A few benefited by the change, but for the mass of people it meant only a change in the character of their servitude. And Christianity, the religion of Kings, with its doctrines of submission and humility, still remained the religious bond of civilization. [2]

But hope for the unprivileged masses was at hand, for on the Fourth of July, 1776, the United States declared its independence of Great Britain, and in its famous Declaration of Independence laid the foundation of a new epoch of civilization, an epoch in which the religion should be the Religion of the People, and its binding principle, Justice. That the American people had not as yet secured all that the Declaration of Independence implied, that is, the equal right of all men to equal opportunity; " to equal care in infancy; equal protection and equal opportunities for mental and physical development in childhood and youth; equal credit according to the powers of his or her individual industry and genius in manhood or womanhood "; and to an equal

[1] *Ibid.*
[2] " The Nature and History of Human Civilization."

certainty of reward in proportion to his or her services through life, with equal security for enjoying what his or her services may have earned,[1] Madame D'Arusmont believed due to the failure of the people of the United States to prevent the transference of the Banking and Funding System of Europe to America, and the failure to square the administrative practice of the Constitution with the principles of the Declaration of Independence.[2]

Fortunately for the future of human civilization, however, America had finally recognized her mistake, and had taken steps to correct it. President Jackson's courageous attack on the Second Bank of the United States had already weakened one of the ties which bound America to Europe. The establishing of the Independent Treasury would break it completely. And then it would be the task of the American people, having thrown off the maleficent influence of the Religion of Kings, to put their administrative practice in accord with the principles of 1776. Of the order of society which should then result Madame D'Arusmont gave her auditors a brief sketch in the last lecture of the series.

In developing her picture of organized society under the Religion of the People Madame D'Arusmont seems to have drawn in part upon the communism of Robert Owen, and in part upon the anarchistic theories of her friend, Josiah Warren, "the first American anarchist," but the greater part of the picture is her own.[3] As a first step in the attainment of this ideal society she proposed "that the whole real property of the State—lands, mines, quarries, buildings and capital of every description be declared forever public

[1] *Ibid.*

[2] *Ibid.*

[3] Madame D'Arusmont met Warren at New Harmony. For a sketch of his life and principles, see Bailie, William, *Josiah Warren, the first American anarchist*, Boston, 1906.

property (as, in the nature of things it is), and administered by the Body Politic for the equal encouragement of all its members." In carrying out this measure, however, all those who had previously held a portion of the public estate were to be compensated by a life revenue in proportion to the amount of their holding. This first step having been taken, the life of the people was to be constitutionally organized in the townships and cities of the nation, for these Madame D'Arusmont considered to be the natural units in the ideal organization of society. In these units the citizen would enjoy employment at all times " according to the choice and capacity of the individual and of the public demand." A record would be " kept on the public books of his ward or Township of the work he executes or of the service he renders," and a salary be given him " proportioned to the service rendered—held payable on demand and in the mode required." His children from an early age would be under the public guardianship, and their education provided for in the public establishments of the township, whence they might advance to the higher schools of county, state, and nation, if merit warranted. And finally the citizen would find " support in old age in that degree of ease or of wealth and honor earned by the services of his life as substantiated in his accompt current with the Body Politic." In return for these advantages of citizenship the individual would owe all to the public, " his energies, his talents, his genius, his devotion."

In this new order of society the people would " finally be relieved from their never ending disputes on the subject of a currency as from the never ending frauds arising out of the use of money," for the wants of the citizens " would be at all times furnished, in the public warehouses and other establishments, in the articles or service required; the same being scored on the books of each separate establishment

and transferred nightly or weekly to the books of the Head
Offices of the wards or Townships." Thus every citizen
would have his open account with the Body Politic instead
of with banks or individual employers, and "wherever he
went he would take his letter of credit with him certifying
precisely what he was worth to the Community and what
was the debt of the Community to him." Gold and silver
would disappear except as a standard of value to be referred
to in the mind, or as a medium for trade with less fortunate
peoples.

As to the public press in this model society there were to
be daily bulletins from each department of human occupation within the township, together with official township,
county, state, and national dailies. In the first two would
be found all the information having to do with each particular industry, art, science and occupation, the account
current between the individual and the occupation in which
he worked, the state of the public fortune, the demand for
labor, raw materials or manufactured products, and the daily
price of labor "whether of the head or of the hand . . . regu-
lated always by the demand, inverse the supply." In the
county, state, and national dailies would appear respectively
the sum of the current affairs of the township, county, and
state, "showing the surplus and wants of each," together
with all information "calculated to enlarge the minds and
stimulate the exertions of the population." The con-
ductors of these several publications were "to be elected by
the citizen-creditors embraced in each division of territory
and population."

The master key to this whole system of sound American
economy, when finally developed, said Madame D'Arusmont, "will be found in the universal application of the
principle of free and frequent election" carried "into every
occupation—practiced in every office, workshop, farm."

Thus "the wheels of administration would move easily, noiselessly, and steadily. All intrigue would be annihilated when the directing officers in each Dep't of labor would ever be chosen by the workers in that Dep't; daily, weekly, monthly, yearly, as it might be." Where the skill required might have a more general bearing "the choice would be decided by the votes of the citizen-creditors generally."[1]

Such was, in brief, the order of society which Madame D'Arusmont believed would arise when the American people put into practice the true principles of their Declaration of Independence. In such an order of society the coercive elements of government would disappear, and the chief duty of government would become the successful administration of the public economy.

Having pointed out to the American people their responsibility for the future of human civilization, and indicated the course of action they must pursue if the Religion of the People was to prevail, Madame D'Arusmont withdrew from the lecture platform for all time. Her efforts to bring about the reform of society, however, were not yet ended, for in 1848 she published, in London, the most pretentious of all her literary works, *England the Civilizer*. In this interesting though somewhat difficult volume she further elaborated the ideas contained in her lectures on "The Nature and History of Human Civilization," and brought out particularly the part played by England in shaping the course of civilization under what she termed the Religion of Kings. She closed the volume, as she had closed her course of lectures, with a description of an ideal state of society. In this description the organization of society was similar to that sketched in her lectures, but the phraseology used was more suited to the European reader.[2]

[1] "The Nature and History of Human Civilization."

[2] D'Arusmont, Frances Wright, *England the Civilizer: Her History developed in its Principles*, London, 1848.

Unfortunately the last few years of this active and interesting life were saddened by domestic troubles which ultimately resulted in divorce. Just where the fault was it would be hard to say. Phiquepal's disapproval of her public life may have had something to do with it, while differences of opinion over money matters also played their part.[1] To the writer, however, the chief cause of trouble would seem to have been incompatibility of temperament. The closing years of her life, which she spent in Cincinnati, were lonely and sad. In the winter of 1851-1852 she fell on the icy pavement and broke her hip.[2] It proved to be an injury from which she never fully recovered. Less than a year later the end came, December 13th, 1852.[3]

So passed Frances Wright, a true " friend to humankind," and one of the most interesting and courageous of nineteenth-century reformers. Just how deeply she influenced American thought it is difficult to say. Many of the principles which she advocated were already the concern of thoughtful Americans, some were far in advance of her generation, and some were chimerical. Probably it would be safe to say that through her lectures and editorials she did much to popularize and stimulate the demand for a more liberal religion, more liberal marriage laws, the protection of the property rights of married women, a more generous system of education, and the abolition of capital punishment and of imprisonment for debt. Slavery she opposed as irrational, and an obstacle to the progress of America, but she was not an abolitionist in the sense that Garrison

[1] Wright MSS. A long letter from Phiquepal to Frances, dated Paris, October 1, 1850, makes it plain that for some years they had been growing apart. Money matters, Sylva's education, Phiquepal's objections to his wife's public life, and a general incompatibility of temperament seem to have been the chief causes of trouble.

[2] Gilbert, pp. 42-43.

[3] *Cincinnati Daily Gazette*, December 15, 1852.

was.   She believed rather that slavery like the other evils which she pointed out would disappear with the growth of a rational society.   For this reason her attacks upon the " peculiar institution " of the South were few.   Perhaps Miss Wright's greatest contribution was to the intellectual emancipation of women.   A pioneer, she was scoffed at, hooted, and reviled, but she showed what the feminine mind was capable of, and having blazed the way, other courageous women were not wanting to follow in her footsteps.

# BIBLIOGRAPHY

## Manuscript Material

What remains of the large collection of letters and other documents left by Frances Wright D'Arusmont is now in the possession of her grandson, the Reverend William Norman Guthrie, Rector of St. Mark's in-the-Bouwerie, New York City. A good part of this collection Dr. Guthrie kindly placed at my disposal. For the remainder, which unfortunately had been misplaced at the time Dr. Guthrie removed from Sewanee, Tennessee, to New York, I was forced to depend upon the carefully made copies taken by Alice Jane Gray Perkins of New York City. Miss Perkins who is best known as the author of *The Honorable Mrs. Norton* at one time contemplated writing the life of Frances Wright and in preparation spent a summer at Sewanee, transcribing much of the material in the Wright collection. These transcriptions Miss Perkins most cheerfully loaned to me.

## The Works of Frances Wright D'Arusmont

*Altorf, a tragedy* . . . , Philadelphia, 1819.
———— *Ibid.*, London, 1822.
*Views of Society and Manners in America; in a Series of Letters from that Country to a Friend in England, During the Years 1818, 1819, 1820.* By an Englishwoman, London, 1821.
———— *Ibid.*, New York, 1821.
———— *Ibid.*, London, 1822.
———— *Ibid.*, 2 vols., Paris, 1822 (in the French).
———— *Ibid.*, 2 vols., Amsterdam, 1822 (in the Dutch).
———— *Ibid.*, New York, 1825.
*A Few Days in Athens; Being the Translation of a Greek Manuscript discovered in Herculaneum*, London, 1822.
———— *Ibid.*, New York, 1825.
———— *Ibid.*, New York, 1835. The edition published by Robert Dale Owen without Miss Wright's consent. It contained the four additonal chapters which first appeared in the *New Harmony Gazette*.
———— *Ibid.*, London, 183–(?). A reprint of the New York edition of 1835, containing the four additional chapters. Published by Austin & Co.
———— *Ibid.*, New York, 1835. Republished from the original London edition.

*Course of Popular Lectures,* New York, 1829.

—— *Ibid.,* New York, 1831. This edition contains three additional lectures, and a reply to the charges against the French reformers of 1789.

—— *Ibid.,* vol. ii, Philadelphia, 1836. This volume contains three lectures: I. Geographical, Political, and Historical Sketch of the American United States; II. Origin and History of the Federal Party; with a General View of the Hamilton Financial Scheme; III. On the Sectional Question — Southern Slavery.

*Introductory Address, delivered by Frances Wright, at the opening of the Hall of Science, New York, on Sunday, April 26, 1829,* New York, 1829.

*Address, containing a Review of the Times, as first delivered in the Hall of Science, New York, May 9, 1830,* New York, 1830.

*An Address to the Industrious Classes; a Sketch of a System of National Education,* New York, 1830.

*Fables,* New York, 1830.

—— *Ibid.,* London, 1842.

—— *Ibid.,* New York, 1854.

*Parting Address, as delivered in the Bowery Theater to the People of New York in June, 1830,* New York, 1830.

*What is the Matter?* New York, 1838.

*Tracts on Republican Government and National Education addressed to the Inhabitants of the United States of America,* New York, 183-(?). Robert Dale Owen wrote the tract on Republican Government and Miss Wright that on National Education.

—— *Ibid.,* London, 1840.

*Biography, Notes, and Political Letters of Frances Wright D'Arusmont.* (From the Dundee, Scotland, *Northern Star*). In two parts, New York, 1844. The first part of this work is in reality a brief autobiography sketching in outline form the life of the author down to the year 1829. It was written while on a short visit to Dundee in 1843. The pages devoted to William Phiquepal D'Arusmont may well have been written by D'Arusmont himself, as the style differs from that of the rest of the book.

—— *Ibid.,* Boston, 1848.

*England the Civilizer: Her History developed in its Principles,* London, 1848.

BOOKS, PAMPHLETS, AND PERIODICALS CITED

Adams, John Quincy, *Memoirs; comprising Parts of his Diary from 1795 to 1848,* 12 vols., Philadelphia, 1874-1877.

*Annuaire Historique Universel,* Paris. For the years 1818-1824.

Anthony, Susan B. and others, *History of Woman Suffrage*, 4 vols., New York, 1881-1902.

*Appleton's Cyclopedia of American Biography*, edited by James Grant Wilson and John Fiske, 6 vols., New York, 1887-1889.

Ashe, Thomas, *Travels in America, performed in 1806*, London, 1808.

Bailie, William, *Josiah Warren, the first American Anarchist*, Boston, 1906.

Beecher, Lyman, *Autobiography, Correspondence, etc.*, 2 vols., New York, 1864-1865.

——, *Works*, 3 vols., Boston, 1852.

Bentham, Jeremy, *Works*, 11 vols., edited by John Bowring, Edinburgh, 1843.

Bernard, Duke of Saxe-Weimar Eisenach, *Travels through North America, during the Years 1825 and 1826*, 2 vols., Philadelphia, 1828.

Bourne, W. O., *History of the Public School Society of the City of New York*, New York, 1873.

Bradlaugh, Charles, *Biographies of Ancient and Modern Celebrated Freethinkers*, Boston, 1877.

*British Annual Register*, London. For the years 1815-1822.

Brownson, Orestes Augustus, *The Convert: or Leaves from my Experience*, New York, 1857.

*Cambridge Modern History*, 14 vols., London, 1902-1912, volume x.

Carleton, F. T., "The Workingmen's Party of New York City," *Political Science Quarterly*, vol. xxii, pp. 401-415.

Channing, William Ellery, *Works*, 6 vols., Boston, 1845.

Charavay, Étienne, *Le Général La Fayette*, Paris, 1898.

Commons, John R. and others, *History of Labor in the United States*, 2 vols., New York, 1918.

*Dictionary of National Biography*, London, 1885-1901.

Domett, Henry W., *A History of the Bank of New York*, New York, 1884.

Ely, Ezra Stiles, *The Duty of Christian Freemen to elect Christian Rulers: A Discourse delivered on the 4th of July, 1827, in the Seventh Presbyterian Church, in Philadelphia, by Ezra Stiles Ely, D. D., pastor of the Third Presbyterian Church in that City. With an Appendix, Designed to Vindicate the Liberty of Christians, and the American Sunday School Union*, Philadelphia, 1828.

Fearon, Henry Bradshaw, *Sketches of America*, London, 1818.

Ferral, S. A., *A Ramble of Six-Thousand Miles through the United States of America*, London, 1832.

Flower, George, *The History of the English Settlement in Edwards County, Illinois*, Chicago, 1882.

Fox, Dixon Ryan, *The Decline of Aristocracy in the Politics of New York*, New York, 1919.

Gilbert, Amos, *Memoir of Frances Wright: the Pioneer Woman in the Cause of Human Rights*, Cincinnati, 1855.

Hall, Basil, *Travels in North America in the years 1827 and 1828*, 2 vols., Philadelphia, 1829.

Hall, J. R., *The Bourbon Restoration*, London, 1909.

Jefferson, Thomas, *Writings*, edited by P. L. Ford, 10 vols., New York, 1892-1899.

——, *Writings ... Being his Autobiography, Correspondence ... and other Writings ...*, edited by H. A. Washington, 9 vols., Washington, 1853-1854.

——, *Correspondence*, edited by W. C. Ford, Boston, 1916.

——, *Letters and Addresses*, edited by William B. Parker and Jonas Viles, New York, 1908.

Lamartine, A. de, *Histoire de la Restauration*, 8 vols., Paris, 1851-1852.

Levasseur, A., *Lafayette en Amérique, en 1824 et 1825*, 2 vols., Paris, 1829. Translated by J. D. Godman, 2 vols., Philadelphia, 1829.

Lockwood, G. B., *The New Harmony Movement*, New York, 1905.

Madison, James, *Writings*, edited by Gaillard Hunt, 9 vols., New York, 1900-1910.

Martineau, Harriet, *A History of the Thirty Years' Peace*, 4 vols., London, 1877.

Mathieson, William Law, *England in Transition*, London, 1920.

Maurin, Albert, *Histoire de la Chute des Bourbons*, 6 vols., Paris, 1849-1852.

Morgan, George, *The True Lafayette*, Philadelphia, 1919.

Myers, Gustavus, *The History of Tammany Hall*, New York, 1901

Nevins, Allan, *The Evening Post*, New York, 1922.

Newspapers :
*African Repository*, Washington.
*Christian Advocate*, Philadelphia.
*The Correspondent*, New York.
*Daily Cincinnati Gazette.*
*Free Enquirer*, New York.
*Genius of Universal Emancipation*, Baltimore and Washington.
*The Minerva*, New York.
*New York American.*
*New York Commercial Advertiser.*
*New York Courier and Enquirer.*
*New York Daily Sentinel.*
*New York Evening Post.*
*New York Journal of Commerce.*
*New York Morning Courier.*
*New Harmony Gazette*, New Harmony, Indiana.
*New Harmony and Nashoba Gazette or Free Enquirer*, New Harmony, Indiana.
*National Intelligencer*, Washington.

*North American Review*, Boston.

*The Observer*, New York.

*The Telescope*, New York.

*The Theophilanthropist*, New York.

*United States Gazette*, Philadelphia.

*Washington Gazette*, Washington.

*Working Man's Advocate*, New York.

Nolte, Vincent, *Fifty Years in Both Hemispheres*, New York, 1854.

Nordhoff, Charles, *Communistic Societies of the United States*, New York, 1875.

*North American Review*, Boston, January, 1822, pp. 15-26. "Views of Society and Manners in America " (Review).

Noyes, John H., *History of American Socialisms*, Philadelphia, 1870.

Owen, Robert Dale, *Moral Physiology; or, A brief and plain treatise on the population question*, London, 1841.

——, *Threading My Way*, New York, 1874.

——, "An Earnest Sowing of Wild Oats," *Atlantic Monthly*, July, 1874.

——, "Frances Wright, General Lafayette, and Mary Wollstonecraft Shelley : a chapter of autobiography," *Atlantic Monthly*, October, 1873.

Palmer, Elihu, *Posthumous Pieces, being three chapters of an unfinished work intended to have been entitled " The Political World " to which are prefixed a Memoir of Mr. Palmer by his Friend Mr. John Fellowes of New York*, London, 1824.

Perkins, Ephraim, *A Bunker Hill Contest, A. D. 1826, between the Holy Alliance for the Establishment of Hierarchy and Ecclesiastical Dominion over the Human Mind, on the one side; and the Asserters of Free Enquiry, Bible Religion, Christian Freedom, and Civil Liberties, on the other . . .* , Utica, 1826.

Royall, Anne, *The Black Book, or A Continuation of Travels in the United States . . .*,3 vols., Washington, 1828.

——, *Mrs. Royall's Pennsylvania, or Travels Continued . . .* , 2 vols., Washington, 1829.

Skidmore, Thomas, *The Rights of Man to Property: Being a proposition to make it equal among the Adults of the Present Generation; and to Provide for its Equal Transmission to Every Individual of Each Succeeding Generation, on arriving at the Age of Maturity*, New York, 1829.

Stanton, H. B., *Random Recollections*, New York, 1886.

Tappan, Lewis, *The Life of Arthur Tappan*, New York, 1870.

Tone, Theobald Wolfe, *The Life and Adventures of Theobald Wolfe Tone, Written by Himself*. Edited by his son, William Theobald Wolfe Tone, Glasgow, no date given.

Trollope, Anthony, *Autobiography*, New York, 1883.

Trollope, Frances Milton, *Domestic Manners of the Americans*, 2 vols., London, 1832.

Trollope, Thomas Adolphus, *What I Remember*, New York, 1888.
Wallas, Graham, *The Life of Francis Place*, London, 1898.
Walpole, Spencer, *A History of England from the conclusion of the Great War in 1815*, 5 vols., London, 1878-1886.

BOOKS, PAMPHLETS, AND PERIODICALS FOUND USEFUL BUT NOT CITED

Adams, A. D., *The Neglected Period of Anti-Slavery in America (1808-1831)*, Boston, 1908.
Alexander, De Alva Stanwood, *A Political History of the State of New York*, 3 vols., New York, 1906.
American Bible Society, *An Abstract of the American Bible Society, containing an account of its Principles and Operations*, New York, 1830.
American Tract Society, *A Brief Survey of the History and Operations of the American Tract Society for fifty years*, Boston, 1859-1860.
Baird, Robert, *Religion in America, or, an account of the Origin, Progress, Relation to the State, and Present Condition of the Evangelical Churches in the United States*, New York, 1844.
Beecher, Lyman, *Lectures on Scepticism—delivered in the Park Street Church, Boston*, Cincinnati, 1835.
Blunt, Reginald, editor, *Mrs. Montagu, "Queen of the Blues," Her Letters and Friendships from 1762 to 1800*, 2 vols., Boston and New York.
Brown, Anne B. A., "A Dream of Emancipation," *New England Magazine*, June, 1904.
Byrdsall, F., *Origin and History of the Loco-Foco Party*, New York, 1842.
Catterall, Ralph C., *The Second Bank of the United States*, Chicago, 1902.
Clark, Joseph B., *Leavening the Nation*, New York, 1903.
Cleaveland, Catharine C., *The Great Revival in the West, 1797-1805*, Chicago, 1916.
Cloquet, Jules, *Recollections of the Private Life of General Lafayette*, London, 1835.
Cunningham, Abner, *Practical infidelity portrayed and the judgments of God made manifest. An address submitted to the consideration of R. D. Owen, Kneeland, Houston, and others of the infidel party in the city of New York*, New York, 1836.
Everett, L. S., *An Exposure of the Principles of the Free Enquirers*, Boston, 1831.
Finney, Charles G., *Memoirs*, New York, 1876.
Forney, John W., *Anecdotes of Public Men*, New York, 1873.
Francis, John W., *Old New York, or Reminiscences of the past Sixty Years*, New York, 1865.
General Union for Promoting the Observance of the Christian Sabbath, *Second Report*, New York, 1830.
Gillett, Ezra Hale, *History of the Presbyterian Church in the United States of America*, 2 vols., Philadelphia, 1864.

Green, Ashbel, *Life*, New York, 1849.

Hale, Sarah J., *Woman's Record, or Sketches of all Distinguished Women*, New York, 1860.

Hammond, Jabez D., *History of Political Parties in the State of New York*, 2 vols., Syracuse, 1852.

Holland, F. M., "Frances Wright," *The Open Court*, September 5, 1895.

Hone, Philip, *Diary, 1828-1851*, 2 vols., New York, 1889.

Hotchkin, James, *History of Western New York, and of the Rise, Progress, and Present State of the Presbyterian Church*, New York, 1848.

Lee, Elizabeth, "Frances Wright, The First Woman Lecturer," *Gentlemen's Magazine*, May, 1894, pp. 518-528.

Lundy, Benjamin, *The Life, Travels, and Opinions of Benjamin Lundy*, compiled by his Children, Philadelphia, 1847.

McMaster, John Bach, *History of the People of the United States*, 8 vols., New York, 1883-1913.

Morton, Samuel G., *Memoir of William Maclure*, Philadelphia, 1844.

Owen, Robert, *Autobiography*, 2 vols., London, 1857-1858.

Owen, Robert Dale, *Prossimo's Experience: On the study of Theology*, London, 1841.

——, *Discussion on the existence of God*, London, 1840.

——, *Outline of the System of Education at New Lanark*, Glasgow, 1824.

——, *Situations; lawyers, clergy, physicians, men and women*, London, 1839.

——, *Galileo and the Inquisition: Effects of missionary labours*, London, 1841.

——, *Darby and Susan, a tale of old England...*, London, 1842.

——, *Wealth and Misery...*, London, 1841.

——, *Address on the Influence of the Clerical Profession*, New York, 1831.

Owen, William, "Diary of William Owen," *Indiana Historical Society Publications*, vol. ix, no. 1, Indianapolis, 1906.

Porter, Sarah Harvey, *The Life and Times of Anne Royall*, Cedar Rapids, Iowa. 1909.

Riley, I. Woodbridge, *American Philosophy; The Early Schools*, New York, 1907.

Putnam, S. P., *Four Hundred Years of Freethought*, New York, 1894.

*The People's Rights Re-claimed; being an Exposition of the Unconstitutionality of the Law of the State of New York, compelling the Observance of a Religious Sabbath Day and erroneously entitled An Act for Suppressing Immorality, Passed March 13, 1813*, New York, 1826.

Robertson, John M., *Short History of Freethought — Ancient and Modern*, 2 vols., New York, 1906.

Spring, Gardiner, *Personal Reminiscences of the Life and Times of Gardiner Spring*, 2 vols., New York, 1866.

Thorburn, Grant, *History of Cardeus and Carver, or the Christian and Infidel Family*, New York, 1847.

———, *Sketches from the Note-book of Laurie Todd*, New York, 1847.

Tuckerman, Bayard, *The Life of General Lafayette*, 2 vols., New York, 1889.

Turner, Frederick Jackson, *The Rise of the New West*, New York, 1906.

Underwood, Sara A., *Heroines of Freethought*, New York, 1876.

Venable, W. H., *The Beginnings of Literary Culture in the Ohio Valley*, Cincinnati, 1891.

# INDEX